L'Homme.
Europäische Zeitschrift für Feministische Geschichtswissenschaft

Herausgegeben von
Ingrid Bauer/Wien und Salzburg, Anna Becker/Aarhus, Mineke Bosch/
Groningen, Bożena Chołuj/Warschau, Maria Fritsche/Trondheim,
Christa Hämmerle/Wien, Gabriella Hauch/Wien, Almut Höfert/Oldenburg,
Anelia Kassabova/Sofia, Claudia Kraft/Wien, Ulrike Krampl/Tours,
Christina Lutter/Wien, Sandra Maß/Bochum, Claudia Opitz-Belakhal/Basel,
Kristina Schulz/Neuchâtel, Xenia von Tippelskirch/Frankfurt am Main,
Heidrun Zettelbauer/Graz

Initiiert und mitbegründet von Edith Saurer (1942–2011)

Wissenschaftlicher Beirat
Angiolina Arru/Rom, Sofia Boesch-Gajano/Rom, Susanna Burghartz/Basel,
Kathleen Canning/Ann Arbor, Jane Caplan/Oxford, Krassimira Daskalova/
Sofia, Barbara Duden/Hannover, Ayşe Durakbaşa/Istanbul, Ute Frevert/Berlin,
Ute Gerhard/Bremen, Francisca de Haan/Budapest, Hanna Hacker/Wien,
Karen Hagemann/Chapel Hill, Daniela Hammer-Tugendhat/Wien,
Karin Hausen/Berlin, Waltraud Heindl/Wien, Dagmar Herzog/New York,
Claudia Honegger/Bern, Isabel Hull/Ithaca, Marion Kaplan/New York,
Christiane Klapisch-Zuber/Paris, Gudrun-Axeli Knapp/Hannover,
Daniela Koleva/Sofia, Margareth Lanzinger/Wien, Brigitte Mazohl/Innsbruck,
Hans Medick/Göttingen, Herta Nagl-Docekal/Wien, Kirsti Niskanen/
Stockholm, Helga Nowotny/Wien, Karen Offen/Stanford, Michelle Perrot/
Paris, Gianna Pomata/Bologna, Helmut Puff/Ann Arbor, Florence Rochefort/
Paris, Lyndal Roper/Oxford, Raffaela Sarti/Urbino, Wolfgang Schmale/Wien,
Gabriela Signori/Konstanz, Brigitte Studer/Bern, Marja van Tilburg/
Groningen, Maria Todorova/Urbana-Champaign, Claudia Ulbrich/Berlin,
Kaat Wils/Leuven

L'Homme. Europäische Zeitschrift für
Feministische Geschichtswissenschaft
35. Jg., Heft 1 (2024)

Ukraïne

Herausgegeben von
Dietlind Hüchtker und Claudia Kraft

V&R unipress

Inhalt

Dietlind Hüchtker und Claudia Kraft
Editorial 9

Beiträge

Yurii Zazuliak
Abducted Women and Anxious Patriarchs. Abduction of Women and
Ambiguities of Noble Honour in Galicia during the Fifteenth Century 17

Nataliia Starchenko
"Treacherous" Women or Opportunistic Men. Volhynian Gentry Women
Accused of Murdering Their Husbands in the Eastern Region of the Early
Modern Polish-Lithuanian Commonwealth 35

Olha Posunko
The Protection of Women's Property Rights in the Courts of Southern
Ukraine from the End of the Eighteenth to the Mid-Nineteenth
Centuries 55

Nataliia Kolb and Nataliia Mysak
The Daughters of Greek Catholic Priests in Galicia in the Late Nineteenth
Century. Between Conservatism and Emancipation 73

Viktoriia Ivashchenko and Yulia Kiselyova
"I Am Stronger Now, I Know I Can Do So Much". Women Academics in
Conditions of Forced Migration during the Russian-Ukrainian War 99

Aktuelles & Kommentare

Tetiana Isaieva
Das Gendermuseum in Charkiv. Ein Dialog über Geschlechtergleichheit und
Menschenrechte – 15 Jahre informelle Bildung 119

„HERstory of the War". Der Krieg gegen die Ukraine in Erfahrungsberichten
ukrainischer Frauen 123

Susanna Burghartz
„Die Vergangenheit ist unendlich reizvoll und bisweilen sogar eine Quelle der
Hoffnung." Nachruf auf Natalie Zemon Davis (1928–2023) 133

Rezensionen

Olena Petrenko
Oksana Kis, Survival as Victory. Ukrainian Women in the GULAG 137

Katharina Wiedlack
Jessica Zychowicz, Superfluous Women. Art, Feminism, and Revolution in
Twenty-First-Century Ukraine 139

Nina Seiler
Maryna Shevtsova, LGBTI Politics and Value Change in Ukraine and Turkey.
Exporting Europe? 142

Maria Tranter
Emmanuelle Santinelli-Foltz, Couples et conjugalité au haut Moyen Âge
(VIᵉ–XIIᵉ siècles) 147

Gabriela Signori
Julia Burkhardt und Christina Lutter, Ich, Helene Kottannerin.
Die Kammerfrau, die Ungarns Krone stahl 149

Claudia Opitz-Belakhal
Katrin Keller, Die Kaiserin. Reich, Ritual und Dynastie 151

Stephanie Lämmert
Corinne T. Field und LaKisha Michelle Simmons (Hg.), The Global History
of Black Girlhood 154

Jiří Hutečka
Christa Hämmerle, Ganze Männer? Gesellschaft, Geschlecht und Allgemeine
Wehrpflicht in Österreich-Ungarn (1868–1914) 158

Margit Reiter
Valérie Dubslaff, „Deutschland ist auch Frauensache". NPD-Frauen im Kampf
für Volk und Familie 1964–2020 161

Anna Leyrer
Grit Bühler, Eigenmächtig, frauenbewegt, ausgebremst. Der Demokratische
Frauenbund Deutschlands und seine Gründerinnen (1945–1949) 165

Abstracts 169

Anschriften der Autor*innen 173

Editorial

Die aktuelle L'Homme-Ausgabe präsentiert neueste Forschungen zur ukrainischen Frauen- und Geschlechtergeschichte in einem breiten Bogen vom Spätmittelalter bis in die unmittelbare Gegenwart. Wir freuen uns sehr, dass sich zahlreiche Kolleg*innen von unserem *call for articles*[1] angesprochen fühlten, die verschiedenen Regionen der Ukraine zu untersuchen und die Komplexität der Geschichte dieser historischen Räume offenzulegen. Ukrainische Geschichte zu betreiben heißt, die vielfältigen Bezüge zu unterschiedlichen Herrschaften und Zugehörigkeiten mitzudenken – von den mittelalterlichen Herrschaftsverbänden des Königtums Polen und des Großfürstentums Litauen über die frühneuzeitlichen Staatsbildungen der polnisch-litauischen Adelsrepublik und des russländischen Reiches bis hin zu den modernen Imperien seit dem späten 18. Jahrhundert, als Russland und die Habsburgermonarchie infolge der Teilungen Polens über große Gebiete mit ukrainischsprachiger Bevölkerung verfügten. Es heißt auch, die ukrainischen Territorien im Kontext europäischer und globaler Ereignisse zu sehen, etwa hinsichtlich der Nationalstaatsbildungen, der Weltkriege und der Eroberungspolitik, die diese Region besonders prägen, und die Folgen der Sowjetisierung in der Nachkriegszeit und den globalen Kalten Krieg miteinzubeziehen. 1991 entstand im Zuge des Zerfalls der Sowjetunion ein durch ein eindeutig ausgefallenes Referendum legitimierter ukrainischer Nationalstaat, der seit 2014 von der Russischen Föderation mit Krieg überzogen wird, einem Krieg, der sich seit 2022 gegen die gesamte staatliche Existenz des Landes richtet. Es war der Überfall auf die Ukraine im Februar 2022, der im Herausgeberinnengremium von „L'Homme. Z. F. G." die Idee entstehen ließ, frauen- und geschlechtergeschichtliche Arbeiten ukrainischer Forscher*innen bekannter zu machen und einem interessierten Publikum vorzustellen. Damit wollen wir die Möglichkeit bieten, auch unter den herrschenden Kriegsbedingungen die Integration der ukrainischen Forschung in die europäische Frauen- und Geschlechtergeschichte fortzuführen. Die Beiträge zeigen die Gemeinsamkeiten der Fragen und Themenfelder und gleichzeitig die Spezifik der ukrainischen Geschichte,

---

1 Siehe https://www.hsozkult.de/event/id/event-128847, Zugriff: 25. 1. 2024.

die durch regionale und/oder alltags-, rechts- und sozialgeschichtliche Zugänge sichtbar wird.

Aus der Resonanz auf den *call for articles* sticht ein Schwerpunkt ganz deutlich hervor: Mehrere interessante Einreichungen nehmen die vormoderne Frauen- und Geschlechtergeschichte in den Blick und werfen in Verbindung damit zentrale Fragen aus einer ebenso rechts- wie alltagshistorischen Perspektive auf. Dabei geht es vor allem um die Rolle adliger Familienbeziehungen, die Historisierung des Verständnisses von Öffentlichkeit und Privatheit, die Fluidität von Normen, die Praxis des Rechtsetzens ‚von unten' und die nicht nur durch Geschlecht, sondern auch durch Stand, Verwandtschaft und Vernetzung mitbestimmten Handlungsräume der historischen Akteur*innen. Damit gliedern sich diese Beiträge in die aktuellen Debatten der feministischen Frühneuzeitforschung ein, die die Diversität betont, mit der Macht und *agency* zwischen den Geschlechtern und in familiären Zusammenhängen ausgehandelt wurden.[2] Die Erforschung der Themenfelder eheliche Konflikte, Gewalt, Eigentumsregelungen und Ehre liefern dazu wichtige neue Einsichten. Wie auch in anderen Teilen Europas waren frühneuzeitliche Geschlechterbeziehungen in den ukrainischen Gebieten jedoch weder statisch noch repräsentierten sie eine dichotomische Geschlechterhierarchie.

Die ukrainische Frauen- und Geschlechterforschung trägt so zur Selbstverständlichkeit bei, mit der intersektionale Perspektiven Eingang in die frühneuzeitliche Geschlechtergeschichte finden. Gleichzeitig verweist sie auf die lokalen und regionalen Spezifika der ukrainischen Gebiete unter unterschiedlicher Herrschaft. Es geht also nicht in dem Sinne um Besonderheiten, dass „die Ukraine" als anders als das restliche Europa präsentiert würde. Im Gegenteil begünstigt der Blick auf die ukrainischen Regionen die Verschiebung von *mental maps* in der Geschlechtergeschichte. Statt das östliche Europa als eine generelle *border region*[3] zu begreifen, unterstreicht die Forschung damit die Diversität europäischer Regionen.

Auch in einem zweiten Schwerpunkt des Heftes, zum Engagement von Frauen im 19. Jahrhundert und zu den Auswirkungen des aktuellen Kriegs auf die Handlungsmöglichkeiten und -optionen von Frauen, werden aktuelle Forschungskonzepte der

---

[2] Vgl. Teresa Phipps und Deborah Youngs (Hg.), Litigating Women. Gender and Justice in Europe, c.1300–c.1800, London 2021; Dorothea Nolde, Gattenmord. Macht und Gewalt in der frühneuzeitlichen Ehe, Köln ²2015; Margareth Lanzinger, Janine Maegraith, Siglinde Clementi, Ellinor Forster und Christian Hagen (Hg.), Negotiations of Gender and Property through Legal Regimes (14th–19th Century). Stipulation, Litigating, Mediating, Leiden/Boston 2021; Alexandra Lutz, Ehepaare vor Gericht. Konflikte und Lebenswelten, Frankfurt am Main 2006. Auch in der ukrainischen Historiografie ist die Alltags- und Rechtsgeschichte der frühneuzeitlichen Adelsgesellschaft inklusive ihrer Geschlechterordnung in jüngster Zeit eingehend untersucht worden, vgl. Nataliia Starchenko, Ukraïns'ki svity Reči Pospolytoï. Istoriï pro istoriju [Ukrainische Welten der Rzeczpospolita. Geschichten über die Geschichte], Kyiv 2021.

[3] Vgl. Teresa Kulawik und Zhanna Kravchenko (Hg.), Borderlands in European Gender Studies. Beyond the East-West Frontier, London/New York 2020.

Frauen- und Geschlechtergeschichte aufgegriffen: Hierbei geht es vor allem um die Erweiterung von Handlungsräumen, die nicht intendierten Folgen der Inkludierung von Frauen in nationale Projekte und die Geschlechterdynamiken im Kontext von Krieg und Gewalt. Die maßgeblichen Studien zu den Feminismen, Frauenbewegungen und ihren Bedingungen im 19. und 20. Jahrhundert sind darauf ausgerichtet, Ordnung und Typisierungen zu entwickeln.[4] Dabei sind polnische und ungarische, gelegentlich auch tschechische und russische Frauenbewegungen durchaus integriert worden, während dies für die ukrainische Frauenbewegung, die sich im habsburgischen Galizien ausgebildet hatte (und Kontakte in die russische Ukraine aufbaute),[5] kaum gilt – von Forschungen zur Habsburgermonarchie abgesehen.[6] Das verweist auf die lange unausgesprochen übernommene Staatsorientierung der nationalen Frauenbewegungen,[7] was durch Fallstudien zur Ukraine jedoch konterkariert wird. So haben letztere schon seit längerem die Imperiengrenzen und regionenübergreifenden Zusammenhänge deutlich gemacht, sind aber in der Forschungslandschaft weitgehend isoliert geblieben.[8] Die Studien zu den ukrainischsprachigen Intellektuellenmilieus der Geistlichkeit haben die besonders prägnanten Verbindungen zwischen feministischem und nationalem Engagement in religiösen Kontexten analysiert und können daher

---

4 Vgl. Karen Offen, European Feminisms. 1700–1950, Stanford 2000; Gisela Bock, Frauen in der europäischen Geschichte. Vom Mittelalter bis zur Gegenwart, München 2000; Sylvia Paletschek und Bianka Pietrow-Ennker (Hg.), Women's Emancipation Movements in the Nineteenth Century. A European Perspective, Stanford 2004.
5 So etwa Paletschek/Pietrow-Ennker, Women's Emancipation Movements, wie Anmerkung 4; Johanna Gehmacher und Natascha Vittorelli (Hg.), Wie Frauenbewegung geschrieben wird. Historiographie, Dokumentation, Stellungnahmen, Wien 2009; dagegen Kateryna Kobchenko, Parallele Geschichten. Die Entwicklung der akademischen Frauenbildung in der Ukraine von der Mitte des 19. bis zum Anfang des 20. Jahrhunderts, in: Ariadne. Forum für Frauen- und Geschlechtergeschichte, 53/54 (2008): Mädchenschulgeschichte(n). Die preußische Mädchenschulreform und ihre Folgen, 110–118; Ganna Gerasymenko, The Development of Feminist Traditions in Ukraine, in: Edith Saurer, Margareth Lanzinger und Elisabeth Frysak (Hg.), Women's Movements. Networks and Debates in Post-communist Countries in the 19th and 20th Centuries, Köln 2006, 383–395; Lyudmyla Smolyar, The Ukrainian Experiment. Between Feminism and Nationalism or the Main Features of Pragmatic Feminism, in: ebd., 397–411.
6 Vgl. Angelique Leszczawski-Schwerk, „Die umkämpften Tore zur Gleichberechtigung". Frauenbewegungen in Galizien (1867–1918), Wien 2015; Dietlind Hüchtker, History as Performance. Political Movements in Galicia around 1900, New York 2021.
7 Vgl. Susan Zimmermann, The Challenge of Multinational Empire for the International Women's Movement. The Habsburg Monarchy and the Development of Feminist Inter/National Politics, in: Journal of Women's History, 17, 2 (2005), 87–117.
8 Vgl. Martha Bohachevsky-Chomiak, Feminists Despite Themselves. Women in Ukrainian Community Life, 1839–1948, Edmonton 1988; Oksana Malančuk-Rybak, Ideolohija ta suspil'na praktyka xinočoho ruchu na zachidnoukraïns'kych zemljach XIX – peršoï tretyny XX st. Typolohija ta jevropejs'kyj kul'turno-istoryčnyj kontekst [Ideologie und soziale Praxis der Frauenbewegung in der Westukraine vom 19. bis zum ersten Drittel des 20. Jahrhunderts. Ihre Typologie und der europäische kulturgeschichtliche Kontext], Černivci 2006.

sowohl einen Beitrag zur Intersektionalität im feministischen Engagement als auch zur Debatte um Typisierungen von feministischen Bewegungen leisten.

Schließlich geht es im vorliegenden Heft auch um die aktuelle Kriegssituation in der Ukraine. Die Analyse ihrer Auswirkungen auf Geschlechterordnungen und Handlungsmöglichkeiten von Frauen ordnet sich dabei ebenfalls in eine bereits länger geführte Diskussion ein.[9] Dazu gehören ukrainische Studien, die vom Holodomor (der durch die stalinistische Zwangskollektivierung verursachten Hungersnot in den 1930er Jahren) über den Zweiten Weltkrieg und die stalinistischen Lager bis hin zum gegenwärtigen Angriffskrieg Russlands reichen, und vermutlich am besten in eine europäisch oder global perspektivierte Frauen- und Geschlechtergeschichte eingebunden sind.[10] So sind ukrainische Forscherinnen unter anderem am internationalen Forschungsnetzwerk Sexual Violence in Armed Conflicts (SVAC)[11] beteiligt. Die vielfältigen Forschungen unterstreichen die Zwiespältigkeit, die dem *Empowerment* von Frauen unter Gewaltherrschaft und Kriegsbedingungen innewohnt.

Zu den Beiträgen

Yurii Zazuliak beleuchtet in seiner Studie über das seit Mitte des 14. Jahrhunderts von Polen dominierte Fürstentum Halyč die Entführung adliger Ehefrauen als Beispiel für die Aushandlung von Geschlechternormen vor lokalen Gerichten und die durchaus vorhandene *agency* von Frauen. Entführungen waren eine Praxis, die zwischen der Ausübung (auch sexueller) Gewalt und einvernehmlichem Handeln der Beteiligten changierte. So peripher solche Fälle erscheinen mögen, so verweisen sie doch auf Widersprüche im zeitgenössischen sozialen und normativen Verständnis von Geschlecht und Familie. Sie zeigen, dass es immer mehrere Weisen gab, wie Feindschaft, Gesetz und Ehre wirkten. Zazuliak macht deutlich, dass Konzepte wie Ehre situativ bestimmt wurden und dass gerade das Gericht zu einem Möglichkeitsraum für weibliche Adlige wurde, um ihre familiären und gesellschaftlichen Positionierungen immer wieder neu zu bestimmen.

---

9 Vgl. Karen Hagemann und Stefanie Schüler-Springorum (Hg.), Heimat-Front. Militär und Geschlechterverhältnisse im Zeitalter der Weltkriege, Frankfurt am Main 2002; Regina Mühlhäuser, Eroberungen. Sexuelle Gewalttaten und intime Beziehungen deutscher Soldaten in der Sowjetunion, 1941–1945, Hamburg 2010.
10 Vgl. Marta Havryshko, Love and Sex in Wartime. Controlling Women's Sexuality in the Ukrainian Nationalist Underground, in: Aspasia, 12, 1 (2018), 35–67; Olena Petrenko, Unter Männern. Frauen im ukrainischen nationalistischen Untergrund 1944–1954, Paderborn 2018; Tanja Penter und Stefan Schneider, Olgas Tagebuch (1941–1944). Unerwartete Zeugnisse einer jungen Ukrainerin inmitten des Vernichtungskriegs, Göttingen 2022; Oksana Kis, Survival as Victory. Ukrainian Women in the GULAG, Cambridge MA, 2022.
11 Siehe dazu https://www.warandgender.net/about/, Zugriff: 25.1.24.

Auch im Beitrag von Nataliia Starchenko stehen adlige Familienbeziehungen im Zentrum. Im Zuge der detaillierten Darstellung eines umfangreich überlieferten Gerichtsprozesses zur angeblichen Ermordung eines Adligen durch seine Ehefrau entwickelt die Autorin eine faszinierende mikrohistorische Perspektive auf das rechtshistorische Material. Anhand der im 16. Jahrhundert vollständig in das Königreich Polen eingegliederten Region Wolhynien legt sie eine sehr genaue Analyse zu gewalttätigem Handeln vor, das in den Gerichtsakten nicht als eine nach Geschlecht unterscheidbare Praxis erscheint, sondern im genauen Nachvollzug der häufig widersprüchlichen Zeug*innenaussagen eher als ein Kontinuum unterschiedlicher performativer Akte. Starchenko geht in ihren Überlegungen nicht von im Untersuchungszeitraum vorherrschenden Geschlechterrollen aus, sondern liest die Gerichtsakten aus den 1580er Jahren als Belege für gesellschaftlich erwünschte Rollen und spürt darin der *agency* nach, die für adlige Frauen aufgrund ihrer gesellschaftlichen Positionierung beträchtlich sein konnte. In ihrer dichten Beschreibung fokussiert sie nicht auf die (Un-)Wahrheit der vor Gericht präsentierten Beweise, sondern wie Aussagen konstruiert wurden und welche Akteur*innen welche Ressourcen mobilisieren konnten. Trotz vollzogener Eheschließung blieben Frauen mit ihren Herkunftsfamilien verbunden und konnten weiterhin über ihr Eigentum verfügen. Der Autorin gelingt es überzeugend ein Postulat mikrohistorischer Forschung einzulösen, nämlich Erklärungen nicht durch eindimensional konstruierte Kausalitäten, sondern durch möglichst genaues Erzählen zu liefern.

Anders als in den beiden vorangegangenen Beiträgen bildet im ebenfalls rechtsgeschichtlichen Text von Olha Posunko das russländische Reich den normativen Resonanzraum. Die Autorin beleuchtet eigentumsrechtliche Regelungen für einen Zeitraum, in dem die sich unter polnisch-litauischer Oberhoheit relativ unabhängig entwickelnden südlichen Territorien der Ukraine unter russisch-imperialen Einfluss geraten waren, der sich im 18. Jahrhundert voll ausgebildet hatte. Sie entwirft ein Panorama von Multinormativität, in der ein neu eingeführtes zentralisierendes Rechts- und Verwaltungssystem noch für längere Zeit mit älteren Rechtsnormen aus der polnisch-litauischen Zeit koexistierte. Dafür wertet Posunko ebenfalls Gerichtsakten, aber auch persönliche Dokumente sowie Bitt- und Beschwerdebriefe an die Gerichte aus. Hatte das aus polnisch-litauischer Herrschaftszeit überkommene Recht das Eigentum adliger Frauen geschützt, so rückte dieses seit dem späten 18. Jahrhundert in den Fokus der adligen Landbesitzer*innen. Mit Bezugnahme auf den vormaligen Eigentumsschutz wurde an der Wende vom 18. zum 19. Jahrhundert versucht, den gesamten adeligen Besitz dem sich verstärkenden staatlichen Zugriff zu entziehen. Es waren also nicht individuelle Eigentumsrechte, die hier zur Disposition standen und verteidigt wurden, sondern das ständische Interesse des besitzenden Adels. Im Laufe der Zeit geriet dieses Interesse weiter in Bedrängnis, denn der im ehemals polnisch-litauischen Recht formulierte Eigentumsschutz von Frauen wurde nicht nur staatlicherseits infrage gestellt, sondern stand zusätzlich in Kontrast zu der religiös begründeten Beschränkung weiblicher (Persönlichkeits-)Rechte, die mit dem wachsenden Einfluss orthodoxen kanonischen Rechts zunahm.

Dass religiös geprägte Kontexte keinesfalls immer zur Einschränkung weiblicher Handlungsräume beitrugen, machen Nataliia Kolb und Nataliia Mysak in ihrem Beitrag deutlich, der den Töchtern von griechisch-katholischen Priestern im späten 19. und frühen 20. Jahrhundert in Galizien gewidmet ist. Sie beschreiben die Aktivierung von Frauen in den Bereichen Bildung und Soziales, aber auch ihr politisches Engagement in einem von ethnischen und konfessionellen Spannungen gekennzeichneten Umfeld. Im Text wird eindrücklich herausgearbeitet, dass die Familien der griechisch-katholischen Geistlichkeit eine mehrfach relevante Sozialisationsinstanz darstellten und im agrarisch-ländlich geprägten ukrainischen Teil des österreichischen Kronlandes in gewisser Weise Funktionen einer sich politisierenden bildungsbürgerlichen Schicht übernahmen. Die Autorinnen zeigen, dass die geistlichen Familienvorstände Bildung für familiäre, aber auch gesellschaftliche Entwicklungsprozesse durchaus als zentral für ihre Töchter erachteten, zugleich aber an traditionellen Geschlechterrollen festhielten. So entfaltet sich eine differenzierte Bildungsgeschichte Galiziens, in der die Priester zum Entstehen neuer gesellschaftlicher Aktionsräume und Rollen beitrugen, weil durch den Aufbau eines ukrainischsprachigen Bildungswesens und der damit verbundenen zunehmenden weiblichen außerhäuslichen Berufstätigkeit die zentrale Rolle der griechisch-katholischen Kirche als wichtigste Instanz für gesellschaftliche Modernisierungsprozesse untergraben wurde.

Im letzten Hauptbeitrag wechselt die Szenerie räumlich wie zeitlich radikal. Viktoriia Ivashchenko und Yulia Kiselyova widmen sich der durch den Angriffskrieg Russlands gegen die Ukraine erzwungenen Migration von Wissenschaftlerinnen auf der Grundlage von semi-strukturierten Interviews, die sowohl die Ereignisse von 2014 als auch von 2022 in den Blick nehmen. Angelehnt an die geschlechtersensible Biografieforschung nach Bettina Dausien beleuchten die Autorinnen den Konstruktionsprozess von Ich-Identität durch die Erzählungen der Interviewpartnerinnen. Ihre Forschung positionieren sie in dem größeren Fragenkomplex zur Ausbildung von Geschlechtsidentitäten von Wissenschaftlerinnen im postsowjetischen Raum. Sie spüren dem Wandel von darauf bezogenen Einstellungen nach und beleuchten die Prozesse der biografischen Konstruktion von Geschlecht. Dabei betrachten sie sowohl die veränderten Handlungsräume als auch die Reflexionen der Interviewpartnerinnen über Konflikte zwischen alten und neuen Selbstkonzepten in Zeiten kriegsbedingter Migration. Besondere Aufmerksamkeit widmen sie dem Wandel der Bedeutung von Ich- beziehungsweise Wir-Erzählungen und der Spezifik der Schilderung interpersonaler Beziehungen. Aus den Interviews geht hervor, dass der durch die Migration veränderte Blick auf sich selbst, aber auch auf die früheren Lebensbedingungen, widersprüchliche Wahrnehmungen zeitigt, von denen die wichtigste zu sein scheint, sich selbst weniger als Opfer, sondern vielmehr als Agentin des Wandels zu betrachten.

In der Rubrik „Aktuelles und Kommentare" stellt Tetiana Isaieva das Gendermuseum in Charkiv vor, das seit einigen Jahren wichtige Impulse für die Verbreitung von Wissen im Bereich der Gender Studies in der Ukraine liefert. Das Museum greift immer wieder historisch wie aktuell relevante Themen auf und setzt sie in Ausstellungen um. Sehr bald nach dem Überfall Russlands auf die Ukraine wurde etwa eine Sammlung von Zeitzeuginnenberichten („HERstory of the War") initiiert, die einen tiefen Einblick in die Erfahrungen von ukrainischen Frauen in Zeiten des Krieges bieten. Wir haben vier eindrückliche Berichte aus diesem Projekt ausgewählt und ins Deutsche übersetzt, um diese Erfahrungen des Krieges sichtbar zu machen.

In einem Nachruf erinnert Susanna Burghartz an die im Herbst 2023 verstorbene Historikerin Natalie Zemon Davis, die mit ihren Arbeiten nicht nur die Frauen- und Geschlechtergeschichte maßgeblich geprägt, sondern auch bahnbrechende Forschungen zur Mikrogeschichte und zur Historischen Anthropologie insbesondere der Frühen Neuzeit vorgelegt hat.

Das Heft beschließen drei themenspezifische Rezensionen, die sich geschlechtergeschichtlichen Forschungen zum Gulag sowie neuesten Entwicklungen in der Ukraine im Bereich der LGBTI-Politik und des feministischen künstlerischen Aktivismus widmen, sowie weitere Besprechungen von Neuerscheinungen im Feld der Frauen- und Geschlechtergeschichte.

Dietlind Hüchtker und Claudia Kraft

Yurii Zazuliak

Abducted Women and Anxious Patriarchs. Abduction of Women and Ambiguities of Noble Honour in Galicia during the Fifteenth Century

1. Contours of local patriarchy: ravishment, female honour and law

The abduction of women was an ambiguous offence in late medieval and early modern Galicia.[1] It was characterised by many uncertainties related to the local contexts of gender relations, violence and legal process.[2] Poorly regulated by the statute law, abduction constantly oscillated between sexual transgression and crime, including rape, ravishment and adultery, on the one hand, and customary marriage and sexual practices, such as female consent and clandestine relationships, on the other. One might think that abductions were only excesses at the margins of legitimate forms and relations of patriarchy. They were few in number, the legal records of them are fragmentary and their meanings are often quite obscure. Yet, however, marginal such cases may seem, they reveal contradictions within the social and normative fields of gender and family, as well as the plurality of ways in which enmity, law, honour, and legal narratives framed the problem of patriarchal power over women.

---

1 The name Galicia is used in this article to refer to the historical region also known in historiography as Red Ruthenia, Halych Rus', or Rus' Palatinate. It encompassed the territories of present-day western Ukraine and south-eastern Poland. Until the mid-fourteenth century, Galicia was a part of the independent Halych-Volynian polity and was conquered by the Polish kings during the second half of the fourteenth century.
2 On the ambiguity of abduction as a crime in medieval societies, cf. Caroline Dunn, Stolen Women in Medieval England. Rape, Abduction, and Adultery, 1100–1500, Cambridge 2013, 6. On medieval ravishment and abduction, cf. also Kathryn Gravdal, Ravishing Maidens. Writing Rape in Medieval French Literature and Law, Philadelphia 1991; Shannon McSheffrey and Julia Pope, Ravishment, Legal Narratives, and Chivalric Culture in Fifteenth-Century England, in: Journal of British Studies, 48 (2009), 818–836; Mary R. Block, For the Repressing of the Most Wicked and Felonious Rapes or Ravishments of Women: Rape Law in England, 1660–1800, in: Anne Greenfield (ed.), Interpreting Sexual Violence, 1660–1800, London/New York 2016. The issue of abduction and rape mentioned in passing in Maria Koczerska's major study of the Polish medieval noble family. Cf. Maria Koczerska, Rodzina szlachecka w Polsce średniowiecznej [The Noble Family in Medieval Poland], Warsaw 1975, 33–34, 36–37.

Abduction cases highlight the central but also ambiguous role of the concept of female honour and gender symbols in the discourse and practice of inimical relations. Gendered meanings were fundamental elements in the process of the formation of the concept of male and female honour in the context of law and violence.[3] Historians have emphasized that male and female concepts of honour were constructed asymmetrically in terms of the importance, attached to norms of appropriate sexual conduct.[4] The constitution of woman's honour depended much more on the constant assessment of the conformity of her sexual behaviour to the communally accepted and imposed moral and legal views of gender roles. Men were regarded as the guardians of a woman's honour and sexuality, and it was through them that a woman secured her position and her honour, as well as her legitimate protection and position in the patriarchal order.[5] The enmity and violence of local noblemen, as essential elements of the contemporary noble culture and identity, constantly articulated issues of gender honour and sexuality, including abduction, and in this way had a powerful impact on the constitution of the local patriarchal order.

As one of the "grey areas" in the exercise of dominant masculinity and patriarchal power, abduction also revealed some of its basic characteristics. A local version of patriarchy in late medieval Galicia displays features that were in many ways typical of pre-modern Europe and the lands of the Polish Crown. It was embedded in a variety moral, legal and social categories and rules, and was expressed through numerous institutional and informal practices, such as ecclesiastical and common law, ecclesiastical instructions and prohibitions, the system of inheritance, household roles and marriage patterns. Law and conflict played a key role in constructing dominant models of gender and family relations, and in institutionalising a variety of legal and extra-legal forms of paternal and marital authority over women within and across families and kinship groups.

In the case of late medieval Galicia, the evidence of legal practice provides the main, and sometimes the only, perspective from which to approach local gender and family relations. A network of the two main types of local courts, the castle courts and the land courts, was introduced in Galicia in the 1430s, after the region's final incorporation into the Kingdom of Poland, and enormously expanded the legal resources available to people involved in enmities. Legal claims based on the accusation of stealing women

---

3 For a brief recent overview of the problem of honour, gender and law from the perspective of defamation and slender cases, cf. Martin Ingram, Law, litigants, and the construction of "honour". Slander suits in early modern England, in: Peter Coss (ed.), The Moral World of the Law, Cambridge 2000, 135–138.
4 Cf. for example, Lyndal Roper, Will and honour: sex, words, and power in Augsburg criminal trials, in: eadem, Oedipus and the Devil. Witchcraft, Sexuality and Religion in Early Modern Europe, London/New York 1994, 65.
5 This point has recently been emphasised, cf. Sandra Cavallo and Simona Cerutti, Female Honour and the Social Control of Reproduction in Piedmont between 1600 and 1800, in: Edward Muir and Guido Ruggiero (eds.), Sex and Gender in Historical Perspective, Baltimore/London 1990, 79.

were accepted and tried in these local courts, which widened the possibilities of pursuing enmities not only through the exercise of violence but also through the law. Seeking justice and redressing wrongs through the courts often meant for the disputants to satisfy their desire for revenge and to manifest the state of enmity.

Local legal practice enabled various normative rules and social moral discourses that served to construct asymmetrical gender roles and secure women's subordination to be rearticulated and reasserted through legal actions and claims to power in the public and private life. In the courtroom men publicized their role as the natural masters of women, endowed with the legitimate power to administer justice to women, and to control and discipline their behaviour and their bodies. "You cannot judge my wife, she is subject to my law, because she eats my bread under my jurisdiction" – claimed a nobleman at the land court of Przemyśl in 1462, protesting against his wife's summons to this court.[6]

In addition, the patriarchal order was inscribed in bodily behaviour, rituals, and gestures that women had to perform as public and legal personae. Some rituals clearly tended to display and enhance women's voluntary obedience to and public recognition of male power. For example, the legal procedure of renunciation of property rights by women over their male relatives required women to perform it with a cheerful face, and without weeping ("leto vultu, non plorando").[7] However, the origins of this legal procedure, which obliged women to take legal action "leto vultu, non plorando", while renouncing their familial property, can be seen in a very different light and lead the interpretation in other directions. It can be assumed, for example, that the reason for its introduction into legal documents was to prevent women from using gestures and showing emotions that could be seen as undermining the legitimacy of the whole legal action. Thus, some legal procedures and public bodily gestures both implied the power to impose and the ability to manipulate paternal authority.

As a result, public behaviour, social customs and legal practices involved in maintaining and reproducing local gender hierarchies could also reveal inconsistencies between public transcripts and private aspirations of men and women. They show that the family and gender, as social sites of power relations, also involved many challenges to the patriarchal authority, including opportunities for women to expand their social roles and positions.[8] Demands for recognition of women's rights and roles through the law or

---

6 Akta grodzkie i ziemskie z czasow Rzeczypospolitej Polskiej, z archiwum tak zwanego Bernardyńskiego we Lwowie w skutek fundacii A. Stadnickiego [Castle and Land Records from the Times of the Polish Republic, from the St. Bernard Archive in Lviv, supported by the A. Stadnicki Foundation] (henceforth AGZ), ed. by K. Liske, vol. 13, no. 4979: "[…] nolite iudicare consortem meam, detis ipsam ad meum ius de mea iurisdictione comedens panem meum alias moya Chleboyeczscha." The evidence was mentioned in: Koczerska, Rodzina szlachecka, see note 2, 69, and similar evidence, 74.
7 AGZ, vol. 13, no. 6559.
8 On the limits of patriarchal authority and women agency in pre-modern Europe, cf. for example Bernard Capp, Separate Domains? Women and Authority in Early Modern England, in: Paul Griffiths, Adam Fox, and Steve Hindle (eds.), The Experience of Authority in Early Modern England,

through private everyday communication were as important to the normative and social foundations of patriarchy as constraints and obedience. From this point of view, disputes and enmities, with their focus on conflicting and violent aspects of human relations, are especially revealing for representing the patriarchal order as a social space of the constant negotiation and tension over its meanings and boundaries.

2. Ambiguous spaces of legal norms and practices

Law and litigation were thus social domains in which the ambiguities and anxieties inherent in the patriarchal order were displayed and manipulated. Regarding the prosecution of abduction, ambiguities primarily concerned the apparent difference between the normative expectations of the royal statutes of the Kingdom of Poland, and the regulation of this type of wrongdoing by the local courts. Abduction became the subject of legal regulation by the statute and royal law comparatively late. A main legal norm in the late medieval Polish statute law concerning abduction was issued in the statutes of Jan Olbracht from 1493 and 1496. This provision, which was worded identically in both statutes, promulgated a penalty of eternal infamy for men found guilty of abducting both unmarried and married women. In addition, the provision also spoke of the potential liability of women. The law stipulated that the abducted woman had to be deprived of all her inheritance rights, including her dowry, if her voluntary consent to the abduction was proven.[9] In this way, the law attempted to address the realities of gender-based violence as well as the agency of women in abduction cases. The result was a rather ambiguous positioning of women, who were treated as both victims and accomplices. It should also be noted that the law did not specify how and by what means the fact of women's consent could be established, nor did it lay down a clear

---

New York 1996, 117–145. As far as Ukrainian historiography is concerned Iryna Voronchuk, in her seminal study, has stressed the key role of patriarchy in shaping family relations and restricting women's public positions, cf. eadem, Naselennia Volyni v XVI–pershii polovyny XVII st.: rodyna, domohospodarstvo, demohrafichni chynnyky [Population of Volyn during the Sixteenth and the First Half of the Seventeenth Centuries. Family, Household, Demography], Kyiv 2012. Cf. also the polemical article by Nataliia Starchenko, "Dzherela svidchat". Kilka zauvah pro doslidzhennia stanovyshcha shliakhtianky v rannomodernomu sotsiumi Volyni ["The Sources Testify". Some Remarks on the Study of the Status of Noblewomen in Early Modern Society of Volyn], Ukrainskyi arkheohrafichnyi shchorichnyk [Ukrainian Archaeography Annual], 19–20 (2016), 239–267.

9 Cf. for example, The Statute of King Jan Olbracht from 1493, in: Stanisław Grodziski, Irena Dwornicka, Wacław Uruszczak (eds.), Volumina constitutionum [Volumes of constitutions], t. I (1493–1549), vol. 1 (1493–1526), Warsaw 1996, 50, § IX. De raptu foeminei sexus: "Item de raptoribus virginum et foeminarum ita volumus esse statuendum ut talis raptor, si fuerit jure convictus, secundum antiquiora statuta, perpetuis temporibus honore privetur et foeminina se rapi consentiens, bonis omnibus haereditaribus et quibuscunque aliis, ipsam concernentibus rebus, videlicet dote, perpetuo privetur." For the Statutes of 1496, cf. ibid., t. I, vol. 1, 80, § 79.

procedure to avoid slanderous accusations, or perjury, which appeared to be common in these court cases.

In contrast to the severity of the norm promulgated in the statutes of King Jan Olbracht, the evidence of local court proceedings paints a very different picture of how these offences were dealt with. During the fifteenth century, no judgement was passed in the local courts against alleged perpetrators in accordance with the above-mentioned provision of the statute law. Some men accused of abduction were able to successfully clear their names and defend their honour with assistance of oath-helpers recruited from the local nobility. In a few cases, the outcome remained unknown. The information on such cases stopped at the stage of accusation, being brought before the court, the bailiffs taking cognisance of it or the potential offender providing guarantors. Some accusations led to divorce without final court verdict. In one case, the parties attempted to reach an amicable settlement.[10] The comparatively small number of cases recorded in local court registers for the fifteenth century may give the impression that law and justice were lenient in cases of abduction. Legal records of local court proceedings provide information on the eight cases that can be classified as abductions and that were recorded between 1427 and 1496. All but one of these cases predates the promulgation of the above-mentioned legal provision in the statutes of King Jan Olbracht. This could also explain the lack of severe punishment for abductors in local legal practice. It is fair to assume that the statutes, although referring to the old law, introduced a new, more severe punishment, which had not been widespread in the local regulation of this offence before its promulgation.

On the other hand, however, there may have been other reasons for the social tolerance and conflicting attitudes towards abduction. The most important of these was the high status of people involved in the offence. The families from which the offenders and victims came belonged to the local nobility. They represented middling sort or rich noble families that often had a prominent position in the social and political hierarchies of the lands of Galicia, which administratively formed a Rus' palatinate. Abduction was part of the social experience of various groups in the noble estate, including the local aristocracy. This could also explain the important role of different forms of communal solidarity and collective actions by relatives, friends or patrons in these disputes, which resulted in the apparent partiality of the contemporary justice and shaped the highly ambivalent perception of gender violence in contemporary society.

The ways in which local legal records were made reinforce the sense of ambivalence of abduction. In contrast to some sixteenth-century abduction cases, such as the cause célèbre of Halshka Ostrogska, described in detail by Polish authors of the time (for example Łukasz Górnicki), the surviving records from fifteenth-century Galicia are

---

10 Cf. the accusation brought by Jan Dawidowski of Horpyn against the brothers from Neslukhiv in 1444. The charges were denied by the defendants and the parties tried to settle the dispute by means of arbitration, AGZ, vol. 14, no. 1236, 1251.

extremely incomplete. This considerably limits the possibility of knowing all the circumstances of abductions, their origins and their course. The legal contexts in which the records were made, as well as the disputing strategies of the parties, greatly influenced the way and language in which the legal records spoke of the abduction. The parties of the dispute and their attorneys ascribed different and often contradictory meanings to the abduction. Accounts of abduction were construed as legal facts, justified by claims of honour and served the interests of the disputants. As a result, the records left too much unsaid and are marked by many obscurities and ambiguities, which can be seen as attempts to misrepresent the realities of gender-based violence, the intentions and actions of the actors, and which makes it difficult to draw a clear line between abduction and rape, between fact and fiction, between slander or perjury and truth in the surviving accounts.[11]

3. Boundaries of gendered violence: rape and ravishment

It is not always clear from the available records, for example, how the practice of abduction was related to the crime of rape. The boundaries between these two offences were often blurred, and abduction could mean a rape. However, they were not considered identical in contemporary legal sources. Rape and abduction were defined differently in local court registers. The language of legal records for rape was precise and direct, described by the Latin words "dehonestatio" or by phrases using the local vernacular, such as "violencia" alias "wsylstwo", "oppression" alias "wsilstwe".[12] Verbs, such as "deflorasset", "sturpasset" were also used to describe the actions of the perpetrators.[13] When speaking of abduction, the wording of the sources seems to have been more oblique and circumscribed. To describe the theft of women, the sources used phrases such as "raptus", "receptio violenta", "vi recipisti" alias "gwaltem" or simply "receptio".[14]

Another significant difference between the offences of rape and abduction concerned the social profile of the victims. Most cases brought, tried and recorded in local courts involved plebeian women accusing noblemen of sexual violence. It is equally important that none of the cases in which noblemen were accused of raping plebeian

---

11 On the problems related to the legal narrative of pre-modern gendered violence and intrafamilial conflicts, cf. for example Dunn, Stolen Women, see note 2, 5, 18; Barbara A. Hanawalt, Whose Story Was This? Rape Narratives in Medieval English Courts, in: eadem, "Of Good and Ill Repute". Gender and Social Control in Medieval England, Oxford 1998, 124–141; Thomas Kuehn, Reading Microhistory. The Example of Giovanni and Lusanna, in: Journal of Modern History, 61 (September 1989), 512–534.
12 Cf. AGZ, vol. 13, no. 4218; vol. 14, Lwów, 1889, no. 3634; vol. 15, Lwów, 1891, no. 45.
13 Cf. AGZ, vol. 14, no. 443; vol. 15, no. 1286.
14 Cf. AGZ, vol. 9, Lwów, 1883, no. XXVIII; vol. 14, no. 1236; vol. 15, no. 786, 1475, 2262, 2515, 3517; vol. 19, Lwów, 1906, no. 2912.

women are known to have ended with a formal verdict in favour of the victims. As a rule, plaintiffs failed in their pleadings against aggressors in court due to some, sometimes minor, procedural errors.[15] In this sense, rape, as it was presented to the local public courts, was also a social crime, which implicitly marked the boundaries between the nobility and plebeians in contemporary Galician society.[16] This was in sharp contrast to abduction cases, which, as mentioned above, mostly involved noblewomen. It could be suggested that local legal language was used to represent the abduction of noblewomen in order to distance such cases from the suspicion of rape, and thus defend the honour of these women.

However, this was not always the case, and abduction can be seen as a form of brutal and arbitrary gendered violence. An example of this kind of narrative representation of abduction is provided by the earliest known record of this offence, dated 1429. It is a formal complaint lodged by the Armenian community of Lviv with the palatine of Cracow, Jan of Tarnow, against Nicholas Zasowski, accusing him of stealing the unmarried daughter of the deceased Armenian noble Gregory.[17] The case must have aroused public interest in contemporary Galicia. The abducted girl was already engaged to another man, a certain Armenian named Abraam, son of Tulag. The plaintiffs emphasised that the engaged couple belonged to the Armenian community, justifying community's action in their defence. The girl was described as "of our stock" and the man to whom she was engaged as "our brother". There was another aspect that made this case especially notorious. Zasowski was related to the Lviv captain Peter Wlodkowic, the highest royal official in the land. The plaintiffs also claimed that the captain's servants and clients, together with the offender's friends, were the main accomplices in the crime. From the royal castle in Lviv, Zasowski, assisted by the captain's men, raided the village of Lashky, the residence of the family of the above-mentioned knight Gregory, captured the girl and took her against her will to the royal curia in the village of

---

15 For example, in 1436 Alexander Rybotycki was accused before the Przemyśl land court of violating and capturing a married woman during a night raid with accomplices on the village of Pnykut. The case was sent for interrogation and the verdict is unknown, cf. AGZ, vol. 13, no. 33. Another example is a case from 1457 before the Lviv castle court. A local nobleman, Jan Dawidowski, was accused by a certain Anna of rape and wounding ("pro oppressione alias wsilstwe et pro illacione vulnerum"). Despite being accused of such serious crimes, Dawidowski won the case on the grounds that the plaintiff had failed to appear at the court hearing, cf. AGZ, vol. 15, no. 45. The lords also defended their officials accused of raping plebeian women by refusing to bring them to trial, cf. AGZ, vol. 13, no. 4218. In 1473, Vivdia, a plebeian woman from Borshchovychi, with the help of the Lviv vice-captain Pelka Lyssakowski, filed a lawsuit against a local nobleman, Jan Baszynski, accusing him of capture and raping here on the free royal road and then abducting her against her will to his estate. In accordance with the rules of contemporary legal process, Baszynski's attorney did not respond to the factual part of the accusation. He simply pointed out that the victim had failed to make the rape known to other people, as prescribed by written law, cf. AGZ, vol. 15, no. 1286. Cf. also AGZ, vol. 14, no. 443.
16 Cf. Dunn, Stolen Women, see note 2, 2–3.
17 Cf. AGZ, vol. 9, no. XXVIII.

Sknyliv. According to the complaint, the raid and abduction were accompanied by violence against other women who lived on the Lashky estate: the mother of the abducted girl was beaten and her maidservants were "oppressed", which most likely meant sexual violence.

The complaint describes next the blatant abuse of law and miscarriage of justice, caused by the close blood ties between the offender and the Lviv captain, which led the Armenian community to appeal to the palatine of Cracow. When the mother of the abducted girl, accompanied by members of the Armenian community, appealed for justice to the palatine of Lviv (the deputy of the royal captain in the administration of justice), Nikel Korc, he rejected their appeal and refused to hear the case in his court because the offender was a brother of the captain.[18] Their appeal for justice to the captain also failed. The pleaders turned to the Lviv magistrate, who accepted their claim. The magistrate's reasoning was quite revealing. It justified its support to the Armenians on the grounds that the case concerned all people who had daughters and sons in all parts of the kingdom. The outcome of the case and the fate of the abducted girl remain unknown.

4. Abduction and broken matrimonial alliances

Other cases are much more ambiguous in their representation of the abduction. In these legal accounts, the fact of the abduction was not taken for granted but was one of the competing versions of events and motives told by the disputants in court. It seems to have been particularly true of accusations of abduction related to the matrimonial intentions of noblemen and controversies over the choice of spouse. The accusation of abduction could be brought by parents against the noblemen whom their daughters preferred as marital partners, thus contradicting the parent's will and their marriage plans. A case brought by Anna Cebrowska of Zhabokruky and Raphael Sieniawski against Wlodek of Bilka before the Lviv castle court in 1492 illustrates the interrelation between abduction and intricacies of the marriage politics.[19] It should be noted that the Cebrowskis, Bilieckis and Sieniawskis were well-established families of the middle-sort nobility, known for their wealth and prestige and with a history of spectacular political careers in the lands of Galicia (Sieniawskis, whose members had been judges and sub-judges of local courts for several generations). The account of the dispute starts with Cebrowska's charges against Wlodek, accusing him of abducting Anna's daughter Agnes. Anna Cebrowska declared that Agnes was already engaged to Raphael Sieniawski. She also claimed that the abduction took place during Wlodek's violent assault

---

18 Cf. AGZ, vol. 9, no. XXVIII: "Qui iusticiam contra illum violatorem ministrare penitus renuit nec quitquam curavit facere ad premissa eo, quod esset frater dicti domini Capitanei [...]."
19 Cf. AGZ, vol. 15, no. 2262.

on the Cebrowska home. Raphael Sieniawski added to the accusations against Wlodek, saying that during his raid Wlodek had looted the house and taken many household items, including the fur coat that Raphael had bought and given to Agnes as a wedding gift.

Wlodek denied the charges. The defendant argued that he had not used violence against Agnes but had taken her as his legitimate wife. In his defence, Wlodek said that Agnes had personally given to him her hand in marriage and that the fur coat had been given to Wlodek voluntary by Anna Cebrowska. Furthermore, Wlodek also claimed that he had sent a carriage to the Cebrowskis house for Agnes as his wife. A court scribe added a brief remark to Wlodek's testimony, stating that Agnes herself admitted the truth of Wlodek's words.

The record thus suggests that Agnes voluntary consented to accept the bonds of marriage, and calls into question the allegation of her violent abduction brought before the court by her mother and her first husband-to-be, Raphael Sieniawski. Agnes's intentions seem much clearer from the record of the consistory court of the Lviv archbishopric, which was entered into the register in the last days of December 1492.[20] It concerns the accusation made by Raphael Sieniawski against Jan, the Roman Catholic parish priest in Bilka. Sieniawski alleged that Jan had acted against the law by giving Agnes of Zaborkruky, the daughter of the deceased Jan Wloch Cebrowski, in marriage to Wlodek of Bilka and consecrating the marriage between them in the village of Hermaniv, the house of another noblewoman, Slotnicka. According to the accusation, Jan had committed a grave offence, because he knew about the marriage between Raphael and Agnes, which had previously been contracted by mutual consent and consecrated by the parish priest of Bibrka. Raphael then asked the court to punish Jan and to make amends for the wrongs he had suffered as a result of the priest's actions, which the plaintiff estimated at 300 florins. The priest defended himself by saying that he had no prior knowledge of the marriage between the two. He claimed that he had only learned about it when he went to collect a priestly dowry, which Agnes had helped him to do. On this occasion, she asked the priest if she had done good deed by breaking with Raphael after contracting a marriage with him in church. If we are to believe the words of the priest, he rebuked her saying that she had done wrong and that he did not approve of her behaviour.

The last record in this case dates from the following year, 1493. It is a testimony given by three local noblemen in support of Wlodek and recorded in the register of the Lviv castle court.[21] In their testimony, the nobles claimed to be witnesses of the following fact: they testified that they had been present in Bilka, enjoying the company of Wlodek, at the same time when the carriage with Agnes had arrived there. According

---

20 Cf. Wilhelm Rolny (ed.), Acta officii Consistorialis Leopoliensis antiquissima [The Oldest Records of the Lviv Consistory Office], vol. 2, Lwów 1930, no. 919.
21 Cf. AGZ, vol. 15, no. 2272.

to the testimony, Agnes came out of the carriage wearing the fur coat to which Raphael Sieniawski had claimed his rights. From this testimony it can be concluded that Wlodek's behaviour in the matter of his marriage to Agnes was non-violent, peaceful and voluntary.

The case was transferred for the final judgement to the diet of the Kingdom in Piotrków, which was to be held in early 1493. In order to secure the transfer, another group of local noblemen were appointed as sureties for Wlodek of Bilka, with a high pledge of 1000 marks, established with the promise to present Wlodek for trial at the king's court during the above-mentioned diet.[22] The outcome of the trial at the king's court is unknown. However, it is noteworthy that it seems to have been the same diet, where the statute of King Jan Olbracht on the punishment of abductors and their female accomplices was instituted. With a certain degree of probability one can speculate that the case of Wlodek of Bilka and Agnes Cebrowska served as a legal precedent for the formulation of the above-mentioned law and that they were probably the first to be punished according to the norm of the statute.

This case shows that some noblewomen were able to resist the matrimonial plans of their relatives and the terms of marriage offered to them. Abduction, if consensual, can thus be included in the range of possible actions taken by women to oppose the will of their parents or husbands. Female disobedience in the face of familial and marital violence or injustice was not random during the period in question, as some other sources suggest. The records of the Lviv consistory court from the late fifteenth century, for example, make it clear that running away from one's husband was perhaps one of the most common ways for women to express their disappointment in marriage. The noblewoman Hedvig Szulikowska admitted in court that she had run away from her husband three times, staying with different noblemen each time, before being chased and brought back by her relatives or her husband.[23] Women like Szulikowska, when summoned to court, justified their flight and refusal to live with their husbands by claiming that they had been forced into marriage, sometimes as minors, by their male relatives, who used threats, violence and brutal coercion.[24]

The case of Agnes Cebrowska suggests that the abduction was both a means of establishing new martial alliances and of breaking the existing marriage ties. From this point of view, the abduction opened up possibilities for divorce, especially when the women's intentions coincided with the interests of their parental relatives. Such a scenario can be found in cases, where married noblewomen found themselves at the

---

22 Cf. AGZ, vol. 15, no. 2263–2265.
23 Cf. Rolny (ed.), Acta officii, see note 20, vol. 2, no. 1977.
24 Cf. Rolny (ed.), Acta officii, see note 20, vol. 1, Lwów 1927, no. 204; vol. 2, no. 1974. On intrafamilial violence against women and its regulation by ecclesiastical courts in the late medieval Kingdom of Poland, cf. Martha Brożyna, Not Just a Family Affair. Domestic Violence and the Ecclesiastical Courts in Late Medieval Poland, in: Isabel Davis, Miriam Müller and Sarah Rees Jones (eds.), Love, Marriage, and Family Ties in the Later Middle Ages, Turnhout 2001, 299–309.

centre of enmities between two related families. Abduction could be one of the steps in such hostile relations that marked the end of the alliance between two families and led to divorce. This is true, for example, of the case of the enmity between Protasiy of Bortnyky and Senko Lopatka of Ostalovychi, recorded in 1450 in the register of the Lviv castle court. The records start with Protasiy's complaint in which he accused Senko of assaulting his house and estate and causing great damage, amounting to the sum of eight hundred marks.[25] Senko vehemently denied these charges as slanderous and unjust. The court bailiff hesitated to confirm Protasiy's accusations, saying that he had not witnessed the violence but had only observed its traces.[26] Senko was then asked to present three groups of oath-helpers to prove his innocence.[27]

In response to Protasiy's accusations, Senko made his own charges, blaming his adversary for breaking the pledge of peace and defaming his honour.[28] An important issue that fuelled the enmity was Fedka, Protasiy's wife and Senko's daughter. Unfortunately, most of the details are missing. Only one record mentions that Protasiy accused Senko of forcibly taking his wife and actually abducting her. Senko denied the accusation. He claimed that he had legally regained his daughter, adding that he had received her from the hands of the captain (the phrase probably meant that a court decision had been made in his favour regarding his daughter: "recepi ipsam de manibus vestris").[29] The enmity and the accusation of abduction led to the formal divorce between Protasiy and Fedka. The divorce was officially proclaimed in the form of a judgment passed at the special session of the castle court presided over by the royal captain Peter of Sprowa and the Ruthenian Orthodox archpriest Vasyl. The judges also adjudicated a special divorce fine to be imposed on Fedka and her father.[30]

Nothing is known about Fedka's role in the enmity between her father and her husband, which ended in her divorce from Protasiy. Apparently, the abduction put her in a position where she had no choice. She was simply returned to her father, and the divorce was decided by the two male enemies. It is well known that marriage in premodern Europe was a crucial instrument of kinship politics, aimed at creating new and maintaining existing inter-familial alliances. In many cases, women were subject to the power and will of their parents and other male relatives who decided on their marriage. From this point of view, women were seen as important assets in the politics of patriarchy and kinship, with its permanent exchange of material goods, land, people and blood. It also gave a wife's family or kin group substantial rights to intervene in the

---

25 Cf. AGZ, vol. 14, no. 2258–2260.
26 Cf. AGZ, vol. 14, no. 2261.
27 Cf. AGZ, vol. 14, no. 2262–2265.
28 Cf. AGZ, vol. 14, no. 2267–2268.
29 Cf. AGZ, vol. 14, no. 2258.
30 Cf. AGZ, vol. 14, no. 2269–2270. On the practice of divorce among the Ruthenian nobility, cf. Kazimierz Sochaniewicz, Rozwody na Rusi halickiej w XV i XVI wieku [Divorces in Halych Rus' during the Fifteenth and Sixteenth Centuries], Lwów 1929.

family life of the spouses to prevent or pacify a crisis in the relationship. It also served as an important precondition for the use of force to assert the rights of the parental family and the rights of their wives in marriages. Official courts sometimes affirmed the right of the members of families and kin groups, to which married women initially belonged, to interfere in the couple's family life, especially to prevent violence against women. For this purpose, for example, sureties were provided by relatives of the spouses, sometimes with the participation of the local royal captain, to guarantee peaceful familial relations.[31]

However, women's capacity for action, though limited, should not be underestimated. Women, as weaker partners in marriage, were most interested in the constitution of the conjugal relationship as a semi-public space, including their right to appeal and settle intra-familial conflicts in public courts or through the intervention of relatives in the event of their husbands' misbehaviour. The enforcement of proper community norms of marital coexistence and the correction of spousal misbehaviour have always been considered one of the fundamental issues of the patriarchal familial politics. Besides ecclesiastical courts, the castle and land courts of fifteenth-century Galicia also played a significant role in providing the community with institutional sites for the control and regulation of intra-familial relations. For example, royal captains could intervene in private marital conflicts and preside over the court proceedings on the question of divorce, and the same fact of divorce could be recorded in the register of the secular court. It should be noted that cases of male marital misconduct came to the attention of the courts no less frequently than those of female misconduct. The intervention of secular courts and their officials in family life sometimes went so far as to force husbands to leave their concubines and return to their legitimate wives under threat of severe punishments.[32] Women could also use the power of their parents and relatives to oppose their husbands.[33]

Thus, the lack of clearly defined boundaries between private and public in intra-familial relations, together with the broad possibilities for communal surveillance and intervention by relatives in the lives of spouses, made abduction a legitimate step in the

---

31 Cf. for example the 1471 case of an agreement between Peter Grochowski and Stanislas Niewczas Drohojowski mediated by the Przemyśl captain Jacob Koniecpolski, concerning the conditions of cohabitation between Grochowski and his wife and sister of Drohojowski, Victoria, cf. AGZ, t. 17, Lwów 1901, no. 672. For another similar case, cf. AGZ, vol. 18, Lwów 1903, no. 4186.

32 Cf. for example the case and verdict against a male representative of the magnate family of the Prochnickis, tried at the Przemyśl castle court in 1470, who was forbidden to communicate with his concubine, a certain Apollonia from Przemyśl, under threat of confiscation of all his property and the death sentence for Apollonia, AGZ, vol. 17, Lwów 1901, no. 272–273, 302. In another case, the court prohibited a man from the village of Sanochok to run away from his wife ("fugere ab uxore"), cf. AGZ, vol. 11, Lwów 1886, no. 1564.

33 Cf. for example the dispute between Jacob Clus of Solowa and Demeter of Spyklosy from 1443, in which Katherine, Jacob's wife and Demeter's daughter took side of her father, AGZ, vol. 14, no. 840.

enmity between two related families. It is not surprising that some noblemen accused of abduction justified their actions in court by referring to their close familial ties to the abducted women. In 1474, for example, the bailiff Janusz testified before the Lviv castle court that he visited Romaniv, the estate of Andreas Romanowski, with two other nobles, he saw Milochna, the legitimate wife of another local noble Matthew Goldacz.[34] According to the record, Romanowski had previously been accused by Goldacz of kidnapping Milochna during a raid on the free road. When interrogated by the bailiff, Andreas Romanowski did not try to deny that he had taken her from Goldacz. He simply argued that he had kept her in the house because she was his sister.[35]

The record does not say whether Romanowski's raid and abduction of a female relative from her husband's house was based on some legal claim and was a way of enforcing the court's verdict. However, such raids could indeed be a form of self-help, and the court's decision was invoked to legitimise its use, especially when other means of its implementation failed. This aspect is highlighted, for example, in the record of the dispute between Jan Piasecki and the Humieniecki family in 1487.[36] It is a record of the testimony of three brothers – Jan, Jacob and Nicolas Humieniecki from Pukiv. The brothers described that they had raided the Piasecki estate in order to recover their cousin Sofia, who had been unjustly seized and held by Jan Piasecki. The report emphasises the non-violent and legitimate nature of the action. It specifically mentions that nothing was damaged or looted during the raid, and that no one was wounded or killed. Their only aim was to recover their sister, whom the nobleman had refused to hand over, ignoring special orders from the king and the captain. The legitimacy of their action was further supported by the presence of a bailiff and some nobles.

5. Enmity, female honour and slander

The existing accounts of the abduction of the married women are also instructive with regard to the ambiguous relationship between honour and slander in such accusations. The alleged kidnapping of two daughters of the late Lviv castellan Nicholas Gologorski stands out as an exceptional instance in this regard. These cases concern women of the highest social standing, members of the local aristocratic elite. The first case, known from a single record dating from 1470, involved the alleged abduction of Elisabeth Gologorska, the wife of Nicholas Grot of Ostrow, a tenant in Vavelnytsia and Holohory. The charges were brought against Michael of Jazlivets', a captain of Chervonohorod and a member of the Buczacki family, one of the most powerful clans of the

---

34 Cf. AGZ, vol. 19, no. 2912.
35 Cf. AGZ, vol. 19, 2912: "[…] quia dum per eundem ministerialem Ianvssium et terrigenas idem Andreas Romanowsky fuit interrogatus de eadem consorte stans ibidem noblis. Andreas Romanowsky vice secunda recognovit: ipsam habeo tanquam sororem in domo."
36 Cf. AGZ, vol. 15, no. 1893.

local magnates. The only record that has survived is the successful compurgation carried out by Nicholas and his oath-helpers in response to the accusation that they had attacked the estate and abducted Nicolas's wife.[37] The case of this alleged abduction can be seen as an episode in the history of Elisabeth's several marriages and divorces.[38] Elisabeth's marriage with Nicholas Grot of Ostrow was her second, concluded after her separation from Nicholas Odrowąż, the son of the Lviv castellan Paul Odrowąż of Sprowa and representative of another powerful family in the region. It is possible that between her two marriages to Nicholas Odrowąż and Nicholas Grot, Elisabeth was also engaged or married to Nicholas Odrowąż's cousin, the palatine of Rus', Andrzej Odrowąż of Sprowa. It is noteworthy that after her abduction, Elisabeth also divorced Nicholas of Ostrow. The divorce could be a clue that gives some weight to the accusations against Michael of Jazlivets'.

The alleged abduction of Elisabeth's sister Catherine cast doubt on the veracity of such claims. In 1471, a member of the local magnate family, Andreas of Sienno, filed a lawsuit in the Lviv castle court against Jan, the son of the Zhydachiv nobleman Iuchno Nagwasdan.[39] Andreas of Sienno claimed that Jan Nagwasdan was guilty of kidnapping his wife (her name was not mentioned in the records). The record states that after seeing his wife abducted by Jan, Andreas arranged a chase, followed the assailant on his last tracks and captured him with some material evidence of his crime (*cum facie*). The report does not specify what kind of evidence Andreas discovered when he captured Jan. It is also silent on what happened to Andreas' wife after the abduction.

The charges made by Andreas of Sienno, as well as the course of events, were vigorously contested by the father of the alleged kidnapper, Yuchno Nagwasdan. Yuchno Nagwasdan claimed that, when his son was captured, he refused to acknowledge ownership of all the items that were, presented as evidence of his crime. Jan Nagwasdan made his protest in the presence of all the inhabitants of the village where he had been captured. In addition, in all the other villages and towns through which Jan had been carried in captivity by the servants of Andreas of Sienno, he publicly protested the illegality of his captivation before the local nobles and commoners who had come to witness the event. The purpose of such protests was to show the onlookers the injustice of his capture and to claim that no evidence of his guilt had been found by Siennowski's familiars during his imprisonment. Yuchno Nagwasdan further specified that, in response to his son's protests, Siennowski's familiars failed to show witnesses the evidence on which Jan had been arrested. All the people, mentioned in Yuchno Nagwasdan's

---

37 Cf. AGZ, vol. 15, no. 3517 (termini regales).
38 Cf. Renata Trawka, Skarb i dziewczyna. O fortunie kasztelana halickiego Mikołaja Gologórskiego i jego córki Elżbiety [A Treasure and a Girl. On the Fortune of the Halych Castellan Nicholas Gologorski and His Daughter Elisabeth], in: Przegląd Historyczny [Historical Overview], t. CXIII, z. 3 (2022), 413–416.
39 Cf. AGZ, vol. 15, no. 786.

speech as witnesses to his son's arrest and protests came to the court and testified to the veracity of Yuchno's account.

The record ends with a formal verdict. Based on the witnesses' testimonies, the judges declared Jan Nagwasdan innocent of the alleged crime and restored his honour. It is noteworthy that Andreas of Sienno did not suffer any penalty for his violent behaviour and his legal claim. It should be added that after the compurgation, Jan Nagwasdan summoned Andreas of Sienno and his wife Katherine of Gologory to court.[40] One can speculate that the charges aimed to avenge the dishonour that Jan had suffered during his capture and trial. Unfortunately, the records do not specify the factual content of Nagwasdan's claims.

In the legal and social contexts of fifteenth-century Galicia, abduction emerges as a social drama in which women were objects of both sexual desire and control, and in which fears and obsessions about gender honour and patriarchal power were revealed. The daily experience and social identity of the local nobility were shaped by the ubiquity of violence, and noblemen competed for women in the same way as they competed for land, dependent peasants and power. Success or failure in such a competition was one of the key criteria by which a noble's honour and status were determined and measured. Legal accounts of abduction often fit into the widespread pattern of the noble enmities in fifteenth-century Galicia, based on the widespread use of violence. Organised raids on opponents' estates, whether or not backed by legal claims, were regularly used as occasions for the abduction of women and for the plundering goods and the threatening or killing of dependent peasants. From this perspective, the abduction of women was an important manifestation of the contemporary masculine culture of the local nobility, with its propensity for enmity and violence.

6. Conclusion

The abduction of women was one of those areas of contemporary gender and family relations whose meanings and functions defied a single definitive explanation. To examine cases of abduction is to deal with aspects and meanings of local patriarchy and social gender relations that were often both elusive and affirmative, real and imagined. On the one hand, they reveal violent aspects and contexts of patriarchy and can be seen in context of other forms of gendered violence, such as abusive guardianship of unmarried women, disputes over women's rights to patrimonial property, violent dispossessions of widows of their dowry, etc. On the other hand, however, cases of abduction not only resulted in the re-establishment of patriarchal hierarchies but also pointed to the possible spaces of action within which women's roles were reordered and

---

40 Cf. AGZ, vol. 15, no. 829–830.

women's agency expanded. They reveal the potential of women to challenge the power of their male guardians, to pursue their own interests in family politics or act as self-assertive individuals. For example, alternative versions of the events leading up to the abduction, when presented in court, offer a picture of more complex relationships, suggesting the possibility of alliances between abductor and abducted noblewomen. The fact that some cases of abduction led to divorce could also suggest the role of this practice in escalating crises in marital relationships and concealing the desire of both partners to separate.

A comparatively large number of failed abduction cases not only leaves an impression of great uncertainty about the realities and imageries of gendered violence, but also suggests the existence of conflicting concepts of honour, which were often played out in an ambiguous and instrumentalised manner.[41] Disputes over abduction show that local courts functioned primarily as forums where honour was displayed, performed, defended and challenged by noblemen. Gaining the upper hand over an opponent in enmity and legal disputes was a way of demonstrating and asserting one's reputation and honour within the community of peers. Such public and performative dimensions of honour could have little in common with the notion of honour as a code of internalised moral convictions. Instead, the games of honour, which were integral part of the enmity and litigation, allowed for a considerable degree of moral and ethical ambivalence and simulation. In other words, they revealed inherent conflicts between *Schein* and *Sein* (between appearance and being) in the public behaviour and public display of noble identity.

It is impossible to be sure, for example, whether in some cases fathers and husbands did not act as unscrupulous slanderers who were prepared to pursue legal action to the end at any cost, including the damage to the honour of their daughters and wives. Accusations, if not proven, raised the suspicion of slander and thus undermined their trustworthiness and reputation, as well as the women's honour. Thus, the enmities that erupted over accusations of abduction demonstrate disruptive power of hostile relationships in contemporary society, which caused considerable damage to the reputations of all parties involved in such disputes. From this point of view, honour as a fundamental value of the noble ethos and identity was framed, manipulated and constantly re-assessed in the contexts of the developed and sophisticated culture of dispute, with highly shifting boundaries between truth and slander, perjury and claims to honour. Collective legal action, social ties and public rituals played a key role in re-

---

41 On conflicting concepts of honour and their ambiguous meanings in early modern European societies, cf. Sibylle Backmann and Hans-Jörg Künst, Einführung, in: Sibylle Backmann, Hans-Jörg Künst, Sabine Ullmann and Ann B. Tlusty (eds.), Ehrkonzepte in der Frühen Neuzeit. Identität und Abgrenzungen, Berlin 1998, esp. 15; Sylvia Kesper-Biermann, Ulrike Ludwig and Alexandra Ortmann, Ehre und Recht. Zur Einleitung, in: eadem (eds.), Ehre und Recht. Ehrkonzepte, Ehrverletzungen und Ehrverteidigungen vom späten Mittelalter bis zur Moderne, Magdeburg 2011, 3–16.

affirming the boundaries of honour in the context of such transgressions. Various social and political networks and actors were mobilised to 'repair' a damaged reputation by supporting the person's claims to honour and re-establishing his/her place in the 'community of honour' as an essential precondition for the belonging to the social group.

Nataliia Starchenko

"Treacherous" Women or Opportunistic Men. Volhynian Gentry Women Accused of Murdering Their Husbands in the Eastern Region of the Early Modern Polish-Lithuanian Commonwealth

The anonymous author of a political treatise from the 1st Interregnum in the Polish-Lithuanian Commonwealth, which began with the death of Sigismund II Augustus on 12 August 1572, made several serious proposals regarding the reforms in the country, before adding that it was also necessary "to make sure that women are not tolerated in the diet (*sejm*), where *sacrosanctus consilii locus*".[1] This phrase, seemingly incongruous with the pathos of the rest of the treatise, seemed to be indicative of certain social anxieties. Shortly before the interregnum, the brilliant author Andrzej Frycz Modrzewski, in his treatise on the improvement of the Polish-Lithuanian Commonwealth, mentioned women's informal influence over men. He castigated the officials who turned to their wives for advice on public matters, noting that this relegates the leadership over other men to women.[2] The era's phobia of the seeming subversion of the traditional gender hierarchy can be seen in a number of satirical texts that demanded women to be removed from the public sphere and consigned to domestic spaces. Some authors presented a "world turned upside down" where women engaged in politics could be elected to the diet and wrote instructions for reforming the state or, more precisely, discussed the "disciplining" of men.[3]

---

1 Jan Czubek (ed.), Pisma polityczne z czasów pierwszego bezkrólewia [Political Writings from the Period of the 1st Interregnum], Kraków 1906, 166.
2 Cf. Andrzej Frycz Modrzewski, O poprawie Rzeczypospolitej księgi czwore [On the Improvement of the Republic of Poland, book four; original title: De Republica emendanda libri quinque], ed. by Mirosław Korolko, Piotrków Trybunalski 2003, 170.
3 Cf. [Andrzej Glaber z Kobylina?], Senatulus to jest sejm niewieści, który niegdy w Rzymie dzierżan był od trzech stanów ich, od małżonek, wdów i (panien) [Senatulus or the Diet of Women that Was Once Upon a Time Held in Rome for Representatives of Their Three Ranks, That Is, Married Women, Widows and Maidens], Kraków 1543; Marcin Bielski, Sejm niewieści [Diet of Women], in: Jerzy Starnawski (ed.), Komedyja Justyna i Konstancyjej [A Comedy of Justin and Constance], Kraków 2001; Seym białogłowski [Diet of the Fair Sex], in: Karol Badecki (ed.), Polska satyra mieszczańska. Nowiny sowiźrzalskie [Polish Bourgeois Satire. Jesters' News], Biblioteka Pisarzów Polskich, Kraków 1950, 61–83; Sejm Panieński albo Rozmowa o biesiadach Mięsopustnych tudziesz o Obyczajach Młodzianów [The Diet of Maidens or a Treatise on Palm Week Conversations on the Customs of Young People], Kraków 1697; Monika Szczot, Literacka satyra obyczajowa czy polityczny program reform? Staropolskie 'sejmy' kobiet i ich antyczne wzorce [Literary Satire of Manners

Male fears of women's overwhelming subjectivity and parity with men seem to have left no room for phobias of another level: fear of a wife as a threat in the husband's own home. Popular literature of the Polish-Lithuanian Commonwealth, unlike the English literature of the time, does not feature texts dealing with mariticide. As Frances Dolan has noted, texts of the period give the impression that English husbands lived in pervasive fear of an attack by the secret enemy in their own homes.[4]

It might seem that violence was a legitimate or quasi-legitimate instrument of maintaining the legal and cultural patriarchal hierarchy in familial relations.[5] A husband's dominance over his wife, be it real or symbolic, not only dictated a gendered mode of behaviour for each spouse but also modes of murder allegedly typical of each gender and tropes for describing that murder. It was traditionally believed that when a husband killed his wife, it was usually the unintended result of using excessive force in the process of quasi-legitimate "disciplinary" practices. The lack of intent was usually proven by a history of violence against the wife which, up to a certain point, had milder consequences. The murder of a husband by a wife, on the other hand, was associated with a different narrative: a physically weaker woman at the mercy of a stronger partner does not openly resist his violence but nurtures resentment and concocts plans of cruel revenge. The murder of a husband is then interpreted as a way of breaking free from the patriarchal power hierarchy and achieving agency through transgression and violence. Murder was a wife's way of asserting her right to change the situation, a violation of the established cultural construct of a woman as a passive creature incapable of taking active steps.[6] In many cases, however, the narrative of a murderous wife had little to do with reality, being modelled on literary topoi or societal expectations rather than on fact. A study of such cases in the early modern period shines the light both on groundless

---

or a Program for Political Reforms? Old Polish 'Diets' of Women and Their Models from Antiquity], in: Monika Anna Kubiaczyk and Filip Kubiaczyk (ed.), Płeć i władza w kontekstach historycznych i współczesnych [Gender and Power in Historical and Contemporary Contexts], Gniezno 2014, 147–57; Barbara Obtutowicz, Świat 'na opak' – ironia, przestroga, rzeczywistość. Literackie wyobrażenie kobiet aspirujących do kierowania państwem [The World Turned Inside Out: Irony, Warning, Reality. Women Aspiring to Run the State in the Literary Imagination], in: Annales Academiae Paedagogicae Cracoviensis, Folia 28, Studia Historica IV (2005), 68–83.

4 Frances Dolan, Dangerous Familiars. Representations of Domestic Crime in England, 1550–1700, Ithaca 1994, 25–26.

5 For an overview of topics related to domestic violence cf. Marianna Muravyeva, 'A King in His Own Household'. Domestic Discipline and Family Violence in Early Modern Europe Reconsidered, in: The History of Family, 18, 3, (2013), 227–237. On rethinking the influence of the so-called "civilisational approach" to marital violence and patriarchal dominance cf. Joanne Baylie and Loreen Giese, Marital Cruelty. Reconsidering Lay Attitudes in England, c. 1580 to 1850, in: ibid., 289–305; Julie Hardwick, Early Modern Perspectives on the Long History of Domestic Violence: The Case of Seventeenth-Century France, in: Journal of Modern History, 78, 1 (2006), 1–36.

6 For an analysis of typical descriptions of wives murdering their husbands in popular early modern English literature cf. the relevant chapter in: Frances Dolan, Dangerous Familiars, see note 4, 20–58; idem, Home Rebels and House-Traitors: Murderous Wives in Early Modern England, in: Yale Journal of Law and the Humanities, 4, 1 (1992), 1–31.

accusations and on a variety of reasons and circumstances for the murders. In essence, this analysis encourages us to discard the strict binary opposition between male and female violence and focus instead on a broad spectrum of similarities.[7]

Therefore, based on court records of the Volhynian voivodeship, I will analyse the following questions: who accused the wives; what was the rhetoric of such accusations; did the descriptions contain stereotypical details; could these accusations be described as gender-motivated? I will highlight the question of the wives' subjugation to their husbands and the resources that changed the balance of power in the family. The majority of these accounts are highly fragmentary and represented by accusations or passing mentions of such accusations, so they will serve as a context for the court case against Nastasia of the Oshchovsky family, accused of killing her husband, Borys Okhlopovsky. This case features every stage of the court trial and attendant extra-judicial acts: an accusation, a trial, manipulation of public opinion, appeals to the royal court, a decree and the woman being acquitted of charges after swearing an oath with sworn witnesses. The trial of Nastasia Okhlopovska is indicative not only of relations within gentry (*szlachta*) families in the Volhynian Voivoideship but also of the fact that marital relations were integrated into a wide circle of para-familial relations.

The first part of the article focuses on the discourse about women in the context of murder accusations, which is what we are dealing with when working with narratives from court records. They are not so much depictions of reality as accounts of "what someone thought should happen, hoped would happen, wanted to pretend had happened – and yet sometimes had not happened at all, or at least not as recorded in the document".[8] And yet the authors sought to influence reality through these texts, and did indeed do so by adopting the instruments provided by the community. Essentially, the tropes used to describe a murder always mobilise the socio-cultural resources of the

---

7 Cf. Trevor Dean, Domestic Violence in Late-Medieval Bologna, in: Renaissance Studies, 18, 4 (2004), 529–530; idem, Theft and Gender in Late Medieval Bologna, in: Gender and History, 20, 2 (2008), 412. For an analysis of possible factors that curbed violence in *szlachta* families of the Volhynian voivodeship cf. Nataliia Starchenko, Dzherela svidchat: kilka zauvah pro doslidzhennia stanovyshcha shliakhtianky v rannomodernomu sotsiumi Volyni [Sources Testify. Several Notes Towards Studying the Status of *Szlachta* Women in the Early Modern Society in Volhynia], in: Ukrainskyi arkheohrafichnyi shchorichnyk. Nova seriia [Ukrainian Archaeographical Annual. The New Series], 21, 19–20 (2016), 242–247.

8 Shannon McSheffrey, Detective Fiction in the Archives. Court Records and the Uses of Law in Late Medieval England, in: History Workshop Journal, 65, 1 (2008), 65–78. Cf. also my foreword Shukaiuchy tochku opertia: doslidnyk mizh dzherelom yak nepevnym opovidachem ta shliakhetskymy konventsiiamy [Finding a Fulcrum. A Scholar between a Source Text as an Unreliable Narrator and *Szlachta* Conventions] to my publication of sources: Nataliia Starchenko, Stratehii ta rytualy konfliktu: shliakhetskyi sotsium Volyni zlamy XVI i XVII st. Dzherela ta interpretatsii [Strategies and Rituals of Conflict. *Szlachta* Society in Volhynia at the Turn of the 16th–17th Century. Sources and interpretations], Kyiv 2020, 6–72.

time and space.⁹ The trial of Nastasiia Okhlopovska provides fertile ground for analysing the performativity of murder accusations. In constructing my text, I embrace the suggestions of microhistorians by introducing explanations through storytelling. Additionally, my conclusions draw on broader explanations of the status of *szlachta* women in the eastern parts of the Polish-Lithuanian Commonwealth. Nevertheless, the main goal of this article is to offer a discursive analysis of judicial narratives about women in liminal situations, without necessarily providing a broader overview of the status of women.

Volhynia was one of the three Ukrainian voivodeships that the king annexed from the Grand Duchy of Lithuania to the Crown of Poland with the Union of Lublin in 1569. The residents of these lands enjoyed fairly extensive autonomy based on the royal privilege granted by the king. They were guaranteed the inviolability of their borders, the status of the Ruthenian (Old Ukrainian) language as the language of courts and the administration, the preservation of the judiciary based on the Second Statute of Lithuania, equality between Catholics and Orthodox Christians (with the latter being the majority of the local population), etc. Volhynia was the informal political centre of the three Ukrainian voivodeships integrated into the Crown of Poland, and the processes typical of early modern Ukrainian nation-building were especially prominent there. The total territory of the three voivodeships was equivalent to half of the Grand Duchy of Lithuania, or, from 1569, half of the Crown of Poland.

1. An enemy in ones bed?

It is believed that the majority of mariticides are preceded by a lengthy history of family violence against the wife. The authors of the Second Statute of Lithuania (1566) offered judges and the community a rigorous narrative scheme to describe mariticides from the beginning to their possible conclusion: "When out of hatred or enmity either side, be it the husband or the wife, kills, murders or poisons the other during a quarrel for whatever reason"[10] is a beginning of a possible story that allowed a spouse of either sex to be suspected in the case of a murder under unclear circumstances. Conflicted coexistence was framed as a motive for the crime and as intent to kill. The victim's sons or relatives were tasked with conducting the case in court. If, for whatever reason, relatives failed to file a lawsuit, court officials could also initiate an investigation. In this case, they were expected to investigate, interrogate the neighbours and other members of the community who might have been familiar with the circumstances of the crime,

---

9 Cf. K.J. Kesselring, Bodies of Evidence: Sex and Murder (or Gender and Homicide) in Early Modern England, c.1500–1680, in: Gender & History, 27, 2 (2015), 245–262.
10 Statut Velykoho kniazivstva Lytovskoho 1566 [Statute of the Grand Duchy of Lithuania, 1566], in: S. Kivalov, P. Muzychenko and A. Pankov (eds.), Statuty Velykoho kniazivstva Lytovskoho u 3-kh tomakh [Statutes of the Grand Duchy of Lithuania in 3 volumes], vol. II, Odesa 2003, 172.

and choose from among them the seven trustworthy gentry men who would point out the murderer under oath.[11] Guilt, therefore, had to be proven, and each case could turn out not to be as straightforward as the conclusion of the story (postulated at the beginning of the legal norm) might have suggested. The adversarial nature of the judiciary at the time dictated that a crime should be understood primarily as a private "offence" against the victim; therefore, all the pre-trial procedures were relegated to the injured party, for without a complaint, there was no crime. Court officials were expected to intervene only if the "common peace" was threatened; their intervention meant that the community and the state at large stood by the accuser alongside the injured party. This demonstrates that mariticide was seen as a socially threatening crime. Similarly to the murder of one's parents, the murder of a spouse was punishable by "dishonourable" death: first, the offender was to be driven around the market while their flesh was torn with pincers, and then they were to be placed into a leather sack with a dog, a hen, a snake and a cat, and drowned in the deepest part of a body of water. The murderer's accomplices were to be punished in a similar way.[12]

It might seem that the legal norm pertained to both spouses, regardless of gender. However, it is worth repeating that covert actions were usually associated with the suspect's subjugated status, which is why it was usually the wife who fell victim to accusations if the husband died under unclear or suspicious circumstances.[13]

That said, court records contain a case of an attempt by a newcomer to Volhynia, Yan Napolsky, who had no property of his own, to treacherously do away with his wife, Fedora of the Hulevych family, who owned the Brany manor after the death of her first husband. Napolsky's attempts to shift the power balance in his favour took the form typical for the resistance of a dependent: he acted by stealth, stooped to stealing documents (theft was considered to be a disgraceful offence) and tried to poison his wife.[14] And yet, let us focus on the eight cases that I discovered in court records where the wife was accused either of attempting to kill her husband (two cases) or of realising this insidious intention (six cases). The earliest case dates back to 1573 and the latest to 1621. Two of these cases resulted in a conviction, which might serve as proof of the woman's guilt.[15] Nevertheless, it remains unclear whether the verdict was carried out or

---

11 Cf. Statut Velykoho kniazivstva Lytovskoho 1566, see note 10, chapter 11, article 16.
12 Statut Velykoho kniazivstva Lytovskoho 1566, see note 10, chapter 11, article 16, 175.
13 It should be noted that, under English law, the wife's murder by the husband was treated as murder, whereas the husband's murder by the wife was treated as treason, cf. Frances Dolan, Home Rebels, see note 6, 5.
14 Cf. Central State Historical Archive in Kyiv (henceforward TsDIAK), 25/1, vol. 34, fol. 183–185^v, 186–188^v).
15 Cf. the court trial of Kateryna Kharlenska, accused of murdering her husband Shchasny Kharlensky: Arkhiv Iugo-Zapadnoi Rossii, izdavaemyi Vremennoi komissiei dlia razbora drevnikh aktov [Archive of South-Western Russia published by the Temporary Commission for Processing Ancient Records] (henceforth AYuZR), ch. 8, t. III, 494–520; cf. also the trial of Kateryna, of the Kolia-

whether, as was usually the case, the families reconciled. All cases share a number of common features, which I will discuss in more detail.[16]

The death of the husband or the accusation of attempted murder against the wife were usually preceded by a family conflict, either recorded in the lawsuit or inferred from circumstantial evidence. However, not a single case mentions physical violence by the husband against the wife. This does not mean that violence was never a part of family life, but it is clear that the community did not perceive it as a legitimate means of disciplining a wife. None of the cases included an attempt by the husband or his relatives to demonstrate their control over the wife. The husband is usually described as an "unwary" person who did not suspect any ill intent, was not known to resort to any behaviour that could sally the *szlachta's* dignity, and spared no effort to maintain peace in the family. It was the wife who was usually described as the cause of all discontent: "having lived with her husband in wickedness for a long while"/"having forgotten fear of God and not wishing to live [with him] courteously, the way other wives live with their husbands",[17] she demonstrated her unprovoked "vitriol and hatred" for her husband in various ways. Moreover, in some cases she would deliberately leave the family home with her belongings without the husband's permission and stay with her parents and/or brothers for long periods of time. For example, in response to her husband's repeated pleas for her to return to the family home, Kateryna Kharlenska resorted to a ritual typical of chivalric culture: she publicly threatened revenge.[18] In essence, the accused wives were allegedly planning to "wickedly and disgracefully" murder their husbands. This was qualified as "treason" because the wife's actions "undermined and broke the trust" sealed by marital vows.

It might seem that the accusations against wives for murdering their husbands contain gender-motivated elements, but a comparison with similar accusations against *szlachta* men for criminal (premeditated) murder demonstrates that these accusations

---

novsky family, and her brothers, accused of murdering Mykhailo Malynovsky (TsDIAK, f25/1, vol. 50, fol. 387ᵛ–389ᵛ; vol. 57, fol. 58–60; 28/1, vol. 34, fol. 65–65ᵛ).

16 Cf. the case of Stepan Khmara, murdered by his nephew Andrii Khmara, who tried to accuse his uncle's wife (TsDIAK, 25/1, vol. 1, fol. 215–224ᵛ); Pavlo Zhlichynsky accusing his wife, Hanna Montovtivna, of attempting to poison him, in order to take hold of his wife's possessions: Zhizn kniazia Andreia Mikhailovicha Kurbskogo v Litve i na Volyni [The Life of Prince Andrej Mikhailovich Kurbski in Lithuania and Volhynia], vol. I, Kyiv 1849, 182–189; TsDIAK, 26/1, vol. 9, fol. 831ᵛ–833; AYuZR, ch. 8, t. III, 469–473; TsDIAK, 25/1, vol. 46, fol. 58–58ᵛ; Prince Lev Voronetsky's testament mentions that his wife attempted to poison and divorce him (TsDIAK, 25/1, vol. 124, fol. 668ᵛ–671); the court record mentions that Yan Rusetsky was murdered, allegedly at the instigation of his wife Marusha (TsDIAK, 25/1, vol. 70, fol. 680–681; 873–874); Nastasia Puzovska was accused of murdering her husband Karpo Puzovsky. The case ended in a reconciliation and Puzovsky's property being handed over and rented to his brothers, the accusers (AYuZR. ch. 8, t. III, 478–484; TsDIAK, 28/1, vol. 34, fol. 186ᵛ); an analysis of accusations against Nastasia Okhlopovska will follow in the next section.

17 TsDIAK, 25/1, vol. 124, fol. 669ᵛ.

18 Cf. AYuZR, ch. 8, t. III, 497–498.

were identical. The common elements include the portrayal of the victim as a peaceful and honest person that had no reason to expect hostility; the murderer acted treacherously, with the intent to kill, resorting to deception and engaging accomplices. Therefore, it seems likely that what the scholars are dealing with are scribal clichés common to all accusations in grave crimes. The wife might be treacherous, but no more so than a male *szlachta* enemy.

In three cases, the accused allegedly used poison. The accusation of poisoning is especially vivid in the complaint filed by the brothers of Shchasny Kharlensky against his wife, Kateryna Monvydivna, who was also accused of using magic to harm her husband.[19] While the use of poison or magic was perceived as a feminine-coded practice, it was also a social marker of the person's subjugated status. Male servants might also have used these instruments.[20]

Notably, based on these accusations, the wives appear as individuals with their own agency, free to choose where and with whom they would rather live, and acting with a sense of purpose. And yet, such portrayals might be not descriptive of the facts, but rather tropes that underline the unfeminine behaviour and disregard for the norms aimed at maintaining the harmonious coexistence of the couple. Complaints rarely mention the wife undermining the standard patriarchal model of relationships, except for the fact that she may have left the home for prolonged periods of time without her husband's permission. However, the husband's authority may have overlapped and clashed with the power of other men: the wife's relatives. The wives' accomplices in their criminal plans, real or not, included their brothers or fathers, who supported the women in conflicts, sheltered them for long periods of time, gave them advice and stood up in their defence in and out of court after the accusations had been made. The sphere of marital relations included the wider family circle, so that the husband who sought to "discipline" his wife in conflicts did not have to face her, but her representatives and protectors, who were equal to him in terms of gender status. Therefore, the husband's traditional power over his wife was affirmed or restored through competition and compromise with other men who might be physically stronger, have a greater symbolic capital or better access to the power resources.

Servants were traditionally seen as instruments in the hands of the treacherous wife, appearing as her allies in family conflicts. In old literature, this narrative had to confirm the belief that the wife was indeed treacherous and willing to resort to seduction and bribery. The complainants constructed their narrative (more or less) according to certain schemes and with the help of established clichés.[21] And yet it is clear that this motif was not just a rhetorical trope: spouses could compete for the allegiance of dependent members of the household. Despite their dependent status, servants could

---

19 Cf. AYuZR, ch. 8, t. III, 497.
20 Cf. for example TsDIAK, 25/1, vol. 27, fol. 102–105.
21 Cf. Dean, Domestic Violence, see note 7, 533 f.

support one spouse in conflict and make the other's life a living hell. The balance of power in the family may have been predetermined by social beliefs and stereotypes, but the spouses' dispositions could change according to individual needs, opportunities and compromises as their relationships evolved or as a result of open confrontation with unpredictable results. Obviously, gender status was not stable either: the woman's status depended on the legal framework, her material possessions, whether she belonged to a certain estate and whether she could get a divorce if her marital choice turned out to be unsuccessful.

Marital conflicts could be particularly dramatic because of the close ties between husband and wife, the deep emotional involvement of each side in the relationship and the view of marital coexistence as a life project that ended in disaster. In times of marital difficulties, negotiations between the husband and his wife's relatives and friends were the first measure to "correct" the husband's behaviour. Court files or other documents describing family conflicts often mention the involvement of similar support groups in mending marital relations. For example, when Ivan Boloban-Osekrovskyi tried to normalise his relations with his wife, Hanna of the Stakorsky family, who had thrown him out of her estate, "forgetting her vows to affirm the marital bond" and appropriating his possession, he sent his friends to her to find out the reasons for her behaviour and try to persuade her to return to marital life.[22] Prince Andrii Ostrozhetskyi also used his friends as intermediaries in his negotiations with his wife. The woman had left home and taken refuge with her mother after being beaten by her husband. When asked by her husband's friends if she would return to her marital home, Nastasia answered: "I will come back when I want to."[23]

However, if the husband systematically abused the wife who, for whatever reason, was deprived of her relatives' support, or if this support proved ineffective, family relations could indeed turn into a war in which the wife was the less powerful party.

Charges against the wife for the murder of her husband, where the wife's guilt was not to be proved, are much more common than those where the wife was reasonably suspected of criminal intent (six to two). The evidence was based on "witness accounts" from neighbours or friends who, at most, might have known of the deceased's family problems. They had to back up this ambiguous knowledge with an oath, by swearing on God's name. Given that the adversarial judicial system did not entail investigations, accusing the wife became a useful tool in the hands of the relatives of the deceased to retaliate or manipulate the wife and to get a better share of the inheritance. The reward could be custody of the deceased's property and children, or depriving the widow of the portion of the estate that the husband had given her during their married life or left her in his testament. These were probably the motives for many of the accusations of

---

22 AYuZR, ch. 8, t. III, 451–452.
23 Almost every scholar of domestic violence in early modern Europe emphasises this fact. Cf. for example Hardwick, Early Modern Perspectives, see note 5, 22.

murder against the wives. The case study I propose for a more in-depth analysis seems to be a vivid example of this phenomenon. It also highlights how accusations were constructed and how shaky the grounds for accusations could be. Therefore, it provides a good basis for analysing another resource on which the accusers relied: the peculiarities of the court system, whose function differed from finding the guilty party and punishing them according to the law.

2. An accident or a treacherous knife

On 10 August 1583, Yona Okhlopovsky's lawsuit was read in the Lutsk court: Yona accused Nastasia Mykhailivna of the Oshchovsky family of murdering her husband, Borys Okhlopovsky, cousin to Yona, Kostiantyn and Sava Okhlopovsky. The accusation had all the typical elements: the wife was portrayed as the cause of the couple's unhappy marriage; she allegedly harboured no sympathy for her husband and was determined to get a divorce; she had made up her mind, "secretly" planned a "shameful" murder of her husband and was waiting for the right circumstances.[24] Nastasia took all her belongings to her brothers and lived with them for a long time. On 18 March 1582, she "shamefully, godlessly and treacherously"[25] stabbed Borys in the throat with a knife, mortally wounding him. Nastasia had persuaded her servants "through weird and evil means"[26] to assist her in murdering her husband: one had held a candle while others stood guard. According to the accusation, Borys "shouted" that it was "treason"[27] in his own home that had pushed him off the mortal coil moments before his death. The plaintiff's father, Yakym Okhlopovsky, who died before the trial began, had allegedly established that Nastasia had killed her husband, but refused to accuse her, a gentry woman, without any firm evidence. At Borys's funeral, he asked her to delay the burial and thoroughly interrogate as many people as possible about the circumstances of his death. Despite his advice, Nastasia refused to give her permission for the "investigation"[28] and left the cemetery, leaving Borys's body behind. Meanwhile, her drunken brothers, Vasyl and Mykyta, had nearly killed Yakym. So, "moved by pity",[29] he testified over the body in the presence of a court usher that Borys had been killed and lodged a lawsuit with the castle court. The Okhlopovsky brothers announced in various castles that held courts that it was Nastasia who was guilty of the murder. Nastasia's brothers were summoned to court along with her.

---

24 AYuZR, ch. 8, t. III, 368.
25 AYuZR, ch. 8, t. III, 369.
26 AYuZR, ch. 8, t. III, 368.
27 AYuZR, ch. 8, t. III, 369.
28 AYuZR, ch. 8, t. III, 370.
29 AYuZR, ch. 8, t. III, 370.

The accusers submitted to the court the testimony of the ushers: the testimony of Stanislav Kolomyisky, who examined the wounded Borys Okhlopovsky, in Lutsk castle court of 10 April 1582, and later testimonies from after Borys's death in the Lutsk, Volodymyr and Kremenets castles. The scribe summarised these testimonies in a few important facts: while her husband was still alive, Nastasia refused to "seize" the servants for "interrogation"[30]; after Borys's death, she refused to postpone the funeral and once again forbade the interrogation of the servants although she had promised to make them available for questioning in court.[31] Appended to the lawsuit were the testimonies of Borys's three sisters, which pointed to servants as the perpetrators, and two letters from the four persons who had allegedly heard Borys say that someone had stabbed him with a knife in his own home while only his family and domestic staff were present. To sum up, Yona Okhlopovsky claimed that all the appended testimonies pointed to the widow as the culprit: she was not interested in an investigation, did not tell her neighbours how Borys had been wounded and did not publicly announce her husband's murder.

Nastasia was represented in court by two lawyers (Matej Stempkovsky and Ivan Porvanetsky), who told a different story. She was not at home when Borys was wounded: her husband had sent her to his sister, and the women had gone to a christening at Mrs. Invalska's in Myrkov; Nastasia did not return home until late at night. In his wife's absence, Borys went to church on that Sunday morning, invited the priest home after the service, got drunk with him and began looking for an adventure. After some protestations, the priest persuaded him to go to bed. When the priest left, Borys took his wife's possessions out of a chest and began hacking at them, eventually breaking his sabre. Then he took a loaded gun, reloaded it and fired a shot. The shock wave was so strong that Borys fell and hit his chest so hard that a bump appeared on the right side of his chest. He also broke a bone in his shoulder and was wounded in the neck, possibly by a splinter from the rifle butt. He bandaged his neck and went to bed. When Nastasia returned home and asked what had happened, Borys said that he did not know, but was not feeling well and wanted to be left alone. Realising that the matter was serious, Nastasia sent her servant Fedir to find a barber surgeon in the town of Horokhiv. As morning approached, she also sent for her brothers, who, seeing that the barber surgeon was not helping, had sent a messenger to Svyniukhy to get a more experienced "professional". A barber surgeon from Svyniukhy attended to the man until he died. That Monday, Borys had sent for his relatives, and on Tuesday, in the presence of many witnesses, he had drawn up a will in which he had made no mention of murder and left his possessions to his wife.

---

30 AYuZR, ch. 8, t. III, 372.
31 Volodymyr court records note that Nastasia had not allowed her servants to be interrogated without her brothers present. The Oshchovsky brothers stated that the Okhlopovsky family could take them to court, but until then they would not allow an interrogation (TsDIAK, 28/1, vol. 15, fol. 216–217ᵛ).

The lawyers proceeded to present their own account of the events at the cemetery during the funeral: while the grave was being dug, Yona Okhlopovsky and Kuzma Porvanetsky with their accomplices drew their sabres, chased away priests and mourners and seized the hearse containing the dead body (the defendants filed a complaint about this with the court of the land gentry). The three priests who were present at the funeral testified at the castle court that Yona Okhlopovsky with accomplices had seized the body on 29 April. In addition, Nastasia's lawyers presented the testament, certified and sealed by Yona himself and by the deceased's brothers-in-law, Kuzma and Klym Porvanetsky. They also presented the written testimony of the Svyniukhy barber surgeon Mykolaj, who stayed at Borys's bedside for almost three weeks and never once heard the wounded man complain of a treacherous attack. Borys died after the barber surgeon tried to drain the pus from the lump on his chest, but after making an incision, the pus poured into his abdominal cavity. This letter of 12 April seems to have been written immediately after the Okhlopovsky family began constructing their own version of events and circulating it in the local community, for example by submitting the testimony of court ushers in all three Volhynian court chancelleries.

The lawyers claimed that Nastasia did not testify at the castle court because she saw no unfair play in her husband's death. Her husband lived for three weeks after being wounded and never accused anybody but himself. Moreover, the wife, being a woman, did not know how best to proceed, and did not seek advice. In summary, the side of the accused requested permission to conduct a *scrutinium,* or an investigation, by presenting the witnesses chosen by the interested party to be questioned in court on the agreed date.[32] Embracing the basic principle of the presumption of innocence ("leaning towards releasing rather than punishing"[33] the accused), the court granted permission to conduct a *scrutinium* during the subsequent hearings. Nevertheless, it was decided that the accused was to remain in the castle throughout the trial, without leaving it. Nastasia's brother and servants were to be incarcerated with her.

Court officials questioned each servant individually as primary suspects. In general, their accounts matched the version presented by Nastasia Okhlopovska's lawyers, despite differences in detail. For example, another protagonist appeared in the story: Borys's nephew Kozhukhovsky, who ran away from the house that night. The wounded Borys allegedly said that he had been attacked by Kozhukhovsky after Nastasia returned home to find him wounded (Kozhukhovsky himself declared himself innocent). The maid said that the master spoke of a knife wound in the neck.[34]

---

32 Cf. Nataliia Starchenko, *Scrutinium* yak inkvizytsiinyi element u sudochynstvi Volynskoho voievodstva (70-ti rr. XVI – pochatok XVII st.) [*Scrutinium* as an Inquisitorial Element in the Court System of the Volhynian Voivodeship (1570s – Early 17th Century)], in: Zapysky naukovoho tovarystva imeni Shevchenka. Pratsi istorychno-filosofskoi sektsii. [Notes of the Shevchenko Scientific Society. Works of the Section for History and Philosophy], vol. CCLXIV, 171–195.
33 AYuZR, ch. 8, t. III, 380.
34 Cf. AYuZR, ch. 8, t. III, 365–383.

Two days later, on 12 August 1583, the testimonies of the servants, obtained under torture, were added to the Lutsk court records, and they differed significantly from their earlier accounts. The maid Votsia, who had initially accused Kozhukhovsky of murdering Borys, now testified that Nastasia, with Kozhukhosky as her accomplice, had murdered Borys in anger because he had damaged her property while all the servants stood by and watched. Fedir Diohot said that he went to bed as soon as he got home, but when he heard that the master was wounded, he decided to visit him. Unfortunately, the lady would not let him go near Borys. Even before being tortured, Vasko Hrytskovych had claimed that Borys was stabbed by his wife while her maids held candles. He claimed to have witnessed the scene through a window, but Yakiv Oshchovsky had forbidden him to disclose this until the time was right. Meanwhile, the maid Paraska testified that the master was murdered by Kozhukhovsky and Fedir.[35] As we can see, the testimony obtained under torture was far from unanimous.

On 19 September 1583, the accused conducted a *scrutinium*. The court released Nastasia from prison on the grounds that everybody should have the right to testify to their innocence in person. The widow's lawyer promised that the defendant would lodge a separate lawsuit against the Okhlopovsky family, accusing them of unlawful imprisonment (the defendants insisted that Nastasia should be kept in prison). A total of 30 witnesses appeared before the court. Each was questioned individually and signed their testimony "according to their ability".

Ten witnesses, including Anton Zabolotsky, had personally heard Borys Okhlopovsky describe his wound as a shooting accident. Anton Zabolotsky wrote the testament at the deceased's request. He testified that the last will was read out in the presence of Yona Okhlopovsky, as well as Klym and Kuzma Porvanetsky, who were dissatisfied with its content and addressed Borys as follows: "You damned your children, leaving everything to your wife and nothing to them."[36] They tried to postpone certifying the testament despite Borys's pleas, and finally refused to sign it and put their seals on it (despite the fact that the defendants had presented a signed testament to the court). According to the will, Nastasia's brothers were to become guardians of Nastasia and her children, while the estate was to go to the widow on good terms. Among the witnesses was the barber surgeon of Svyniukhy and his brother-in-law, who was present at Borys Okhlopovsky's bedside almost continuously until his last breath.

Other so-called "witnesses" had heard various people describe Borys's wound as accidental under different circumstances. Six persons were given the information by Vasyl Olizarovsky, a representative of the accusers, whose testimony was supposed to prove Nastasia's guilt. Tellingly, this group of witnesses included Vasyl's own brothers: Fedir, Andrii and Levko Olizarovsky. Another witness said they had heard a similar account from another representative of the accusers, Kuzma Porvanetsky. One person

---

35 Cf. AYuZR, ch. 8, t. III, 383f.
36 AYuZR, ch. 8, t. III, 389.

heard at a market on 25 March that Borys was wounded in the absence of his wife. Four people relayed an account from the barber surgeon of Horokhiv that Borys was wounded accidentally during his wife's absence; two others quoted a similar account from Father Karpo. In his testimony, Adam Rudavsky added that Yona Okhlopovsky had allegedly abducted the priest who had certified the testament. The servants of the men, who met Borys in person, were an important source of information; witnesses also quoted rumours that Nastasia was innocent of her husband's murder. In the end, the defendant's lawyer requested permission for Nastasia and six witnesses to swear an oath to prove her innocence,[37] adding that the persons who participated in the *scrutinium* were also ready to swear the oath.

However, the accusers objected and offered to present their own account, which the court allowed despite the defendant's protests. They presented the testimony of a court usher who had questioned Yakub, the barber surgeon of Horokhiv. He allegedly said that he had refused to treat Boris because the stab wound in his throat was fatal. The surgeon from Svyniukhy corroborated the verdict of his "colleague". The accusers subsequently presented a letter from the Volodymyr chamberlain, Yan Boki Pechykhvostsky, who had visited Borys, but the man had been too weak and barely spoke to the guest. The three Porvanetsky men confirmed that Borys had been wounded, but they did not know by whom. Another witness, Bohush Lyplensky, testified that Borys's life with his wife had not been easy, and that Nastasia was known to leave her husband for prolonged periods of time to stay at her brother's house. Once, when Borys came to pick up his wife at her brother's house, sat down next to her and tried to hug her, she moved further away from him before fleeing the room. When Borys asked why the Oshchovsky family allowed his wife to stay with them, they attacked him and he barely managed to escape. Lyplesky also testified that he had tried to find out what had happened and what Borys himself had said after the accident. Ivan Kholonevsky claimed that he had heard Borys say: "They say that I was drunk. I was drinking with the priest and fooling around. They also say that I must have stabbed myself with a knife."[38] Another witness said that he had not personally heard Borys claim that he had been attacked, but other people quoted him saying that he had been treacherously wounded by an unknown attacker.

---

37 Cf. AYuZR, ch. 8, t. III, 401. In requesting that Nastasia swore an oath with six witnesses to acquit herself, the lawyer quoted an article referring to a crime of a different kind: highway robbery. That article did indeed suggest that an accused nobleman who faced a death sentence should his guilt be proven could acquit himself by swearing an oath with six co-swearers. The lawyer used this argument by analogy. For the relevant article (paragraph 11, article 23 of the Second Statute of Lithuania), "Should a nobleman perpetrate highway robbery against another nobleman", cf. Statut Velykoho kniazivstva Lytovskoho 1566, in: Kivalov/Muzychenko/Pankov (eds.), Statuty Velykoho kniazivstva Lytovskoho, see note 10, vol. II, 177.

38 AYuZR, ch. 8, t. III, 404.

As we can see, none of the witnesses directly named Nastasia as the perpetrator. The difference between the accounts provided by the two sides was that Nastasia's witnesses authoritatively described Borys's wound as the result of an accident, while the witnesses for the Okhlopovsky brothers allowed for the possibility of foul play. This did not stop the Okhlopovsky brothers from declaring in their closing speech that every witness had pointed to the widow's guilt, and that the same version had allegedly been confirmed by the testimony of the servants under torture. The accusers requested permission to take an oath to prove their accusations.

In response, Nastasia's lawyer argued that the Okhlopovsky men had abducted the servants and fabricated their accusations in order to force Nastasia to agree to their guardianship. Finally, the lawyer appealed to the presumption of innocence, which meant that the accused had the burden of proof, appealing to chapter 4, article 30 of the 2nd Statute of Lithuania.[39] Taking into account the ambiguous nature of the complaint and the testimony of the accusers' witness, the court ordered Nastasia to take an oath with six co-swearers. In response, the accusers asked for permission to appeal to the king, and the judges agreed. Nastasia's oath was postponed pending the decision of the royal court while the witnesses on her side swore that their testimony had been truthful.[40]

On 17 December, before the hearing of the royal court, Yona Okhlopovsky, on behalf of himself and his brothers, lodged a protest with the castle court, "revealing" the treacherous plan of Nastasia and her guardians. They were said to have gathered their friends and others, including "simple peasants", and persuaded them to give the necessary testimony in court:

> "They hosted them for two days, beseeching them passionately and weeping loudly, and possibly even offering them gifts, in order to bend them to their will and to lead them to court, where they willingly presented before the court a false, untruthful, unjust, very contradictory, erroneous and highly doubtful *scrutinium,* unbefitting the circumstances."[41]

As a result of these manipulations, the court wrongly allowed Nastasia to swear an oath. Whether by choice or by order of the judges, the scribe had failed to record in the minutes many facts that were necessary for the accusers to appeal to the royal court. Moreover, to cover their tracks, the culprits had tried to get rid of the accusers and had

---

39 This article, "How parties should behave in court according to their lawsuits", contains no mention of the presumption of innocence. Despite that, the principle of the presumption of innocence was crucial in the judiciary and was often voiced during trials: e.g., "When in doubt, the court should lean towards releasing rather than punishing" (TsDIAK, f28/1, vol. 22, fol. 626ᵛ). The article does contain another important principle, namely, *nullum crimen sine lege:* the judges "should not judge and punish as they see fit; they should act only according to the Statute, as is specified in it", cf. Statut Velykoho kniazivstva Lytovskoho 1566, in: Kivalov/Muzychenko/Panko (eds.), Statuty Velykoho kniazivstva Lytovskoho, see note 10, vol. II, Odesa 2003, 106f.
40 Cf. AYuZR, ch. 8, t. III, 384–408.
41 AYuZR, ch. 8, t. III, 411.

begun to do away with the servants. Court officials did not offer any protection to the servants, while the Okhlopovsky family did not have the resources to do so, as they were "of poor stock, incapable of providing servants and guards".[42] The servants were very ill after the torture, so it came as a surprise when they disappeared from the castle one night. Soon after, the body of the maid Votsia was discovered in a well on Demian Pavlovych's land, with a stone around her neck. Pavlovych's servants, who discovered the body, had allegedly seen the maid in the courtyard of the Oshchovskys' associate. Friends wasted no time in informing Yona Okhlopovsky of the discovery, spreading the news "in many quarters".[43]

The court usher who examined the body that Yona Okhlopovsky had brought to the Lutsk castle court said that "one could tell that it was a woman".[44] These words suggest that the body was not ideally preserved. This raises the question of whether the body had been positively identified as Votsia's, or whether Yona had used the opportunity to frame the "discovery" as proof of the guilt of Nastasia and her brothers. Later, another court usher noted that the dead woman's hair was shorn, and that her body bore signs of torture. However, given the state of decomposition of the body, this too could be Yona's interpretation: after all, the interested parties often coached court ushers to provide the testimony they needed. Nevertheless, the discovery had no consequences.

In the end, the trial concluded, as ordered by the royal court's decree, with Nastasia and six members of the gentry accompanying her swearing an oath on 20 February 1586, almost four years after Borys Okhlopovsky's death. The woman swore that she had not stabbed her "drunken sleeping" husband with a knife, had not conspired in any way with the servants and had not been involved in his death "by advice, knowledge or assistance". The concluding words of her oath were: "If I have sworn untruthfully, oh God, don't help me, and kill me, God, in this life and the next, body and soul."[45] Breaking an oath was seen as a "great dishonour to God, because He, the incarnation of truth and righteousness, is being implicated in confirming a lie".[46] The divine punishment for perjury was the destruction of the evildoers' entire family.

To summarise, let me note that in most cases it does not seem possible to reconstruct the events based on contemporary court accounts, or at least to attempt to reconcile highly contradictory details. The account given in court by both sides were not entirely reliable. Therefore, it is best to leave aside the question of the cause of Borys Okhlopovsky's death, whether it was a knife wielded by his treacherous wife or an accident that freed her from an unhappy marriage. This question cannot be answered without relying too much on the subjective assumptions of the scholar. Moreover, the people

---

42 AYuZR, ch. 8, t. III, 410.
43 AYuZR, ch. 8, t. III, 412.
44 AYuZR, ch. 8, t. III, 412.
45 AYuZR, ch. 8, t. III, 414f.
46 Innokentii Hisel, Myr z Bohom choloviku [Peace with God to Man], in: Larysa Doyha (ed.), Vybrani tvory u 3-kh tomakh [Selected Works in 3 Volumes], vol. 1, Book 1, Kyiv/Lviv 2012, 212f.

who appeared before the court did not seem to care much about the facts of the case. For the Okhlopovsky family, the priority was to prove the widow's guilt at any cost: this was the only way they could regain control of their cousin's property. Nastasia and her brothers needed to be exonerated. Borys's nephew Kozhukhovsky, the servants, the woman's body found with a stone around her neck, the priest who disappeared without a trace, a bloody knife and a gun, and new witnesses who appeared as the story unfolded, soon got lost among other elements in these contradictory accounts. For those involved in the trial, much of this remained white noise. For a historian, however, they are proof that the sides did not seem overly concerned with evidence, contradictions in testimony or reconciling differing accounts. In the end, it remained unclear which wound – the chest or the neck – was the direct cause of Borys's death. On the eve of the trial, a court usher testified that he had been told by the barber surgeon of Horokhiv that "there was no other wound, only a stab wound on the right side of the throat" (for some reason, this information did not appear in the minutes).[47] What is perhaps of paramount importance to the scholar, however, is how each side "constructed" their witness accounts and testimony, and what resources were involved in the process. In the absence of an independent investigation as part of the trial process, witnesses appeared as the main argument. It was the testimony of a witness and the rhetorical skills of the lawyer that played the decisive role in court. I will focus on these factors in more detail, starting with how the accusations against the widow were constructed.

The Okhlopovsky brothers began their information campaign to discredit the widow after Borys's death by accusing her of refusing to interrogate the servants. The official accusation of murder was not made in court until a year later (as was typical in similar trials). The majority of witnesses on Nastasia's side presented the information received during the early stages of Borys's illness (between 18 March, when the accident happened, and 25 March, the market day, when the information began to circulate widely). Some witnesses presented the testament as conclusive evidence that the deceased, despite his complicated marriage, did not see his wife as a possible murderer. Witnesses for the accusers referred to the period immediately before Borys's death. Since the testimonies referred to different time periods, Borys's accounts may have changed. It is quite possible that the visitors who flocked to Borys's bedside to discover the circumstances of the accident may have "implanted" the idea of a premeditated attack in the mind of the ailing man with memory gaps. Some of these visitors may have been interested in proving Nastasia's guilt while others may have been impartial. Bohush Lyplensky, a witness presented by the accusers, quoted Borys's words as reported by Ivan Kholonevsky: "They say I must have stabbed myself with a knife." Thus, a witness may have heard different versions of the tragic event from Borys himself over the nearly three weeks of his illness: (1) in the first weeks, Borys *did not know for sure*

---

47 TsDIAK, 25/1, vol. 30, fol. 404ᵛ–405, 18 September 1583.

how he had received the wound, and believed that it resulted from a shooting accident; the testament was written at that time, and the testimony of Nastasia's witnesses referred to this period; (2) in the days before his death, Borys *began to suspect* that he had been wounded by a relative or a servant, and the Okhlopovsky brothers based their case on accounts from that period; the fact that Borys spoke of a treacherous murder, mentioned by the Okhlopovsky brothers in the first court session, was not supported by any witness. Therefore, "witnesses" on both sides could have been perfectly sincere in swearing an oath to support their testimony. Moreover, the witnesses who relayed *what* they had heard and swore an oath to support their testimony did not necessarily state that this was *all* they had heard. It is likely that uncomfortable information may have been omitted.

As witness testimonies demonstrate, an information campaign was an important part of a successful trial. It is no coincidence that this contradictory narrative often mentioned that certain facts were well known in the community, with the information being circulated not only by the gentry but also by servants. Of course, the role of the scribe, who could favour one side or the other by collating information in a certain way, should not be overlooked.

Nastasia's imprisonment violated a fundamental right of the gentry: no one could be imprisoned without a court verdict. Servants were treated as their master's property: it was up to him to allow or forbid their interrogation. If he refused an interrogation, he himself became a suspect, and could be brought to court. Interrogation under torture not only violated property rights and the established community practices but also went against the law that prohibited dependents, such as servants, from testifying for or against their masters.[48] Manipulation of servants' testimonies/accusations was rather common. Wrongful accusations against the gentry carried legal penalties, while accusations against their dependents accomplished the goal of damaging their master's honour while decreasing the accuser's risk of being sued for libel. Such accusations were good arguments in battles for honour.

A good example of this is Andrii Dobrynsky's accusation of 3 June 1571 against Nastasia Dzhusianka, Olekhno Tesovsky's widow, who had allegedly persuaded Dobrynsky's maid Bohdana to poison the accuser, his wife and their servants. Bohdana had been adding the poisonous herbs he had received from Dzhusianka to their food and drink for several days, with no result. Tesovska sent a more powerful poison, but Bohdana's treachery was discovered by chance, and she had pointed out the mastermind of the crime, allegedly of her own free will.[49] Nevertheless, on 12 June, a court usher relayed the account of the maid imprisoned in the castle tower: "While I was in his power, Andrii Dobrynsky beat me, tortured me, did whatever he wanted with me and

---

48 Cf. Statut Velykoho kniazivstva Lytovskoho 1566, see note 10, vol. II, chapter 4, article 53, 116.
49 Cf. TsDIAK, 25/1, vol. 458, fol. 172^v–173^v.

handed me over to the torturer who tortured me."[50] It seems that Bohdana was the victim of a conflict between the gentry.

In the first story, the Okhlopovsky brothers seemed to have used the servants' testimony not so much to establish the circumstances of their cousin's death but to put pressure on the Oshchovsky family. Contradictions in the servants' testimony, obtained under torture, suggest that the servants may have changed their stories again once they were no longer in physical danger. Both sides benefited from the servants' disappearance: it benefited the defendant because the accusers lost an opportunity to further manipulate the servants' testimony while the accusers used the servants' disappearance as an additional argument in their information campaign against Nastasia once the accusation began to fall apart.

Of course, the Okhlopovsky's aim was not to find the real culprit; they went to court to prove Nastasia's guilt. Did they evaluate their chances of success before accusing the widow? Or did they expect to undermine the Oshchovsky's reputation in the community, forcing them to negotiate and eventually surrender some of their property and custodial rights in exchange for a settlement? The length of the trial suggests to the latter. It is quite possible that the Oshchovsky family would have been more willing to negotiate had the families' power been equal. In any case, the Okhlopovsky men had made a mistake. The Oshchovskys' social capital and resources for mobilising support made their position much stronger. Obviously, the family's position, numerical strength and marital alliances played a role. It is likely that the Okhlopovskys' position was further undermined by the damaged reputation of Borys himself, with his excessive drinking and unstable character. In sum, this story illustrates a statement made by a Volhynian nobleman in the midst of an argument that described the Volhynian gentry society as a community of honour, along the lines of: "I'm better than you because I have men who stand by me, and you don't."[51]

3. Conclusion

Obviously, other accusations against women for murdering their husbands also require detailed analysis. And yet, stereotypical descriptions and a stable set of components of this narrative allow us to assume that the majority of the accusations were instrumentalised. What do these materials, namely masculine accusatory narratives, tell us about gender bias against women? Indirectly, the ease with which such accusations appeared demonstrates that women's position was precarious. On the other hand, the paucity of such cases may indicate that men were reluctant to use this instrument,

---

50 TsDIAK, 25/1, vol. 458, fol. 182ᵛ.
51 TsDIAK, 25/1, vol. 34, fol. 924ᵛ–925 (835ᵛ–836 – dual pagination).

which could easily backfire. Marriage did not symbolically separate a woman from her family: she retained the family surname and usually had her own seal.

There were, of course, other factors that could alleviate family tensions. The property of the spouses in a *szlachta* family was not united: the wife was legally entitled to at least one-third of the husband's real estate, or to a portion equal to twice her dowry in money terms. This share could not become the object of the husband's property transactions without the wife's special permission. In reality, in 2/3 of the families, the wife owned a half or more of the couple's property. In this context it is clear that the question of an aggrieved *szlachta* man to his neighbour, whose wife, the land owner, initiated border skirmishes, was clearly rhetorical: "Do you live as you wife's hireling […] if you have no property or power in that estate?"[52] This rhetorical question resonates with the answer given by the widow of Prince Yanush Porytsky to his brothers when settling an inheritance conflict: "I was no cook to His Highness Prince Yanush Porytsky, but his wife."[53]

The husband represented the family in the public sphere, but he was not necessarily the family's only representative, or at least not in every scenario and not without multiple limitations. Last but not least, marriage was treated as a public pact, and the Orthodox Christian Church was fairly lenient in granting divorce, including in cases of marital conflict. This could mitigate confrontation within the family and offer acceptable strategies for either side. Divorce cases did not always reach the ecclesiastical court: a simple pact between the parties was often sufficient. For example, when Tomylo Chelevych noticed that his daughter's marriage was unhappy, he approached his son-in-law through friends and settled for a divorce that allowed each spouse to remarry.[54] The possibility of getting a divorce and leaving behind a life of conflict was a reasonably effective precaution against violence against women. The two cases where the ecclesiastical court did not grant a divorce concerned Catholics, who were a minority in these lands during the period under study.

Importantly, in marital conflicts, the husband had to contend not only with his wife but also with a wide circle of her male relatives. In the early modern period, the community (relatives, friends and neighbours) exercised fairly strong control over family violence, so that family conflicts soon became public and subject to negotiation between various groups.[55] The woman herself often had her own support group through her own social network, consisting of, to name just one example, the neighbours. In some cases, the abused wife turned to her mother for help. The woman was

---

52 TsDIAK, 28/1, vol. 4, fol. 135.
53 TsDIAK, 28/1, vol. 5, fol. 50ᵛ.
54 Cf. TsDIAK 21/1, vol. 35, fol. 209, 1592.
55 On family violence as a public matter and on the "privatisation" of the family sphere in the latter half of the eighteenth century cf. Hardwick, Early Modern Perspectives, see note 5, 19, 35; Susan Dwyer Amussen, Punishment, Discipline, and Power: The Social Meanings of Violence in Early Modern England, in: Journal of British Studies, 34, 1 (1995), 19–23.

not alone in case of marital conflict, even within her own home: servants were a resource she could also call upon.

Finally, I would like to point out that the specificity of the functioning of the court system is an underappreciated factor in studies of family violence. The adversarial system turned a trial into a verbal duel between the parties based on shaky evidence. Therefore, the complainant did not necessarily come to court expecting a verdict: he often intended to defame the defendants and force them to negotiate and settle the conflict through property concessions. After all, the gentry were only considered guilty as long as the often material demands of the complainants remained unsatisfied. Note how Matias Yendrykovych described the "innocence" of Prince Stanislav Voronetsky, whom he had previously accused of wounding him and other abuses: "as an honourable man, he restored justice to me and offered me a sufficient reward that I liked".[56] The main aim of the judiciary was to make sure that "each stayed with their own, certain and assured of keeping what belongs to them".[57] Admittedly, it also encouraged the conflicting parties to make peace through out-of-court mediation.

The approach, which takes into account every aspect of how this society functioned, can shed light on relationships within families that are rarely revealed in documents, despite the fact that the line between what was private and what was public was often blurred in the early modern period.

---

56 TsDIAK, 25/1, vol. 55, fol. 5.
57 TsDIAK, 25/1, vol. 124, fol. 779ᵛ.

Olha Posunko

The Protection of Women's Property Rights in the Courts of Southern Ukraine from the End of the Eighteenth to the Mid-Nineteenth Centuries

Property rights are one of the indicators of women's socio-economic status in society. The extent of these rights and the possibility of exercising and protecting them are extremely important for gender studies. Even if women were "invisible" in economic processes, they were still an essential part of them. The problems of identifying sources of information and approaches to the study of women's economic activity in the early modern and modern periods are of concern to researchers from different countries.[1] It is noteworthy that a recent issue of the "Journal for Eighteenth-Century Studies", entitled "Women and Property in the Long Eighteenth Century", was dedicated to this topic.[2]

These problems are also relevant to Ukrainian historiography, where the analysis of the scope of women's property rights and their implementation has not actually been the subject of a separate study. The issue is researched in a variety of other contexts: the general legal status of women, the development of customary and written law and sometimes court practice.[3]

There is also an uneven level of scholarly interest in different regions and periods. The history of Ukraine until the twentieth century was marked by the fact that for a long time its territory was divided between different states. This led to certain regional particularities and differences. Accordingly, a regional approach to the study of many issues is more often used in relation to the period of the eighteenth and nineteenth

---

1 Cf. Michelle Lamarche Marrese, A Woman's Kingdom. Noblewomen and the Control of Property in Russia, 1700–1861, Ithaca 2002, 296; Sheilagh C. Ogilvie, A Bitter Living. Women, Markets, and Social Capital in Early Modern Germany, Oxford 2003, 394.
2 Journal for Eighteenth-Century Studies, 44, Special Issue 4 (2021): Women and Property in the Long Eighteenth Century, ed. by Rita J. Dashwood and Karen Lipsedge, at: https://onlinelibrary.wiley.com/toc/17540208/2021/44/4, access: 15 December 2023.
3 Cf. Марина Гримич, Інститут власності у звичаєво-правовій культурі українців XIX–початку XX ст. [Maryna Hrymych, The Institution of Property in the Customary Legal Culture of Ukrainians of the Nineteenth and Early Twentieth Centuries], Kyiv 2004, 588; Олександр Кривоший, Материзна. Жінки в правовій культурі українського народу (X – перша половина XVII ст.) [Oleksandr Kryvoshyy, Materyzna. Women in the Legal Culture of the Ukrainian People (X – the first half of the XVII Century)], Zaporizhzhya 2001, 95.

centuries. Southern Ukraine[4] of the late eighteenth and first half of the nineteenth century, which is the subject of this article, is often perceived as a region under strong imperial influence. For this reason, researchers tend to focus on those areas where Ukrainian legal traditions have been preserved for a longer period of time (for example Right Bank and Left Bank Ukraine). The situation is further complicated by the problem of historical sources, which will be discussed below.

An obvious and popular way to study property rights is to analyse the legislative framework. However, life practices often turned out to be either different from the legislator's vision or extremely variable. For my research, the works that focus on the experience of the Russian Empire, which included Ukrainian territories, are important.[5] Of particular interest is the monograph by the American historian Michelle Lamarche Marrese "A Women's Kingdom"[6], which, in a broad comparative context, outlines the property rights of noble women. At the same time, Marrese examines various elements of property rights: ownership, inheritance and disposal. This approach is a combination of legislative analysis, judicial and life practice, which seems to be relevant and has been used to the maximum possible extent in this article.

The source base of my research was primarily archival documents from judicial institutions of various levels in the region, namely materials from both central (in Kyiv) and five regional archival repositories, first and foremost from the Dnipropetrovsk and Odesa regions. I would like to note that the archives of Southern Ukraine suffered disastrous losses during the Second World War. This has led to a situation where researchers, aware of the fragmentation of the source base, avoid certain scientific topics. For this reason, the surviving documents of the courts and various structures that cooperated with the judicial system were used as much as possible to write this paper.

Most of the material covering women's property issues relates to civil proceedings. In terms of form, these include lawsuits, court records with testimony, property registers and court decisions. However, litigants also used wills, deeds of gift and personal letters as evidence of property.

It was common practice in this period to appeal to various high-ranking officials, noble leaders, the emperor and the senate in parallel with court proceedings. Therefore,

---

4 Southern Ukraine is a historical and geographical region often associated with Steppe Ukraine; today it includes the territories of Dnipropetrovs'k, Zaporizhzhia and most parts of the Mykolaiv, Kherson, Kirovohrad, Donets'k and Luhans'k oblasts (regions).

5 Cf. Светлана Ворошилова, Гражданско-правовое положение женщин в России (XIX – начало XX века) [Cvetlana Voroshilova, The Civil and Legal Status of Women in Russia (Nineteenth to Early Twentieth Century)], Saratov 2010, 222; Елена Татаринова, Гражданско-правовой статус женщин в России в XVII – первой половине XIX века: дис. ... канд. юрид. наук [Yelena Tatarinova, The Cvil and Legal Status of Women in Russia in the Eighteenth to the First Half of the Nineteenth Century], PhD law thesis, Saratov 2017, 196.

6 Мишель Ламарш Маррезе, Бабье царство: дворянки и владение имуществом в России (1700–1861) [Michelle Lamarche Marrese, A Woman's Kingdom. Noblewomen and the Control of Property in Russia, 1700–1861, authorized translation by Nina Luzheckaja], Moscow 2009, 368.

documents of this type were also used: complaints against the courts, personal appeals to officials and requests for guardianship of estates. The published documents include legislative acts (laws, decrees of the senate, emperors); materials of higher state institutions, which were the last resort.

This article aims to identify the regional specificities of women's property rights in the late eighteenth and the first half of the nineteenth century, using Southern Ukraine as an example. Women's economic rights depended on their social status, regional traditions and social gender stereotypes, which underwent certain changes during this period. These factors will be examined in this article through the prism of court proceedings.

1. Regional and historical features

The study focuses on the territory of Southern Ukraine in the late eighteenth and early nineteenth centuries. The Zaporozhian Cossacks had lived here from the sixteenth century.[7] Their relations with Moscovia[8] varied from the mid-seventeenth century, but they were finally incorporated into the Russian Empire in 1734. An active struggle for Russia's access to the Black Sea began during the reign of Empress Catherine II. Cossack military units helped the empire in this struggle. After successful military campaigns, the imperial authorities liquidated the Zaporozhian Sich[9] (1775) and later annexed the Crimean Khanate[10] (1783). It was then that the active phase of the final incorporation of the vast territory into the Russian Empire began. This process included the unification of the administrative and territorial system and the system of public administration. In 1783, these lands were subject to the "Regulations for the Administration of the Governorates of the All-Russian Empire" of 1775, which were the legal basis for an administrative reform by Catherine II.[11] Along with the new administrative division, a new judicial system was established in the south of Ukraine. Notably, it was also new to Russia itself, as it was just being implemented.

---

7 Cf. Cossacks, at: https://www.encyclopediaofukraine.com/display.asp?linkpath=pages%5CC%5CO%5CCossacks.htm, access: 9 November 2023.
8 Cf. Muscovy (Moskoviya), at: https://en.wikipedia.org/wiki/Muscovy, access: 9 November 2023; https://www.britannica.com/place/Grand-Principality-of-Moscow, access: 9 November 2023.
9 The Zaporozhian Sich was the military and administrative centre of the Zaporozhian Cossacks, a kind of fortified military base. In a broader sense, it is the territory that belonged to the Cossacks from the time when they were part of the Polish-Lithuanian Commonwealth. The siege by Russian troops and the capture of the fortified Sich in 1775 meant the end of the existence of the Zaporozhian Cossacks in their previous form and the expropriation of Cossack lands and property by the authorities.
10 The Crimean Khanate was a Crimean Tatar state of the Geray dynasty. It existed from 1441 to 1783.
11 Полное собрание законов Российской империи, Собрание первое [Complete Collection of Laws of the Russian Empire, 1st Collection] (henceforth ПСЗРИ-1), vol. 21, № 15696, St. Petersburg 1830, 889.

The Katerynoslav[12] Viceroyalty was established in 1783 and covered a vast territory. In addition to the lands that belonged to Southern Ukraine, it included some territories of neighbouring Ukrainian regions such as the Hetmanate[13] (Left Bank Ukraine) and Sloboda Ukraine[14]. The administrative and territorial system became stable in the early nineteenth century. At that time Southern Ukraine included the Katerynoslav and the Kherson Governorates and a small mainland part of the Taurida Governorate.

Each of the territorial components had its own specific historical development and legal traditions, especially during the time of the Katerynoslav Viceroyalty (1783–1796). This also affected women's property rights as well as the opportunities to exercise and protect them. The imperial authorities had to take this into account. Accordingly, the laws of the Russian Empire were considered the basic ones within Southern Ukraine, with some exceptions. Exceptions were made for the districts (*povets*) of the former Hetmanate, for foreign colonists and for internal migrants, who were still allowed to rely on their own written and customary law in the field of civil law for some time. While ethnic communities exercised their rights within the framework of special proceedings,[15] residents of the Left Bank of Ukraine applied to general courts, but appealed to the provisions of the Third Statute of Lithuania of 1588 and sets of the Magdeburg Law.[16] These norms prevailed from the time when the Left Bank was part of the Polish-Lithuanian Commonwealth.[17]

Michelle Marrese wrongly assumes that these laws were applied to these territories because of the presence of people from Polish noble families.[18] However, after Bohdan Khmelnytsky's Ukrainian-Polish war in the mid-seventeenth century and the transfer of Left Bank Ukraine to the nominal rule of the Russian tsar (1654), most of the Polish elite left. And the new Ukrainian elite (Cossack *starshyna*)[19], who demanded noble rights, did not consider it necessary to abandon the Lithuanian Statutes. Only a few norms of state law were changed, and serfdom was abolished. In fact, the Hetmanate was autonomous. Radical changes in governance and judicial proceedings took place in

---

12 The centre of the governorate was the city of Katerynoslav, now Dnipro.
13 The Hetmanate was a semi-official but common name for the Ukrainian state that existed from the mid-seventeenth century until its dissolution (1764) during the reign of Catherine II. Within the Russian Empire, these lands were called Little Russia. The Hetmanate was located on the territory of Left Bank Ukraine, that is on the left bank of the Dnipro River, so this term is also often used.
14 Sloboda Ukraine *(Slobozhanshchyna)* is a historical and geographical region that borders Southern Ukraine in the north-east. It covers what are today Kharkiv, Sumy, parts of the Donetsk and Luhansk oblasts of Ukraine and the Voronezh, Kursk and Belgorod oblasts of Russia. The Cossack system was abolished during the reign of Catherine II in 1765.
15 For example, the Greeks in Mariupol had their own national court (1779–1869).
16 Cf. ПСЗРИ-1, see note 11, 20, № 14609, 522–523; 22, № 16334, 539.
17 Cf. The Commonwealth of Poland (the Polish-Lithuanian Commonwealth), at: https://www.britannica.com/place/Poland/The-Commonwealth, access: 9 November 2023.
18 Cf. Маррезе, Бабье царство, see note 6, 22.
19 The Cossack *starshyna* (officers) were the military and administrative leaders of the Cossacks, and in the reality of the eighteenth century, the ruling elite of the Hetmanate.

the eighteenth century, but the norms of marriage, family, inheritance and property law for this Ukrainian territory had their own specificities in Russian legislation until the 1840s.

Thus, the courts of the Katerynoslav Viceroyalty were characterised by two powerful and, to some extent, divergent legal practices.[20] Later, the administrative units of Southern Ukraine excluded the districts of the former Hetmanate. However, Ukrainian legal traditions were "invisibly" penetrating to the south, as a significant part of the Left Bank nobility became officials in Southern Ukraine, received land and established estates here.

The judicial system implemented in the Russian Empire after 1775 was rather complicated. It combined both the principle of class proceedings and the principle of universality and inclusion of all classes. At the level of the districts, which were the primary units in the governorates, separate courts were established for the nobility and the peasantry. Magistrates performed judicial functions for burghers. A separate institution was the court of conscience.[21] Over time, during the reign of Paul I, the courts for peasants – lower and upper rozpravy (courts) – ceased to exist and the cases of both peasants and nobles were heard in general courts, which are the subject of this study.

It will come as no surprise that in the courts of this period, the vast majority of cases involving women's property rights specifically concerned the privileged class. It was an extremely important time for the imperial nobility. During the eighteenth century, the rules governing their existence were gradually changing, and the Charter to the Nobility of 1785 became especially significant, as it completed the formation of class rights and privileges. However, the real estate of the nobility was still divided into "family" and acquired property. Only the acquired property could be sold and bequeathed at will, while the family property was inherited exclusively by law. After some time it became clear that the inviolability of the property of the nobility (namely family property) could be violated by the state, so the nobility concentrated their efforts on strengthening their own economic rights. The nobility lobbied for the adoption of laws that would help remove their property from the state control. Often this could only be done by expanding the scope of property rights for noblewomen.

The nobility of the former Hetmanate, the Cossack *starshyna*, were granted the right to equality with the imperial nobility. And in the last years of the eighteenth century,

---

20 Cf. Ольга Посунько, Використання норм ІІІ Литовського статуту у спадкових спорах останньої чверті XVIII ст. (на судових матеріалах Катеринославського намісництва) [Olha Posunko, The Use of the Norms of the III Lithuanian Statute in the Inheritance Disputes of the Last Quarter of the Eighteenth Century (Based on Judicial Materials of the Ekaterinoslav Province)], in: Scriptorium nostrum. Electronic History Journal, 2, 11 (2018), 234–244, at: https://chtyvo.org.ua/authors/Posunko_Olha/Vykorystannia_norm_III_Lytovskoho_statutu_u_spadkovykh_sporakh_ostannoi_chverti_KhVIII_st_na_sudovyk/, access: 9 November 2023.

21 Cf. Валентина Шандра, Совісні суди в Україні (остання чверть XVIII – середина XIX ст.) [Valentyna Shandra, Conscientious Court in Ukraine (Last Quarter of the 18th to the Mid-19th Centuries)], Kyiv 2011, 266.

they concentrated on the process of ennoblement. The nobility of Southern Ukraine was still in its infancy. Massive distributions of land formerly owned by the Zaporozhian Cossacks began to attract both Russian authorities and various ranks of officers. Officers of the Russian army, whose military units were present in large numbers in the region, could obtain noble status by receiving land and settling on it. A genuine 'land rush' began. In each of these options (for Cossack officers and for Russian officials/officers), there were 'female plots' in the processes of obtaining/consolidation/preserving land ownership. But the 'initial conditions' of these processes were different.

2. Women's economic rights in the counties of the former Hetmanate

These territories were formally part of the Katerynoslav Viceroyalty for a short period of time and did not belong to Southern Ukraine. Nevertheless, I believe it is necessary to describe women's property rights in this part of the Viceroyalty since it is here that the Ukrainian legal tradition is represented.

When, in 1784, the provincial judicial institutions of the Katerynoslav Governorate were opened, performing audit and appeal functions in relation to the district courts, the first cases they received were from the districts of the former Hetmanate. The judicial system and civil law norms that had prevailed since the days of the Polish-Lithuanian Commonwealth continued to operate there, and Ukrainian courts had previously worked quite effectively. Accordingly, when the four districts were transferred to the Katerynoslav Viceroyalty, their courts had cases ready for trial and appeal.

The vast majority of these court files were deposited in the fonds of the Katerynoslav Supreme Zemstvo (local) Court. Of the 50 surviving cases of the civil section, 37 relate to land disputes of the former Hetmanate. Among these, there are many conflicts where women were either plaintiff or defendant (and sometimes both). However, women's property rights are also most frequently mentioned in other cases, especially inheritance cases. They describe property and the principles of its division through the female line, both ascending and descending.

Some women were extremely active in business. For example, Tekla Tarnovska, the widow of Colonel Ivan Tarnovski, had up to a dozen cases in several courts of the Kyiv and Katerynoslav Viceroyalties at the same time. There were cases concerning debts (hers and his), real estate and promissory notes. One of the most high-profile lawsuits in which she was involved was a conflict with the famous Kapnist family. Her correspondence with the Kapnist brothers demonstrates that she had several lawyers in court cases and kept everything under her control.[22]

---

22 Cf. Інститут Рукопису Національної бібліотеки України імені В. І. Вернадського [Manu-

The examples from the Left Bank of Ukraine illustrate a long tradition of women's ownership, inheritance and disposition of property. These stories highlight the difference between the Ukrainian tradition enshrined in written law on the Left Bank and the Russian imperial law implemented in Southern Ukraine.

The Third Lithuanian Statute of 1588, to which the residents of the former Hetmanate appealed, contained a number of provisions and even a separate section on women's property rights, namely Chapter Five, "On the Right to *Posah* and *Vino*", the provisions of which were very popular in the courts. Again, two out of the 22 articles in this part of the Lithuanian Statute were the most popular. The latter are article 2 on *vino* (property registered by the husband to the wife) and article 14 on the division of *materyzna* (maternal property) and father's property.[23] These three terms are key to understanding women's property. When a young girl married, she received a *posah* (dowry) from her parents, which became the joint property of the spouses. However, on the death of her husband or in the event of divorce, the woman could reclaim the dowry. A man, on the other hand, "registered" a *vino* for his wife, a part of his own property, which was usually twice the amount of the dowry. In the event of the husband's death or divorce through his fault, the *vino* became the full property of the wife. There was even a term: "a widow with a *vino*", which meant a widow who was well off and had legally registered property. On the death of their parents, children received two types of inheritance from them: paternal and maternal *(materyzna)*. The specificity was that, according to the law, if there was no other will, the father's real estate went to his sons. However, *materyzna* was divided equally among all children, regardless of gender. These are the main characteristics, although there were many other legal nuances and peculiarities.

The legal foundations and the peculiarities of life in Cossack Ukraine shaped the tradition, when both husbands and wives could run the household almost equally. The men's military service and their long absences forced women to take the household into their own hands. Of course, there were various male trustees who managed the estate in the absence of the owner. But this was done under the strict control of the owner's wife. The peculiarities of land ownership also contributed to women's economic activity. Often, the villages owned by a family were scattered over large areas. In such a situation, the family divided its efforts to manage the property. Correspondence and court documents show that spouses could live apart for a long time and maintain their financial situation quite autonomously. The husband was most often responsible for making large purchases for the household, hiring craftsmen for work and other im-

---

script Institute National Library of Ukraine named after V. I. Vernadskyi], fund III, storage unit 24188, sheet reverse 21.

23 Cf. Статут Великого князівства Литовського 1588 року, в: Сергій Ківалов, Петро Музиченко (eds.), Статути Великого князівства Литовського [Statute of the Grand Duchy of Lithuania of 1588, in: Serhiy Kivalov and Petro Muzychenko (eds.), Statute of the Grand Duchy of Lithuania], vol. III, book 2, Odesa 2004, 197, 203.

portant tasks. However, he often only paid for the work carried out by his wife (and often gave her a loan).[24]

In most cases, the wife's property was controlled by her husband after the marriage. Judicial practice shows that when it came to the second or third marriage of one or both partners in a couple, the separate disposal of property was a more acceptable option. I assume this happened because the widow already had a part of her late husband's property and his relatives could control that their property remained with the family heirs. An example of such management was Marfa Lalosh (Ostrohradska during her first marriage), the wife of the first Katerynoslav nobility leader, Kostiantyn Lalosh. It was the first rather late marriage for the husband and the second for Marfa.[25] Marfa's correspondence with her husband shows that she was active both in her own financial and economic affairs and in settling them in court. She also had her own ways of getting an audience with important officials.[26] Everyone ran their own household, looked after their own property and helped each other. After Marfa's death, the property associated with the Ostrohradskys passed to the children of her first marriage.

The limits of a woman's economic freedom in marriage were determined more by the traditions of a particular family and the personal relationships between the spouses and their relatives. While women had certain opportunities and rights under the law (legal capacity for rights), in practice they were often unable to use them (legal capacity to act) in confrontation with male relatives. Widows were not always able to return their family property or *vino* and to manage their properties independently. Sometimes brothers prevented their sisters from receiving their share of their deceased parents' property.[27] There have been cases of sons pressuring parents to make a will.[28]

Wealthy families on the Left Bank, where the initial phase of land distribution had long since been completed, faced more complicated trials. Here, judges had to deal with family inheritance histories, sales and purchases, cessions and records spanning several generations. For example, what initially appeared to be an inheritance dispute revealed a history of redistribution and changes in property status. Families had a practice of registering women's property in the name of their husbands. The so-called "concessions", that is the exchange of plots of land, which could be unequal, were widely used. All this led to changes in the legal status of property and the transformation of women's property.

---

24 Cf. Державний архів Дніпропетровської області [The State Archives of Dnipropetrovsk Region] (henceforth ДАДО), fund 467, inventory 1, file 13, sheet 5–6.
25 Cf. Ольга Посунько, Перший предводитель катеринославського дворянства К. Лалош: сюжети до біографії крізь призму судового процесу [Olha Posunko, The First Leader of the Katerynoslav Nobility K. Lalosh. Plots to a Biography through the Prism of the Trial], in: The Universe of History and Archaeology, 26, 1–2 (2018), 14–22.
26 Cf. ДАДО, see note 24, fund 467, inventory, 1, file 13, sheet 14.
27 Cf. ДАДО, see note 24, fund 467, inventory 1, file 23, sheet 11.
28 Cf. ДАДО, see note 24, fund 467, inventory 1, file 4, sheet 2.

Court proceedings often lasted 10 to 20 years or more, with new circumstances emerging. And in all these vicissitudes, female owners were always mentioned. For example, in the early 1790s, the case of Varvara Maksymovych[29] was heard by the Katerynoslav Supreme Zemstvo Court. 35 documents were transferred from a povet court to this institution. The case had been dragging for more than 40 years. The case involved three (!) generations of women trying to claim an inheritance. Initially, in the first generation after Andrii Bilukha (Varvara's grandfather), it was an inheritance from the father, and then this property became *materyzna* for Andrii's grandchildren.

The case is rich in 'women's stories'. On the one hand, there is evidence of women's significant rights: in each generation, they claimed not only maternal but also separate shares of their father's property, which had been bequeathed to them by will. In particular, there is a copy of Fedir Levenets's (Varvara's father) testament from 1780, in which it is stated that "in addition to my wife's inheritance, *a quarter* of my own inherited estate should be allocated to my daughters".[30] Levenets also had three sons, but he was not concerned about their rights, as they were better protected by law. The available court documents include examples of changes in property status, inheritance by daughters and part of the father's family property specifically by will.

Usually, the closest male relatives most often acted as representatives of women in court. However, there are cases where women also acted as trustees for men. In 1791, for example, Hanna Myloradovych reported that her husband had gone to the capital "and entrusted me with the defence of all his property".[31] Of course, women did not appear in court in person. Instead, they hired lawyers.

Sources provide much evidence of women having some money and *movable* property of their own. Jewellery, clothing and utensils were traditional components of 'female' property. Marfa Lalosh's purchase record shows that she was not only a housewife who regularly attended fairs in Kharkiv and Romny on business.[32] Her expense accounts also indicate that she constantly bought clothes, utensils and jewellery.[33] In the case of Vasyl Starytskyi's estate in 1795, it is mentioned that a register of his loans included four women among his seven creditors.[34] This means that married women had their own money and were free to use it as they wished.

The property rights of rural women cannot be adequately characterised on the basis of the material from the judicial institutions of Southern Ukraine. Some cases relate exclusively to districts in Left Bank Ukraine, where the plaintiffs/defendants were free people, defined in the new realities as state settlers, Cossacks and state peasants. These cases dealt exclusively with the division of *materyzna* and the allocation of dowries,

---

29 Cf. ДАДО, see note 24, fund 375, inventory 2, file 29.
30 ДАДО, see note 24, fund 375, inventory 2, file 29, sheet 19.
31 ДАДО, see note 24, fund 375, inventory 2, file 48, sheet reverse 1.
32 Cf. ДАДО, see note 24, fund 467, inventory 1, file 13, sheet 5–6.
33 Cf. ДАДО, see note 24, fund 467, inventory 1, file 13, sheet 18.
34 Cf. ДАДО, see note 24, fund 375, inventory 2, file 48, sheet reverse 33.

which was also done according to the Lithuanian Statute. They tried not to divide their paternal property.

For state peasants in other parts of the southern Ukrainian region, it is reasonable to conclude that the law had little impact on their property rights within the family. Disputes were resolved by the customary norms of the village community. Peasants rarely went to court, which acted according to the law. The legal historian Oleksandr Nelin points out that most researchers consider peasant family land ownership to be exclusively a *joint property*.[35] Even a son often could not get a share of his father's land. A daughter-in-law, in the event of her husband's death, was forced to stay with her in-laws, because even if she had land, it was impossible to get a share of it.[36] This situation was caused by the status of the family land plot (its indivisibility), small or meagre plots of land and the lack of land cultivation equipment. Therefore, the further development of property rights for these segments of the population depended on changes in the socio-economic situation of the country.

3. Southern Ukrainian experience under imperial law

The kind of activity displayed by the women of the Left Bank was not typical of women in Southern Ukraine, at least not in the late eighteenth century. As one of the participants in a trial in the 1780s wrote in a letter of credence to her husband: "It is inconvenient for me to enter into all this myself […] because of my female sex."[37] This was not least due to the peculiarities of the region. There was an active process of settlement in the region, and cities were just being established. Since the reform of 1775 had created administrative-territorial units based on population, it often took almost a whole day to travel from a mansion to a district or governorate city. A large number of soldiers who took part in the Russian-Turkish wars (1787–1792; 1806–1812) lived in these cities. Certain areas of the region were quite deserted and had a high crime rate. Thus, regional specificities were added to the traditionally lower presence of women in judicial and government institutions. Women's cases in courts were handled by husbands, brothers and fathers.

From the beginning of the nineteenth century, most of the territories of Southern Ukraine were relatively homogeneous in terms of the application of rule of law, with certain ethnic and religious communities, military settlers, etc. still excluded. However, there was a high degree of standardisation, especially in the case of the nobility. The same applies to women's property rights.

---

35 Cf. Олександр Нелін, Правове регулювання спадкових відносин в Україні (IX–XIX ст.) [Oleksandr Nelin, Legal Regulation of Inheritance Relations in Ukraine (nineteenth and twentieth centuries)], Kyiv 2014, 247, 183.
36 Cf. Нелін, Правове регулювання, see note 35, 181.
37 ДАДО, see note 24, fund 467, inventory 1, file 14, sheet 3.

Since the law of the Russian Empire was largely characterised by causality and the prevalence of case law, a great number of decrees and orders regulated and clarified the range of women's rights. There were, however, several laws that became decisive in the development of property rights in general and women's rights in particular. First and foremost was Anna Ioannovna's personal decree of 17 March 1731, which repealed Peter the Great's legislation on sole inheritance and significantly expanded women's rights to the property of deceased husbands and in-laws.[38] A widow received 1/7 of her husband's real estate and 1/4 of his movable property, and was their full owner even after remarriage. The widower received the same shares. That was the gender equation. On the other hand, this approach was soon criticised because, in the absence of other heirs, all property that was not included in the shares defined by law fell into the category of escheat.[39] The system of wills in the Russian Empire was still quite underdeveloped and did not apply to family lands.[40] This was also different from the Ukrainian tradition of the Hetmanate, where the practice of wills (including women's wills) was highly developed.[41]

The next significant step in the extension of women's property rights was the decree of 30 July 1740 on the division of Admiral Holovin's estate. The senate equalised the rights of sons and daughters to family inheritance.[42] Previously, the law had stipulated that sisters could not inherit from their father's family property if there were brothers. The decree stipulated: "It should be understood that daughters are as much children to their fathers and mothers as sons" – by all accounts an obvious fact.[43] However, there were differences in the shares that daughters could claim. If the deceased had only sons or only daughters, they inherited equally. If the heirs were of different sexes, daughters inherited 1/14 of the immovable property and 1/8 of the movable property, and the rest was equally divided between the sons. But even here there were reservations. In cases where a daughter could receive a larger share than a son, the law was no longer followed. These rules concerned family property and their emergence was determined by the struggle of the nobility to keep landed property within the family. Nevertheless, it is

---

38 Cf. ПСЗРИ-1, see note 11, 8, № 5717, 396–398.
39 Cf. Татаринова, Гражданско-правовой статус, see note 5, 106.
40 The first legal act to unify the rules of inheritance by will was the decree of Nicholas I of 1 October 1831 "On spiritual wills". Before that, there were only separate decrees of the monarch and the Senate.
41 Cf. Ірина Кривошея, Жіночі тестаменти родин козацької старшини XVII – XVII ст., в: Емінак [Iryna Kryvosheia, Women's Testaments of Cossack Officers' Families, 17th–18th Centuries], in: Eminak, 37, 1 (2022), 7–24, 7.
42 Cf. Елена Татаринова, Влияние государственно-правовой традиции на наследственные права женщин в XVII–XVIII веках, в: Вестник Саратовской государственной юридической академии [Yelena Tatarinova, The Influence of State-Legal Traditions on Women's Inheritance Rights in the 17th Century], in: Bulletin of the Saratov State Law Academy, 2 (2016), 85–88, 88, at: https://cyberleninka.ru/article/n/vliyanie-gosudarstvenno-pravovoy-traditsii-na-nasledstvennye-prava-zhenschin-v-xvii-xviii-vekah/viewer, access: 14. November 2023.
43 ПСЗРИ-1, see note 11, 11, № 8190, 206.

undeniable that eighteenth-century Russian legislation was significantly democratised in the area of women's inheritance rights. Each of the above-mentioned decrees is reflected in the court records of Southern Ukraine.

Also of great importance was the Senate Decree of 14 June 1753, which regulated the procedure for registering real estate as personal property, regardless of gender. This document enshrined the possibility for women to own and acquire separate property by purchase, gift and inheritance.[44] Thus, a woman could also sell property separately from her husband.

The introduction of the principle of property separation was one of the major achievements of Russian law of this period. Many foreigners were surprised by the extent of noblewomen's property rights in the Russian Empire at the beginning of the nineteenth century.[45] On the one hand, women were effectively absent from public life, had limited rights to education and were often oppressed in the family. On the other hand, there are many examples of successful female entrepreneurship and economic freedom. All of this led to various hypotheses as to how it was possible to legitimise such a large number of rights in a patriarchal society. For example, the famous Prussian economist and agricultural researcher August von Haxthausen, who visited the Russian Empire in 1843–1844 (he also visited Southern Ukraine), noted a fairly high proportion of women landowners. He estimated that they made up 20 to 25 per cent of the total number of landowners and concluded that this was due to the circumstances of life in the empire. There were many opportunities in the country to get rich quickly and easily. What was gained in this way was not valued, and this often led to excessive spending. Accordingly, in an attempt to save some of the property of the nobility, the legislator was forced to recognise the separation of property and the rights of women.[46]

However, Michelle Marrese's conclusions seem more convincing. She argues that the economic reasons for implementing the principle of property separation are not clearly visible here. In her opinion, the political context was more typical of Russia. Even in the first half of the nineteenth century, the legislator did not provide guarantees of the inviolability of noble titles and property, and thus the nobility protected its rights and privileges in this way (separation of property).[47] In other words, the principle of property separation was implemented not in the context of the struggle for the extension of women's rights or the principles of economic freedom in general, but as a part of a number of measures to protect class privileges.

---

44 Cf. ПСЗРИ-1, see note 11, 13, № 10111, 852–856.
45 Cf. Илья Оршанский, Исследования по русскому праву семейному и наследственному [Ilya Orshanskij, Studies on Russian Family and Inheritance Law], St. Petersburg 1877, 346–347.
46 Cf. Август Гакстгаузен, Исследования внутренних отношений народной жизни и в особенности сельских учреждений России [August Gaksthausen, Studies on the Internal Relations of People's Life and in Particular the Rural Institutions of Russia], Moscow 1870, vol. 1, 30.
47 Cf. Маррезе, Бабье царство, see note 6, 90–91.

It is undeniable that the principle of property separation was used to save real estate in all sorts of critical situations. In the southern region of Ukraine, the risks were even greater. Huge government projects implemented in the region provided exceptional opportunities for officials and landowners to enrich themselves. But it was just as easy to lose the patronage of the higher authorities and all the property one had acquired, to engage in dubious business and risk one's property. In the early 1790s, this happened to the Paskevych family, whose property was inventoried "to repay the state debt E. Petro Paskevych failed to fulfil his financial obligations for renting state-owned salt deposits".[48] In order to save something, the family urgently began to distribute the inheritance to the widows of Petro's two brothers on the basis of the decree of 17 March 1731.[49] This had never happened before these events, and Paskevych administered and disposed of the undivided property "amicably". Both widows, Motrona and Hanna, actively participated in the process and personally appealed to the senate.[50]

Widows representing the interests of their children also appealed to the 1731 decree when they tried to claim a share from their deceased husband's family, sometimes even when they remarried. Perhaps this is what gave them support and confidence in their case. For example, Ivan Bolshoi Shabelskyi's daughter-in-law, Pelaheia Bulhakova, who had already remarried in 1795, initiated and won a lawsuit over the allocation of land for her son in the Bakhmut district.[51]

Over time, the principle of property separation was abused. In 1825, the senate granted the possibility of sale and purchase agreements between husband and wife.[52] Real estate thus registered in the wife's name could not be seized for the husband's debts. This concealed the true size and value of the property and prevented it from being seized. A compromise was reached in 1846 when it was decided that the wife's property acquired from her own husband ten years before the bankruptcy was also subject to seizure and confiscation.[53]

It is important to realise that women's property rights were not equal to those of men, but the scope of these rights was significantly extended. Widows felt most free, but even here there could be restrictions related to guardians who were appointed if there were minor children. There are examples of fairly free disposal of property without interference from guardians, but there are also examples of strict and even excessive control by guardians.

Nevertheless, court documents of civil proceedings show an increase in cases involving women. More precise data for certain years was obtained by analysing a number of case records from the Novorossiysk Governor General's Fund. For example, a

---

48 ДАДО, see note 24, fund 375, inventory 1, file 36.
49 Cf. ДАДО, see note 24, fund 375, inventory 1, file 3, sheet reverse 37.
50 Cf. ДАДО, see note 24, fund 375, inventory 1, file 3, sheet 181.
51 Cf. ДАДО, see note 24, fund 375, inventory 2, file 17.
52 Cf. ПСЗРИ-1, see note 11, 40, № 30472, 443–447.
53 Cf. Маррезе, Бабье царство, see note 6, 92–93.

detailed record for 1824 shows the following data: a total of 146 cases were filed, 43 of which concerned the resolution of various real estate issues. Women were present in 20 of them (46.5 per cent). In 15 cases, a woman initiated the lawsuit (securitisation/land survey, inheritance claims); two cases concerned conflict situations between a man and a woman; in one case, both the plaintiff and the defendant were women. In one of the lawsuits, it was clearly stated that the husband represented his wife's interests, and one case was related to a woman's inheritance.[54] It is therefore fair to say that noblewomen were actively involved in the struggle for economic interests, albeit in many cases only formally. It is noteworthy that the data I have obtained are similar to those Michelle Marrese calculated based on the senate's materials. She found that during the first half of the nineteenth century, 48.5 per cent of lawsuits were between men and women; 13.3 per cent were between women on both sides.[55] Although the representation of men was higher, women were not significantly less represented.

4. The role of the mother as an impetus for the protection of property rights

The role of wife and mother could, curiously enough, also take women beyond the confines of internal family life into the realm of protecting economic interests. This seems to have been the case in many countries in the first half of the nineteenth century. Scholars of the status and rights of married women point out that the modernisation of life brought about some changes in the understanding of women's roles in the family. Richard Chused, describing the American experience, noted that during the first half of the nineteenth century there was a cultural focus on women's households and the development of children. This had to lead to a rethinking of women's economic rights.[56] Michelle Marrese also noted that the content of maternal purpose and role changed in the first half of the nineteenth century, with implications for women's economic claims. A good mother was expected not only to raise and educate children, but above all to provide for their material support.[57] This social 'trend' is confirmed by court documents.

The cases of Mariia Rodzianko[58] from the Novomoskovsk district of the Katerynoslav Governorate and Anastasia Lukina[59] from the Bobrynets district of the

---

54 Cf. Державний архів Одеської області [The State Archives of Odesa Region] (henceforth ДАОО), fund 1, inventory 190, 1824, sheets 12–28 reverse.
55 Cf. Маррезе, Бабье царство, see note 6, 278.
56 Cf. Richard H. Chused, Married Women's Property Law. 1800–1850, in: The Georgetown Law Journal, 71, 5 (1983), 1359–1425, 1423, at: https://digitalcommons.nyls.edu/cgi/viewcontent.cgi?article=1279&context=fac_articles_chapters, access: 14 November 2023.
57 Cf. Маррезе, Бабье царство, see note 6, 278.
58 Cf. ДАОО, see note 54, fund 1, inventory 152, file 83.
59 Cf. ДАОО, see note 54, fund 1, inventory 190, file 2.

Kherson Governorate in the early 1840s are illustrative. The former fought for a share of her husband's property to support herself and her daughter. The man was aggressive and disrespectful towards his wife, and spent the family's money on homosexual relations. Lukina's husband was mentally ill. Local court officials took advantage of this and took the family's land from him for nothing. The women were forced to fight an unequal battle against the system. In their appeals, they emphasised that they could have put up with the way their husbands managed their property ("I used to think I had to tolerate it"[60]), but maternal duty did not allow it: "A mother's feelings compel her to protect the children's property",[61] "mother's sacred duty is to protect my daughter's future".[62] It was only after a personal appeal to the Grand Duke Mikhail Romanov, which she managed to deliver during the emperor's trip in September 1847, that Lukina made any headway in the case.[63] Mariia Rodzianko also did not dare to solve the problem through the courts, but appealed to the governor, the leader of the nobility.

In general, there is a widespread view in historiography that women's independence in the Ukrainian regions of the Russian Empire decreased during the eighteenth century, which is explained by the influence of Russian law.[64] I do not agree with this statement. In the first half of the eighteenth century, women from the privileged classes of the Hetmanate undoubtedly had some advantages over Russian noblewomen. But dynamic changes in Russian legislation 'levelled' the situation. In my opinion, the idea of the economic 'disenfranchisement' of the Russian noblewoman is based on the impression of her family subordination, which was less evident in the Ukrainian tradition. Serafim Shashkov, one of the first researchers and publicists to describe the situation of women in Russia in the second half of the nineteenth century, wrote that: "[…] even in England they envy the property rights of our women". But this only concerned property rights. Otherwise, the situation of women "can only cause a feeling of deep regret".[65]

Russian scholar Inna Krasnova's point about the imbalance between women's property and personal rights in the Russian Empire seems reasonable. Women's economic rights were determined by secular legislation, which was constantly evolving. Their personal status was determined by family law relations, which were regulated by canon law. It was based on religious postulates, was conservative and did not undergo

---

60 ДАОО, see note 54, fund 1, inventory 152, file 83, sheet reverse 11.
61 ДАОО, see note 54, fund 1, inventory 190, file 2, sheet 111.
62 ДАОО, see note 54, fund 1, inventory 152, file 83, sheet reverse 11.
63 Cf. ДАОО, see note 54, fund 1, inventory 190, file 2, sheet 108.
64 Cf. Ірина Капустяк, Людмила Шапенко, Правове становище жінки в Україні: від минулого до сучасності, в: Порівняльно-аналітичне право [Iryna Kapustyak and Lyudmyla Shapenko, The Legal Status of Women in Ukraine. From the Past to the Present], in: Comparative and Analytical Law, 1 (2016), 41–44, 42.
65 Серафим Шашков, История русской женщины [Serafim Shashkov, The Story of a Russian Woman], St. Petersburg 1879, 352, 264.

significant changes.⁶⁶ Until the eighteenth century (before the final subjugation to the empire), marriage relations in Ukraine were regulated mainly by the community on the basis of customary law, and for the nobility on the basis of secular law. The Ukrainian tradition focused on the marriage contract between the parents of the future spouses and the wedding procedure, while the church wedding was of secondary importance. From the end of the eighteenth century, marriage and family relations were almost entirely controlled by the Russian Orthodox Church, which was actively supported by the state. It can be assumed that these new circumstances did not contribute to the democratisation of society's attitude to women's economic activity.

There has always been a problem of correspondence between the legal capacity for rights and the legal capacity to act as a legal person. If a woman grew up or married into a family with strong patriarchal foundations, whatever her legal rights were, she was not immune to the arbitrariness of her father/husband/father-in-law. Her husband could abuse her, misappropriate her property or ruin the household. Society might sympathise with her but offered little support. The more peripheral the judicial institution where a case had to be initiated, the less sympathetic officials were towards women. Despite the laws, court officials often treated various regulations as a formality. Scholars from other countries have also found that judges ignore or arbitrarily interpret the law in relation to women's rights. For example, Constance Bachouse, analysing the Canadian experience, notes that judges even deliberately sabotaged certain legislative initiatives that went against their personal ideas about the family and women's place in it.⁶⁷ Therefore, laws could be changed, but it was important to change people's minds and attitudes.

Ignoring women's rights, men sold or mortgaged their property without informing their wives. Even if the property was jointly owned according to the documents, the wife's position could be ignored. This happened in the case of Hanna Isaieva (1810–1815), who challenged her deceased husband's will. It turned out that he had independently disposed of the joint property. The Kherson Chamber of Civil Affairs replied that the joint ownership had only been "formally" registered once.⁶⁸

---

66 Cf. Инна Краснова, Гражданская правоспособность женщин в России в имперский период, в: Вестник ЮУрГУ. Серия "Право" [Inna Krasnova, Civil Legal Capacity of Women in Russia in the Imperial Period], in: Bulletin of Ural State University, 18, 2 (2018): Law, 90–93, at: https://cyberleninka.ru/article/n/grazhdanskaya-pravosposobnost-zhenschin-v-rossii-v-imperskiy-period/viewer, access: 14 November 2023.

67 Cf. Constance B. Bachouse, Married Women's Property Law Nineteenth-Century Canada, in: Law and History Review, 6, 2 (Fall 1988), 211–257, 241, at: https://www.cambridge.org/core/services/aop-cambridge-core/content/view/4DD51B94F0367BC0A2AA28F103DCC971/S0738248000010178a.pdf/married-womens-property-law-in-nineteenth-century-canada.pdf, access: 14 November 2023.

68 Архив Государственнаго Совета [Archive of the State Council], vol. 4: Царствование императора Александра I (с 1810 по 19 ноября 1825 гг.) [The Reign of Emperor Alexander I (from 1810 to 19 November 1825)], part 3, 144.

Problems often occurred during the husband's lifetime when he sold property without his wife's knowledge. The justification given by judicial officials was that notices of sale were officially submitted to the capital's newspapers and posted on the doors of institutions. However, as court records demonstrate, information was sometimes "withheld", and sales were not advertised in cases where officials were involved in fraud and profited from it.

It was not uncommon for an estate to be ruined by the behaviour of an owner who was addicted to gambling or alcohol, indiscriminate with his acquaintances and involved in dubious businesses. There was virtually no protection against this. Appeals to the leaders of the nobility to take charge of the property were not always effective. Women in distress often lacked the resources to mount a full legal challenge. As the above-mentioned Anastasiia Lukina wrote: "I am not able to conduct this case in a formal manner, to transfer it from one institution to another to appeal, because it requires high costs and I have nothing left but five children".[69]

5. Conclusion

When analysing women's property rights in Southern Ukraine in the late eighteenth and early nineteenth centuries, a scholar of legal practice will most often find documents relating to noblewomen. In other words, the scope and possibilities of judicial protection of women's (and also men's) property rights correlated with their social class. It is important to note, however, that the rights of privileged sections of the population became a kind of benchmark and model for the legislator to follow in relation to other social groups. At this stage, both noblewomen and peasant women were united by their economic dependence on men and families, albeit to different degrees.

The empire's legislation in this area changed quite dynamically. The extended economic rights of noblewomen were, to a certain extent, a tool to ensure the inviolability of the interests and privileges of the nobility. Women's rights as an independent value did not play a role. Accordingly, the implementation of laws at the local level depended on regional traditions and customs. Women's economic activity in the former Hetmanate was determined by the previous rules of custom and law and was culturally ingrained. Women's activity in Southern Ukraine was encouraged by the active economic processes in the region, but was also hampered by the instability of relations and the dangerous living conditions in the region. Noblewomen were most actively involved in the process of acquiring landed property, but this was often to protect the family's real estate from fines and creditors and did not mean financial and economic freedom for women. However, there were exceptions to every rule.

---

69 ДАОО, see note 54, fund 1, inventory 190, file 2, sheet 111.

There are other issues that still need to be clarified in order to fully understand the scope, exercise and protection of women's property rights in Southern Ukraine in the late eighteenth and early nineteenth centuries. The entrepreneurial activities of nobles of both sexes are in general poorly studied. There is little information on the economic activities and rights of women who lived in cities. Therefore, there is a need to bring new sources into scholarly circulation and to conduct a broad comparative analysis with other regions and practices.

Nataliia Kolb and Nataliia Mysak

The Daughters of Greek Catholic Priests in Galicia in the Late Nineteenth Century. Between Conservatism and Emancipation

1. Introduction and Contextualisation

The invigoration of women's movements with their slogans of gender equality, which was characteristic of many countries in Europe and North America in the nineteenth and early twentieth centuries,[1] also became a prominent feature of social life in Galicia at the end of the nineteenth century. Galician feminism combined the general characteristics of women's movements around the world with specific, regional traits, determined by the political and socio-economic specificities of the region.

Galicia became part of the Habsburg Empire in 1772, following the First Partition of the Polish-Lithuanian Commonwealth. The region was marked by a relatively diverse ethnic structure of the population: Ukrainians,[2] Poles, Jews and compact groups of Germans, Czechs and Armenians lived there.[3] The largest groups were Poles and Ukrainians. National differences were consolidated territorially: Poles dominated in the western part and Ukrainians in the eastern part of Galicia. The poly-ethnic character of Galicia gave rise to the struggle of Poles, Ukrainians and Jews for the realisation of national rights, sometimes accompanied by inter-ethnic conflicts. It also determined the originality of the women's movements in the region, which was formed on a national basis. Accordingly, Polish, Ukrainian and Jewish national women's movements developed in Galicia. Despite their similar ideological basis, strategy and

---

1 Cf. Karen Offen, European Feminism, 1700–1950. A Political History, Stanford, CA 2000, 77–249.
2 In the article, we use the modern term "Ukrainian" instead of "Rusyn", which was used at the time. From the beginning of the twentieth century, the position of rejecting the latter has gained more and more supporters because of its similarity to the ethnonym "Russian", and, therefore, a false identification of Galician Ukrainians with Russians. The outbreak of the First World War resulted in the official adoption of a new name for Galician Ukrainians. For more details cf. Ірина Орлевич (ред.), Русь, Малоросія, Україна. галицькі українці у пошуках власного імені (XIX – перша половина XX століть) [Iryna Olrevych, Rus', Malorosiia, Ukraine. Galician Ukrainians in Search for Their Own Name (19th – First Half of 20th Centuries)], L'viv 2021, 464ff.
3 Cf. Wiadomości statystyczne o stosunkach krajowych, wydane przez Krajowe Biuro Statystyczne [Statistical News on National Relations, ed. by the National Statistics Office], Lwów 1909, XXI/II, 208.

social and political implementation mechanisms, they hardly cooperated. Moreover, the Polish-Ukrainian struggle for national rights completely determined the nature of the relationship between the women's movements of both nations – from veiled competition to mutual distancing and even ignoring.[4]

The women's movement in Galicia intensified at the end of the nineteenth century as a result of the gradual liberalisation policy in Cisleithania, and was accompanied by the challenge to stereotypes about the social role of women. In the Ukrainian context, these processes coincided with the intensification of the struggle for national rights. Moreover, the Ukrainian women's movement not only used general ideas of emancipation and gender equality but also national slogans (guaranteeing equal rights and opportunities for Ukrainians and Poles, primarily in education, judiciary, etc.).[5] From the end of the nineteenth century, Ukrainian women demanded an increase in the level of women's education and an expansion of the scope of their social activities. A significant part of the representatives of this movement consisted of women from Greek Catholic priestly families – the wives and daughters of priests.[6]

This was related to the social status and the role of the clergy in the socio-political and cultural life of the region. At the end of the eighteenth and during the first half of the nineteenth century, the majority of Ukrainian society consisted of peasants (more than 90 per cent of the population). The Ukrainian secular intelligentsia was in its infancy and very small. The Uniate clergy was the only social group that could claim the role of the intelligentsia. Therefore, the Austrian authorities relied on priests as the official representatives of the Ukrainian people to implement their policies in Galicia. Vienna took several steps to strengthen the status of the clergy and the Ruthenian Uniate Church, giving it a new name – the Greek Catholic Church – and putting it on an equal footing with the Roman Catholics (1784), restoring the Galician metropolis and the administrative structure of the Church (1808). At the same time, special educational institutions for the clergy were established – the Greek Catholic seminaries

---

4 Cf. Оксана Маланчук-Рибак, Жіночий рух [Oksana Malanchuk-Rybak, Women's Movement], in: Ярослав Ісаєвич, Микола Литвин, Феодосій Стеблій (ред.), Історія Львова [Yaroslav Isayevych, Mykola Lytvyn and Feodosii Steblii (eds.), History of L'viv], 3 vol., L'viv 2007, 2, 289; cf. eadem, Ідеологія і суспільна практика жіночого руху на західноукраїнських землях XIX – першої третини XX ст.: типологія та європейський культурно-історичний контекст [Ideology and Social Practice of the Women's Movement in Western Ukraine during the 19th and the First Third of the 20th Centuries. Typology and the European Cultural and Historical Context], Chernivtsi 2006, 163–166.

5 Chronologically, the emergence of Ukrainian women's movement in Galicia coincided with the beginning of the third (political) stage in the development of the national movement (according to the periodisation of Czech historian and political scientist Miroslav Hroch).

6 Cf. Іванна Черчович, Емансипаційні ідеї vs консервативні практики. жінки у середовищі української інтелігенції Галичини зламу XIX–XX століть [Ivanna Cherchovych, Emancipatory Ideas vs Conservative Practices. Women Among the Ukrainian Intelligentsia of Galicia at the Turn of the 19th and 20th Centuries], in: Оксана Кісь (ред.), Українські жінки у горнилі модернізації [Oksana Kis (ed.), Ukrainian Women in the Crucible of Modernisation], Kharkiv 2017, 32–51.

in Vienna (the so-called Barbareum, which existed from 1774 to 1784) and in L'viv (from 1783) the theological faculty of the University of L'viv (from 1784).[7]

For this reason, in the first half of the nineteenth century the clergy took over the functions of the educated middle class – the intelligentsia – often determining the development vectors of the socio-political life of Ukrainians. Priests were writers, musicians, scientists and even politicians.[8] They played a leading role in the revolutionary events of the "Spring of Nations" in 1848.[9] Under the conditions of the growing national movement within Ukrainian society in Galicia, the belief took root that the clergy, as the "natural leaders of the people", were obliged to take an active part in the public and political life of the Ukrainians. The same view prevailed among the priests themselves (although, of course, it was far from unanimous).[10] For them, the main motivation for playing an active role in civil society was patriotic: a sense of duty to their people and a belief in the rights of Ukrainians to national development. Presbyters not only took practical steps to organise the national movement but also took the legislative initiative. Priests represented the interests of the Ukrainian population in the Vienna Parliament and the Galician Sejm.[11] The formation of a secular intelligentsia somewhat weakened, but did not eliminate, the social influence of the clergy. An important factor in maintaining of the clergy's influential position was the spread of anti-church social ideologies such as liberalism, radicalism and socialism in Galicia at the end of the nineteenth century.[12] In both public and private discourses, priests were forced to respond to challenges to the authority of the Church and to public morality.

As a result, Greek Catholic priests were one of the most active strata of Ukrainian society in Habsburg Galicia, and until the 1880s, before the emergence of the secular intelligentsia, they dominated the intellectual elite. They were highly educated people, conscious of their vocation, open to service, and their homes were centres of the

---

7 Cf. Svjatoslav Pacholkiv, Emanzipation durch Bildung. Entwicklung und gesellschaftliche Rolle der ukrainischen Intelligenz im habsburgischen Galizien (1890–1914), Wien/München 2002, 36–43.
8 Pacholkiv, Emanzipation, see note 7, 230–232.
9 Cf. Oleh Turii, Die Griechisch-Katholische Kirche und die ukrainische nationale Identität in Galizien, in: Thomas Bremer (ed.), Religion und Nation. Die Situation der Kirchen in der Ukraine, Wiesbaden 2003, 25–32.
10 Cf. John-Paul Himka, Galician Villagers and the Ukrainian National Movement in the Nineteenth Century, Edmonton 1988, 125.
11 Cf. Ігор Чорновол, Українська фракція Галицького крайового сейму. 1861–1901 (нарис з історії українського парламентаризму) [Ihor Chornovol, The Ukrainian Faction of the Galician Regional Diet. 1861–1901 (Essay on the History of Ukrainian Parliamentarism), L'viv 2002, 56f.
12 Cf. John-Paul Himka, Religion and Nationality in Western Ukraine. The Greek Catholic Church and the Ruthenian National Movement in Galicia, 1867–1900, Montreal/Kingston/London 1999, 6f.; Oleh Turii, Der "ruthenische Glaube" und die "treuen Ruthenen". Die habsburgische Politik bezüglich der griechisch-katholischen Kirche, in: Hans-Christian Maner (ed.), Grenzregionen der Habsburgermonarchie im 18. und 19. Jahrhundert. Ihre Bedeutung und Funktion aus der Perspektive Wiens, Münster 2005, 123–132.

cultivation of national traditions, culture and love for the homeland.[13] They raised their children in the same way.[14] Therefore, at the turn of the nineteenth and twentieth centuries, a powerful cohort of young, educated and nationally conscious Ukrainian intelligentsia emerged from priestly families. And the daughters of priests played an important role among them. They actively participated in the social life of the region, increasingly entering traditionally 'male' spheres of activity and expanding the generally accepted ideas about the limits of women's competence in society.

In this article, we aim to explore the nature of the phenomenon whereby daughters from priestly families, who might have been brought up in a conservative environment, managed to find their place outside the family, in the professional and public spheres. At the same time, they were the initiators and activists of a women's movement in Galicia. To achieve this goal, we have divided this article into two thematic blocks – theoretical and practical. In the first section, we aim to trace how in public discourse the clergy outlined the role of women in public life, to find out whether there were different opinions on this matter, whether these views underwent transformations, and, if so, in which direction and what factors influenced the process. In the second section, we analyse gender relations in priestly families in practice: what were women's duties and tasks inside and outside the family, how influential was their activity, by what standards, principles and ideals were daughters brought up, what were the attitudes towards their education and opportunities in life. Finally, we will try to trace what women from priestly families thought about the expansion of their social roles and the struggle for gender equality.

---

13 Cf. Наталія Колб, "З Богом за Церкву і вітчизну": греко-католицьке парафіяльне духовенство в Галичині у 90-х роках XIX століття [Nataliia Kolb, "With God for the Church and the Country". Greek Catholic Parish Clergy in Galicia in the 1990s.], Zhovkva 2015, 324 ff.

14 A characteristic of the Greek Catholic Church as the Church of the Eastern Rite was the right of future presbyters to enter the state of priesthood as married persons. This right was highly valued by the Greek Catholic clergy. Thus, in 1900, 76.8 per cent of all priests in the Galician Greek Catholic metropolis were married, 19.7 per cent were widowers and only 3.3 per cent were celibates. Cf. Наталія Колб, Роль жінки (матері/дружини) в житті греко-католицького парафіяльного духовенства в Галичині наприкінці XIX – на початку XX століття (на прикладі о. Ісидора Глинського) [Nataliia Kolb, The Role of a Woman (Mother/Wife) in the Life of the Greek Catholic Parish Clergy in Galicia at the End of the 19th and the Beginning of the 20th Centuries (on the Example of Fr. Isydor Hlyns'kyi)], in: Kazimierz Z. Sowa (ed.) Galicja i jej dziedzictwo [Galicia and Its Heritage], Rzeszów 2016, 24; Jolanta Kamińska-Kwak, Szczepan Kozak and Dariusz Opaliński (eds.), Kobieta w Galicji. Nowoczesność i tradycja [The Woman in Galicia. Modernity and Tradition], Rzeszów 2016, 195–197.

2. Sources and literature

A variety of sources have been used for this article. For example, the basis for studying the public position of the clergy regarding the role and tasks of women in society was Greek Catholic priest periodicals of the late nineteenth century, namely: "Ruthenian Zion" *(Рускій Сіонъ)* (1872–1885), "Pastor" *(Душпастырь)* (1887–1897), "Flag" *(Прапор)* (1897–1900), "Cornfield" *(Нива)* (1904–1939), "Catholic East" *(Католицкий Всхід)* (1906–1907) and "Church East" *(Церковный Востокъ)* (1911–1914). The editors and the contributors to these periodicals were priests, and the publications formed a common position of the Greek Catholic clergy in pastoral and socio-political activities. The magazines reached a large clerical audience (although always far from the entire clergy of the metropolis) and were also in the field of attention of the Ukrainian secular community. The memories of pastors proved to be a fruitful source for the analysis of gender relations in priestly families.[15] At the same time, the memoirs of a priest's daughter and wife, Osypa Bobykevych-Nyzhankivs'ka (1869–1952), were of particular importance for the study, as they allow us to see various aspects of a woman's life in a priest's family in the late nineteenth century "through her own eyes".[16] The work of one of the leading figures, the founder of the Ukrainian women's movement, Nataliia Kobryns'ka (1851–1920), vividly illustrates the position of women in the clergy. They reveal the limitations faced by women on the way to self-realisation and at the same time outline strategies for the development of the Ukrainian women's movement in Galicia. The works of modern historians helped to shed more light on the lives and activities of the daughters of priests such as Nataliia Kobryns'ka,[17] Konstantyna Malyts'ka (1872–1947),[18] Sofia Morachevs'ka (Okunevs'ka) (1865–

---

15 Cf. Олексій Заклинський, Записки пароха Старих Богородчан [Oleksii Zaklyns'kyi, Notes of the Pastor of Stari Bohorodchany], Toronto 1960; Олекса Пристай, З Трускавця у світ хмародерів. Спомини з минулого й сучасного [Oleksa Prystai, From Truskavets' to the World of Skyscrapers. Memories from the Past and Present], II, L'viv/NewYork 1935; Степан Венгринович, Моя рідня. Спогади [Stepan Venhrynovych, My Family. Memories], Melbourne 1994.

16 Осипа Бобикевич-Нижанківська, Спомини з моїх років [Osypa Bobykevych-Nyzhankivs'ka, Memories from My Years], in: Олекса Бобикевич, Твори [Oleksa Bobykevych, Works], L'viv 2000, 152–181.

17 Cf. Алла Швець, Жінка з хистом Аріадни: Життєвий світ Наталії Кобринської в генераційному, світоглядному і творчому вимірах [Alla Shvets', A Woman with the Abilities of Ariadne. The World of Nataliia Kobryns'ka in Generational, Global and Creative Dimensions], L'viv 2018; Ірена Книш, Смолоскип у темряві. Наталія Кобринська й український жіночий рух [Irena Knysh, A Torch in the Darkness. Nataliia Kobryns'ka and the Ukrainian Women's Movement], Winnipeg 1957.

18 Cf. Лідія Бурачинська, Непохитна (Спроба життєпису) [Lidia Burachyns'ka, Unshakable (Biographical Attempt)], in: Виховниця поколінь Константина Малицька. громадська діячка, педагог і письменниця [The Educator of Generations Konstantyna Malyts'ka. Social Activist, Teacher and Writer], Toronto 1965, 7–32.

1926)¹⁹ and Solomiia Krushel'nyts'ka (1872–1952).²⁰ An important addition were several studies on the development of women's education in Galicia. And the inclusion of reports from the Regional School Council, the directorates of girls' secondary schools, and materials from the L'viv Regional State Archives made it possible to determine the number of priests' daughters in certain secondary and higher educational institutions. Works devoted to the Ukrainian women's movement, especially the monographs by Oksana Malanchuk-Rybak[21] and Marta Bohachevs'ky-Chomiak,[22] were of particular importance for the study. Bohachevs'ky-Chomiak was almost the first to raise the issue of the Ukrainian women's movement, particularly its development in Galicia during the Austro-Hungarian Empire, in a broad academic discourse. In particular, she emphasised the role of women from priestly families in this movement and highlighted the characteristics of the Ukrainian women's movement in Galicia, which she described as "pragmatic feminism". Its essence consisted in "an emphasis on self-help, cooperation between socio-economic classes and […] nationalities living in the area, lack of interests in theoretical discussion of the women's question, practical orientation of women's activities, avoidance of ideology […] subordination of women's goals to those of the nation or the prevalent ideology".[23] In this article, we will underline her statements and at the same time outline the new features, in particular by comparing the public discourse and the private practices of the clergy regarding the social role of women. The need to explain the specificities of the social and political life of Galician Ukrainians at the turn of the nineteenth and twentieth centuries and the role of the Greek Catholic clergy in these processes led us to include historical research on these issues.

---

19 Cf. Ганна Скорейко, Феномен Окуневських [Hanna Skoreiko, The Okunevs'ky Phenomenon], in: Дмитро Ліщук, Лікарі Окуневські в історії України та Буковини [Dmytro Lishchuk, The Okunevs'ky Doctors in the History of Ukraine and Bukovyna], Chernivtsi 2022, 8–11.
20 Cf. Галина Тихобаєва (ed.), Соломія Крушельницька. Міста і слава [Halyna Tykhobaieva, Solomiia Krushel'nyts'ka. Cities and Glory], L'viv 2009.
21 Cf. Маланчук-Рибак, Ідеологія, see note 4.
22 Cf. Martha Bohachevsky-Chomiak, Feminists Despite Themselves. Women in Ukrainian Community Life, 1884–1939, Edmonton 1988.
23 Bohachevsky-Chomiak, Feminists, XX–XXI, see note 22.

3. "It is impossible to deny women the right to have their own position in human society"[24]. The role and limits of women's competences in the public discourse of the Greek Catholic clergy

The emergence of the women's movements in Europe and their growing popularity in Galicia prompted the Greek Catholic Church to respond to this phenomenon. However, the position of a significant part of the clergy on women's involvement outside the family was quite conservative. In public discourse, the Church considered the primary role of a woman to be that of a wife and mother. Employment was seen as a means of survival only in situations where a woman lost the material support of her husband or family. The system of home and school education for girls, social norms and rules regarding women were adapted to this standard. However, the challenges of the time – the development of the Ukrainian national movement in Galicia,[25] the rapid aggravation of social issues (particularly the financial support of priests' widows and orphans[26]), emancipation processes and the popularity of the women's movement – led the clergy to consider the creation of wider opportunities for Ukrainian women, primarily access to a thorough education.

An analysis of Greek Catholic priest journals shows that during the last quarter of the nineteenth century the "women's question" was very rarely found in the public discourse of the clergy. The main theme of the few publications was the desire to emphasise the importance of improving educational opportunities for priests' daughters. At the same time, there were different interpretations among the clergy of the role and tasks of a woman in society, and therefore the level of her education and qualifications.

Fr. Porfyrii Bazhans'kyi (1836–1920), for example, expressed a conservative opinion on this question. He stated that the main sphere of a woman's self-realisation was the family and the upbringing of children. In his view, this was a vocation given by God. Therefore, the main task of women was to become "Christian wives, housewives and future mothers who should raise their generation in the same spirit".[27] Therefore,

---

24 Дещо про жіноче питанє [Something about the Women's Issue], in: Нива [Cornfield], 21–22 (15 November 1912), 716.
25 Cf. Маланчук-Рибак, Ідеологія, see note 4, 171–177.
26 Financial support for priests' widows and orphans was extremely poor. After the breadwinner's death, the family lost the right to live in the parish and benefit from its income. In fact, the family was left without any resources. The state did not provide any financial support for priests' widows and orphans, they could only count on a meagre pension from the Church's Fund for Helping Widows and Orphans of Greek Catholic Priests and on the kindness of relatives, cf. Bohachevsky-Chomiak, Feminists, see note 22, 52.
27 Порфирій Бажаньскій, Домашнû института дѣвочû [Porfyrii Bazhan'skii, Domestic Girls' Institutes], in: Душпастырь [Pastor], 15 (3 August 1892), 341.

the education of girls had to be aimed at realising this vocation. The priest considered private girls' institutes run by nuns of the Order of Saint Basil the Great[28] in Yavoriv and L'viv to be the most appropriate. At the same time, Bazhans'kyi suggested that pastors who were unable to pay the tuition fees for such schools should unite and independently establish informal educational centres, where priests and their wives would act as teachers. The curriculum of such schools should include basic subjects and catechism, as well as housekeeping, needlework and piano playing. The knowledge acquired in these centres would enable the girls to take private examinations in public girls' schools and obtain the appropriate qualifications. The priest described the education of girls based on Christian principles and values as an essential condition for the formation of a healthy, moral Ukrainian society and a guarantee of its happy future.[29]

Another option for educating girls was promoted by the catechist of the women's pedagogical seminary in L'viv, Fr. Oleksandr Stefanovych (1847–1933).[30] He emphasised that the lack of quality education for Ukrainian girls had a negative impact on their life prospects: "[T]he stagnation in the development of our girls in the present time, when the whole world is moving forward, has become very noticeable and is the reason for frequent contempt for them, limiting their best destiny and happiness."[31] The priest stressed that the belief that education was an exclusive monopoly of men was disappearing, and that with the help of knowledge girls could not only support themselves financially but also achieve a certain social position. So Stefanovych convinced the priests that their daughters should receive a thorough education. This would enable Ukrainian women to feel "on equal terms" with Polish intellectual women, to be active in public life and to find a way of earning money in difficult circumstances. Stefanovych considered the women's pedagogical seminaries in L'viv and Przemyśl to be the educational institutions that met these requirements and were distinguished by the fact that the curriculum of these schools included a wide range of disciplines: religion, history, geography, psychology, Ukrainian, Polish and German languages, arithmetic, geometry, physics, natural science, drawing, singing, home economics, gymnastics and needlework. If they wished, the girls could also study music and

---

28 The order of Saint Basil the Great was the female branch of the Basilian monastic order. Until 1892 it was the only female monastic formation of the Greek Catholic rite in Galicia.
29 Cf. Бажаньскій, Домашнŭ института дѣвочŭ, see note 27, 341–345.
30 During the 1870s, the journal "Ruthenian Zion" published three articles on the education of Ukrainian girls in pedagogical seminaries. Although only one of them mentions Stefanovych as the author, it is fair to assume that the other two were also written by him. After all, one of the articles practically repeats the information later presented in an authorised article, and the other talks about the discussion at the teachers' meeting, the initiator and active participant of which was Stefanovych. Cf. Зъ села. Въ дѣлѣ образованя дѣвиць [From the Village. On the Matter of Girls' Education], in: Рускій Сіонъ [Ruthenian Zion], 11 (15 May 1975), 342–345; Допись. Зъ Львова [Post. From L'viv], in: Рускій Сіонъ, 23 (1 December 1877), 729–731; Александръ Стефановичъ, Зъ Львова. (Въ дѣлѣ образованья дѣвиць) [Oleksandr Stefanovych, From L'viv. (On the Matter of Girls' Education)], in: Рускій Сіонъ, 12 (15 June 1879), 359–361.
31 Зъ села, see note 30, 342.

French. Stefanovych particularly highlighted the study of subjects such as the Ukrainian language, the Greek Catholic catechism and church singing. For him, Ukrainian women could not only preserve their national identity but also develop it. The catechist stated that unlike Polish families, Ukrainian families of the intelligentsia made very little use of the opportunity to study in women's pedagogical seminaries. In 1879, out of 280 female students at the L'viv seminary, there were only 32 Ukrainian women (11.4 per cent). At the same time, there was a positive dynamic in this aspect, as in 1875 there had been only five.[32]

From the beginning of the twentieth century, the attention of Greek Catholic clerical journalism to the "women's question" increased significantly. The impetus for this was the constant strengthening of the position and influence of the women's movements in Europe, with their demands for gender equality, which found a certain (although still rather insignificant) echo among Ukrainian women. This coincided with the growing popularity of socialist ideas and atheism in Galicia, especially among young people. In these circumstances, there was a growing awareness in priestly circles of the need to pay more attention to the women's movement. "Nowadays it is no longer possible to avoid the women's issue. Now we have to work with a great cultural movement, which is trying, not without reason, to be taken seriously", urged the priest who wrote for the journal "Cornfield".[33] Another presbyter from the journal "Catholic East" emphasised: "The position of women in society depends on the solution of the women's issue, and thus on the direction in which the further historical development of humanity will go."[34] Thus, on the one hand, clerical journals tried to acquaint their readers with the nature of the women's movement as such. At the same time, in many articles the authors reflected on the trends in the development of Ukrainian women's organisations in Galicia, the real and future role of women from priestly families in them, and rethought the role and tasks of women in society, taking them beyond the boundaries of the family and making them active participants in the struggle for the national rights of Ukrainians.

For example, the journals "Catholic East" (1905) and "Cornfield" (1912) published extensive articles on the women's movement, outlining the reasons for its emergence and development, its branches and demands, pointing out the increase in the percentage of women in various professions in the United States of America, countries in Europe and Asia and the social impact of such trends. The aim of these publications was to explain the Church's attitude and the main areas of its activity regarding this social phenomenon. The authors of the articles, reflecting on the demands of women for

---

32 Cf. Стефановичъ, Зъ Львова, see note 30, 360.
33 Дещо про жіноче питанє, see note 24, 704.
34 Онуфрій Волянський, Християнський і антихристиянський світогляд, а природна нерівність і зависимість жіночого пола [Onufriy Volyans'kyy, Christian and Anti-Christian Worldviews, and the Natural Inequality and Dependence of the Female Sex], in: Католицкий Всхід [Catholic East], 1 (1905), 8.

greater rights in society – access to higher education, professional fulfilment, economic independence, participation in political activity – recognised them as justified to a certain extent. At the same time, they rejected the principle of equal rights for men and women in all areas of social life, proclaimed by radical feminists, as contrary to God's revelation. The priests emphasised that men's and women's roles in society were determined by their different nature (physical and psychological characteristics). Therefore, they consistently insisted that a woman's highest and noblest vocation remained that of a mother, wife and housewife, and that her upbringing and education should be adapted to the fulfilment of these tasks. There is no doubt that they considered the role of mother and wife to have priority over women's social activities. As a result, women's claims to higher education or political participation were regarded as rather dubious. Although such aspirations were neutral and did not contradict the dogmas of the Church, they could be an obstacle to marriage, distract a woman from fulfilling her family duties and even provoke misunderstandings and competition between men and women. The priests emphasised that the demands of the women's movements for co-education and equal educational opportunities for children of both sexes were wrong, since each should acquire the amount of knowledge and skills appropriate to their social roles. In the same way, the presbyters advocated a clear demarcation between the professional spheres of men and women and their relationship to the natural endowments of the individual. The clergy saw a great danger in the radicalisation of the Ukrainian women's movement and its transition to liberal and socialist ideological platforms, as these undermined the authority of the family as an institution and "devalued" the role and dignity of women. Therefore, the Church's task was to oppose the radical women's movement firmly, but at the same time to support the moderate wing as much as possible and to encourage its development in the Christian spirit.[35]

The strengthening of left-wing movements with their anti-clerical and atheist slogans led the clergy to emphasise the importance of instilling strong Christian values in women as a priority task in the education of girls. Special expectations in this regard were expressed for women from priestly families. The wives of priests had to ensure that family life was based on the principles of practical Christianity (joint prayer, reading the Holy Scripture and devotional literature, fasting) and patriotism. The standards for raising sons and daughters had to be different. From an early age, mothers had to eliminate from their daughters' lives anything that might provoke frivolity in their behaviour, to control their studies, social relations and leisure time. Instead, it was necessary to cultivate in girls such traits as tenderness, intelligence, a responsible attitude to the fulfilment of duties, aestheticism, truthfulness, sensitivity and mercy,

---

35 Cf. Дещо про жіноче питанє, see note 24, 710–716; Волянський, Християнський, see note 34, 248–252.

altruism, the ability to persevere and to endure trials in a submissive manner.[36] At the same time, it was the Christian and patriotic duty of women from priestly families to help their husbands and fathers in the religious and educational work for the parish.[37]

This emphasis prompted the clergy to reconsider approaches to the religious education of priests' daughters. In one of his articles for the journal "Cornfield", Fr. Onufriy Volyans'kyi (1880–1911) noted that the religious education of girls from priests' families was too primitive, traditional and not very conscious, not designed for public promotion and protection of the Christian worldview. This isolated them from active participation in the religious life of the parishes, and sometimes led them to be prejudiced against the priestly state, preferring to marry secular people rather than seminarists. Therefore, Volyans'kyi emphasised the need to reorient the upbringing of priests' daughters from patriotic to spiritual and religious values, so that they would be "as passionately and sincerely attached to the Church as, for example, to Ukraine",[38] be aware of church and theological issues, be able to defend Christian values in society and become Christian teachers, writers, public figures and consecrated persons.[39]

Among other things, the clergy saw the role of women from priestly families as being to "Christianise" the development of the women's movement, which was becoming increasingly liberal in character. To achieve such goals, the priests recognised the membership of pastors' daughters and wives in general women's organisations as appropriate, in order to channel women's cultural and economic demands in a Catholic direction and to provide a strong counterweight to those members who supported left-wing views. They emphasised the participation of women from priestly families in the most prominent Ukrainian organisation of the time, the Women's Community (Жіноча Громада), founded in L'viv in 1909, which aimed to develop the national consciousness of Galician-Ukrainian women through the organisation of educational courses, performances and concerts. Instances of the organisation of anti-church and anti-religious lectures in the Women's Community, the refusal of individual members to marry in church or baptise their children, and the growth of such tendencies in the women's environment caused concern among the clergy. At the same time, the clergy

---

[36] Cf. Данило Танячкевич, Сьвященича мати [Danylo Taniachkevych, Priestly Mother], in: Нива, 22 (1 November 1907), 686–689.

[37] Cf. Сестры Служебницѣ, а брошурка "Руска женьщина и ѣѣ обовязки" [The Servant Sisters and the Brochure "The Ruthenian Woman and Her Responsibilities"], in: Прапоръ. Мѣсячникъ суспôльно-політичный и економічный для руско-католицкого Духовеньства [Flag. The Socio-Political and Economic Monthly for the Ruthenian Catholic Clergy], 7 (July 1899), 216; [Ц-ский Г.М.], Задачі священичого жіноцтва в нашій церковно-суспільній праці [Cskyy H. M., The Task of Priestly Women in Our Church and Social Work], in: Нива, 14–15 (1 July 1911), 417–424.

[38] Онуфрій Воляньский, В справі релігійного осьвідомлюваня нашого сьвященичого жіноцтва [Onufrii Volians'kyi, On the Matter of Religious Awareness of Our Priestly Women], in: Нива, 15–16 (15 June 1909), 467.

[39] Cf. Воляньский, В справі релігійного осьвідомлюваня, see note 38, 465–468.

emphasised the need for women from priestly families to leave the organisation if it continued to distance itself from Catholic principles and promote atheistic views.[40]

The priests saw the creation of Catholic women's societies as a counterbalance to feminism. The Western European Catholic women's movement was to become a model for them.[41] There were already examples of such organisations in Ukraine. For example, at the end of the nineteenth century, on the initiative of the parish priest and member of the Austrian Parliament Fr. Danylo Tanyachkevych (1842–1906), the Women's Society of St. Ol'ha (*Жіноче товариство св. Ольги*) came into being. However, it did not gain significant popularity and declined at the beginning of the twentieth century. In 1906, the Greek Catholic spiritual authority approved the charter of the Sisterhood of Priests' Wives of Stryi Deanery (*Сестринства священничих дружин стрийського деканату*).[42] All wives, adult daughters and widows of priests as well as the wives of catechists of this deanery could join. The purpose of the Sisterhood was to help priests in their pastoral and educational work, namely: to care for the cultivation of piety among the parish women, fight alcoholism and engage in charity and enlightenment of the population.[43]

However, women from priestly families were increasingly dissatisfied with such limitations of personal and social fulfilment. Exposure to modern public opinion and in particular the achievements of the European women's movements, the expansion of educational opportunities and the desire for self-realisation encouraged women to go beyond the family circle and occupy influential and financially independent positions in society.

4. "A woman is a human being and has the right to a free and independent life"[44]: The position of women in priestly families, a practical dimension

Awareness of the role of women as an important factor in the spiritual, religious and national development of Ukrainian society led the Greek Catholic clergy to take real steps to improve educational opportunities for girls.[45] However, there is no doubt that a

---

40 Cf. [Ц-ский Г.М.], Задачі священичого жіноцтва, see note 37, 16 and 17, 481–490.
41 Cf. Софія Станьчак, В справі жіночої часописи [Sofiia Stan'chak, On the Case of Woman's Magazines], in: Нива, 18–19 (15 July 1909), 687; Йосип Сабарай, В справі організації нашого сьвященичого жіноцтва [Yosyp Sabarai, Regarding the Organisation of Our Priestly Women], in: Нива, 4 (15 February 1910), 121.
42 A deanery was an administrative unit in the structure of the Greek Catholic Church, comprising up to 20 parishes and subordinate to a priest-dean.
43 Cf. Амвросій Полянскій, Къ вопросу о организаціи священничихъ женъ [Amvrosii Polianskii, On the Question of the Organisation of Priests' Wives], in: Церковный Востокъ [Church East], III (1911), 40–46.
44 Cf. Книш, Смолоскип у темряві, see note 17, 35.

strong impetus to be more attentive and open to the "women's issue" also resulted from the fact that most of the pastors were married.[46] In practice, the very question of the self-realisation of wives and daughters, the possibilities of developing their talents and intellectual potential, in many cases prompted priests to go beyond the clichéd positions and standards offered by society in general and the public church discourse in particular.

At the beginning of the nineteenth century, as a result of the reforms of Joseph II, the lifestyle of priestly families underwent a significant change, moving from rural to middle-class urban standards, which was reflected in the style of dress, the decoration of the home and in the organisation of daily life: culinary traditions, etiquette and the organisation of family leisure.[47] The quality of children's education also improved. As a result, the established life strategies of children from priestly families also changed. As early as the late nineteenth century, there was a clear trend for the sons of priests to choose secular careers,[48] and for daughters to be less willing to consider seminarists as marriage prospects.

This was largely due to the fact that the priest's choice of state automatically determined his family's lifestyle – life in the village, far from the centres of cultural movement and educated society, periodic moves from parish to parish, often modest material conditions and a close connection of family's daily life with the village routine (agriculture, etc.). Thus Osypa, the daughter of the parish priest Yosyp Nyzhankivs'kyi (1835–1912), recalled: "Neither the house of my relatives nor the house of any priest was a model of a good life for me. Village life, farming, constant failure."[49] This was the reason why she initially refused to marry the seminarist Oleksa Bobykevych (1865–1902).

The division of responsibilities in the priestly family was such that priests devoted most of their time to performing pastoral and public duties, while wives had to take care

---

45 Cf. Bohachevsky-Chomiak, Feminists, see note 22, 57.
46 Statistics show that the number of married presbyters clearly dominated in the Galician Greek Catholic metropolis at the beginning of the twentieth century. By 1900, out of 2,243 parish pastors of the metropolis 1,724 (76.8%) were married, 444 priests (19.7%) were widowers and only 75 (3.3%) were celibates, cf. Шематизм всього кліру Греко-католицького єпархії Станіславської, Станіславів [Schematism of the Entire Clergy of the Greek Catholic Stanislaviv Diocese of 1900], Stanislaviv 1900, 191; Шематизм Всечесного кліру греко-католиц. Митрополичої архідієцезії Львівської [Schematism of the Reverend Clergy of Greek Catholic Metropolitan Archdiocese], L'viv 1900, 249; Шематизм всього кліру греко-католицького єпархій об'єднаних Перемишльської, Самбірської і Сяніцької [Schematism of the Entire Clergy of the Przemyśl, Sambir and Sianok United Greek Catholic Dioceses], Przemyśl 1900, 411.
47 Cf. Pacholkiv, Emanzipation, see note 7, 13–16.
48 Cf. Ярослав Глистюк, Генеральна греко-католицька духовна семінарія у Львові 1848–1914. Інституційна та соціальна історія [Yaroslav Hlystiuk, General Greek Catholic Theological Seminary in L'viv 1848–1914. Institutional and Social History], Дисертація на здобуття наукового ступня кандидата історичних наук [dissertation], L'viv 2008, 109.
49 Бобикевич-Нижанківська, Спомини, see note 16, 154.

of organising the family life and raise children. At the same time, with the development of the national movement and the processes of modernisation in the clergy, the awareness that a woman is also an active participant in social life, a man's helper in various spheres of his ministry, took root more and more deeply.[50] This development is vividly reflected in the memoirs of two parish priests – Oleksiy Zaklyns'kyi (1819–1891) and Oleksa Prystai (1865–1944). The first, when he planned to marry in 1851, was looking for a girl who "would not be an extraordinary beauty, but a pleasant woman; not educated according to French fashion, but who would know housework and the duties of a married woman; not excessively rich, but who would also be able to support me before ordination and in my first post".[51] Meanwhile, Prystai, who married in 1893, recalled: "I knew too well what I was doing when I chose a life partner. Not only myself and not only my happiness needed her! […] My church also needed my wife, who was to be the ornament of those many peasant women who were the mothers of the future generation […] their guide and adviser."[52] As early as the 1870s, there are many examples of the educational activity of women from priestly families in local reading centres, in organising Sunday Ukrainian readings for peasants, in the practice of giving Ukrainian-language books to the children of parishioners and in teaching needlework to peasant women.[53]

An important factor in the emancipation of women from priestly families was their active participation in Ukrainian public and political discourse: they read European and Ukrainian fiction and political newspapers; they participated in the discussion of political and social issues in the family and intellectual society, which sometimes met in parishes; they took part in the activities of local Ukrainian societies and in the organisation of Ukrainian cultural and patriotic events. The influence of such an environment on the formation of the views of women from priestly families is vividly illustrated by the biographies of the feminist activists Nataliia Kobryns'ka and Olena Kysilevs'ka (Simenovych, 1869–1956). Kobryns'ka came from an old priestly family in which national traditions were carefully cultivated. Her father, Fr. Ivan Ozarkevych (1826–1903), was an active public figure, a member of the Galician Diet and the Vienna Parliament, a poet and an intellectual, and very tolerant of his children's liberal views. Nataliia's three brothers, who studied at the University of Vienna, introduced her to the latest European literature, including books on socialism and feminism. Representatives of the Ukrainian intelligentsia often gathered in Ozarkevych's house, and Kobryns'ka participated in their conversations and discussions on socio-political

---

50 Cf. Bohachevsky-Chomiak, Feminists, see note 22, 49–50, 54–55.
51 Заклинський, Записки, see note 15, 79.
52 Зъ села, see note 30, 87.
53 Cf. Наталія Кобринська, Руське жіноцтво в Галичині в наших часах [Nataliia Kobryns'ka, Ruthenian Women in Galicia in Our Times], in: Перший вінок. Жіночий альманах [The First Wreath. Women's Almanac], L'viv 1887, 96–101.

and cultural topics.[54] The family home also became a place for Kysilevs'kato to become acquainted with the latest views. At the age of 14, due to the death of her father, she had to interrupt her schooling and was educated at home under the guidance of her brother Volodymyr Kysilevs'kyj, a student of the L'viv Academic Gymnasium (*Львівська академічна гімназія*). He belonged to the democratic student youth and was personally acquainted with the famous poet, writer and publicist, sympathiser of liberal and socialist ideas, Ivan Franco (1856–1916). He introduced Kysilevs'ka with new European literature and talked about social (including feminist) views. Later, Kysilevs'ka remarked: "In general, my upbringing, my education, my fondness for reading, my interest in public affairs and my character were most influenced and developed by my brother Volodymyr, who is 12 years older than me. He also made me, a young girl, interested in the issue of women's emancipation."[55] At the same time, priestly families paid more and more attention to educating their children in the spirit of Ukrainian nationalism.[56]

Awareness of the importance of a good, thorough education for their daughters gradually grew among priestly families. From the beginning of the twentieth century, more and more Greek Catholic priests sought to give their children the opportunity to go to university. This situation is vividly illustrated by the letter of the parish priest Fr. Oleksiy Volians'kyi (1862–1947) to the ethnographer Volodymyr Hnatiuk (1871–1926). Speaking of his children, the pastor remarked: "Well, Vlodzia[57] is doing well, because she should be fine with what she is at the university and in a big city with freedom, without worrying about a piece of bread."[58] The success story of the world-famous opera singer Solomiia Krushelnyts'ka was the result of her parents' unprecedented support for their daughter's educational aspirations. To make her dream come true, her father, parish priest Amvrosiy Krushelnyts'kyi (1841–1902), dared to break off his daughter's already announced engagement – a real scandal at the time – and took a loan from the bank, mortgaging his house, to pay for her studies at the L'viv Conservatory (the family had seven children).[59] Sometimes mothers were the initiators of their daughters' education. For example, Olena Malyts'ka[60], a priest's daughter and widow, also supported her daughter's desire to study. She made every effort to ensure

---

54 Cf. Bohachevsky-Chomiak, Feminists, see note 22, 72f.
55 Швець, Жінка, see note 17, 39–47.
56 Сf. Бобикевич-Нижанківська, Спомини, see note 16, 154.
57 The eldest daughter of Fr. Oleksiy Volians'kyi, Volodymyra Volians'ka (1893–1953), studied at the Faculty of Philosophy at the Chernivtsi University in the early twentieth century.
58 Львівська національна наукова бібліотека України імені В. Стефаника, Відділ рукописів [L'viv National Scientific Library Vasyl' Stefanyk, Department of Manuscripts], f. 34, des. 115, ang. 49.
59 Cf. Тихобаєва (ed.), Соломія Крушельницька, see note 20.
60 Biographical data could not be established.

that her daughter Kostantyna Malyts'ka, who later became a famous teacher and activist in the women's movement, received a pedagogical education.[61]

The educational opportunities for girls were positively influenced by the school reforms of Franz Joseph I in the late 1860s, especially the introduction of compulsory primary education in 1869[62] for all children aged 7 to 14, regardless of sex, nationality or religion.[63] Many priestly families made every effort to send their daughters to school. For instance, Fr. Volodymyr Venhrynovych (1867–1947), personally took his four children (two sons and two daughters) to school in Yavoriv because there was no school in his parish.[64] Another example was the wife of Nyzhankivs'kyi. In order to take care of the children during their studies, she moved with them to Drohobych, where the sons went to the *gymnasium* (grammar school) and the daughter, Osypa, went to a girls' school.[65] Despite the above, coeducation in primary schools was unacceptable to many priests, which they justified by gender and psychological differences between boys and girls, the need for different forms, methods and content of their education and the cognitive inability of women to master higher education in general.[66] They were also resentful of the fact that in practice the system of primary education did not allow Ukrainians to exercise their right to study in their mother tongue, since this possibility was prevented by Polish officials in the Galician education administration.[67]

---

61 Cf. Бурачинська, Непохитна, see note 18, 7–12.
62 It should be noted that nominally compulsory primary education in Austria had already been introduced by the General School Regulations for German Elementary and Normal Schools (Allgemeine Schulordnung), approved by Maria Theresa in 1774. The implementation of this legislative act in Galicia began only in 1777, mainly due to the insistence of Joseph II. However, it was not possible to implement compulsory education in practice due to various reasons. The most important of these were the lack of a clear system of local educational administration institutions, the division of functions among them, the reluctance of the population to perceive education as an integral part of life in the new circumstances and the resistance to Germanisation, cf. Larry Wolff, The Idea of Galicia. History and Fantasy in Habsburg Political Culture, Stanford 2010, 56. Practically, it was possible to implement this only with the foundation of the National School Council in Galicia (1867) and the adoption of the Law on the Principles of Education in Elementary Schools (Reichsvolksschulgesetz) dated 14 May 1869.
63 Cf. Ustawy i Rozporządzenia w zakresie szkół ludowych [Acts and Regulations Regarding Elementary Schools], Lwów 1900, 1–3.
64 Cf. Венгринович, Моя рідня, see note 15, 5.
65 Cf. Бобикевич-Нижанківська, Спомини, see note 16, 152.
66 Cf. Анна Вараниця, Гендерний аспект виховання у Східній Галичини другої половини XIX – початку XX століття [Anna Varanytsia, The Gender Aspect of Education in Eastern Galicia in the Second Half of the 19th and the Early 20th Centuries], in: Наукові записки Тернопільського національного педагогічного університету ім. Володимира Гнатюка. Серія: Історія [Scientific Notes of Ternopil' National Pedagogical Volodymyr Hnatiuk University. Series: History], 2, 1 (2013), 26–34.
67 Cf. Józef Miąso. Z dziejów szkolnictwa ukraińskiego w Galicji (1867–1914) [On the History of Ukrainian Education in Galicia (1867–1914)], in: Rozprawy z dziejów oświaty [Papers on the History of Education], (1991), XXXIV, 58.

A significant part of the priests therefore preferred to educate their daughters in private women's institutions. At the end of the nineteenth century, the Greek Catholic clergy avoided sending their children to private Polish girls' boarding schools, as they educated young people in the Polish patriotic spirit.[68] Instead, from the 1870s, boarding schools run by nuns of the Order of Saint Basil the Great[69] in L'viv and Yavoriv became popular among presbyters because they taught in Ukrainian.[70] In 1898, the number of Ukrainian girls' schools was supplemented by the first eighth-grade girls' school[71] named after Taras Shevchenko(1814–1861)[72], founded under the auspices of the Ukrainian Pedagogical Society (Українське педагогічне товариство). Committed to educating Ukrainian women in the national and patriotic spirit, the priests opposed violating the right of Ukrainian women to learn their native language in educational institutions and took measures to include Ukrainian in the list of subjects taught in girls' primary schools.[73]

The situation regarding secondary education for girls was more difficult. Until the early twentieth century, there were no secondary schools for girls in Galicia. As a result, their functions were, to a certain extent, carried out by pedagogical seminaries,[74] whose aim was to train teachers for primary education. These educational institutions in L'viv and Przemyśl became very popular among the clergy, due to the thorough level of education, the relatively low cost and the possibility of exemption from fees, especially

---

68 Cf. Зъ села, see note 30, 343.
69 Cf. Соломія Цьорох, Погляд на виховну діяльність монахинь Василіянок [Solomiya Tsiorokh, On the Educational Activities of the Nuns of the Saint Basil the Great Order], Rym 1964.
70 Cf. Світлана Турків, Діяльність Сестер Чину Святого Весилія Великого у Східній Галичині наприкінці XIX – у першій половині XX століть [Svitlana Turkiv, The Activities of the Nuns of the St. Basil the Great Order in East Galicia from the End of the 19th to the First Half of the 20th Centuries], Дисертація на здобуття наукового ступня кандидата історичних наук [dissertation], Ternopil' 2020, 126.
71 According to the 1873 Law on the Organisation of Public Schools, the primary education system in Galicia consisted of eight categories of educational institutions – eighth-grade, seventh-grade, sixth-grade, fifth-grade, fourth-grade, third-grade, second-grade and first-grade (or basic) primary schools. Eighth-grade schools were usually called separate schools, the rest were simply public schools.
72 Taras Shevchenko was the most famous Ukrainian poet and painter of the nineteenth century, one of the founders of the modern Ukrainian literary language.
73 Cf. Bohachevsky-Chomiak, Feminists, see note 22, 58.
74 Pedagogical seminaries were established in Galicia in 1870. Officially, these educational institutions were not secondary schools, which meant that young people could not continue their education at university after graduation. However, the great popularity of these schools among the population and their prominent role in the educational system contributed to the fact that seminaries were referred to as secondary educational institutions in the press of the time. Enrolment took place on a competitive basis and the course of study lasted four years, cf. Наталія Мисак, Педагогічна освіта в Галичині наприкінці XIX – на початку XX ст. місце та роль у ній українського населення [Nataliia Mysak, Pedagogical Education in Galicia at the End of the Nineteenth and the Beginning of the Twentieth Centuries. The Place and Role of the Ukrainian Population in It], in: Гілея [Hileia], 51, 9 (2011), 19–24.

for poor female students.[75] However, at the turn of the nineteenth and twentieth centuries, such education was rarely considered by priests as a career prospect for their daughters. At that time, there was still considerable prejudice against such a life scenario, which was perceived as a certain "status mesalliance" or evidence of the family's extreme financial hardship. This is vividly illustrated by an episode from the story "The Spirit of the Times" (*Дух часу*) by Kobryns'ka, where the main character, Mrs. Shumins'ka, who was the wife of a priest, categorically rejects her granddaughter's wish to become a teacher, and says: "Are you so poor that you have to earn your own living?"[76] Similar conclusions were also suggested in an article in the clerical journal "Ruthenian Zion", in which the author, urging priests to send their daughters to study at the pedagogical seminary, stated among other things,: "[O]f those who enrol in this school, few intend to become teachers; Polish girls mostly attend it only for their education. And Ruthenian girls get a double benefit from this school: first, an education and, if necessary, a good salary as a teacher."[77] However, the popularity of the teaching profession among Ukrainian women grew,[78] which led to an increase in the number of women's pedagogical seminaries. By 1914, there were four public women's pedagogical seminaries in Galicia: one in Polish (in Kraków) and three in Polish and Ukrainian (in L'viv, Przemyśl, and Berezhany).[79] On the initiative of the secular and clerical intelligentsia, three private Ukrainian women's pedagogical seminaries (in L'viv, Kolomyia and Stanislaviv) and two Polish-Ukrainian seminaries (in Yavoriv and Sambir) were also established in Galicia before the First World War.[80] These schools were also

---

75 Cf. Василь Благий, Шкільництво в Галичині на початку XX ст. Історико-соціологічний аспект [Vasyl' Blahyi, Schooling in Galicia at the Beginning of the Twentieth Century. Historical and Sociological Aspect], L'viv 1999, 14.
76 Наталія Кобринська, Дух часу [Nataliia Kobryns'ka, Spirit of the Times], in: Наталія Кобринська, Дух часу. Оповідання, повість [Spirit of the Times. Story, Novel], ed. by O. M. Kozakevych, L'viv 1990, XX–XX, 32.
77 Зъ села, see note 30, 344. It should be noted that the pedagogical work of women was marked by discrimination, as female teachers received lower salaries and pensions than male teachers. Financial difficulties deprived female teachers of the opportunity for cultural development. Moreover, their choice of profession often affected their personal lives. When they worked in rural primary schools, they often could not find a partner from an educated background. Statistics show that in 1910/11 55.2% of male teachers and only 23.8% of female teachers in Galicia were married, cf. Sprawozdanie c.k. Rady szkolnej krajowej o stanie wychowania publicznego w roku szkolnym 1910/11 [Report of the i.r. Provincial School Council on the State of Public Education in the School Year 1910/11] CII, Lwów 1912; Bohachevsky-Chomiak, Feminists, see note 22, 59.
78 Cf. Bohachevsky-Chomiak, Feminists, see note 22, 61.
79 Cf. Степан Баран, Галицьке шкільництво в цифровім освітленню [Stepan Baran, Galician Schooling from a Statistical Perspective], in: Діло [The Deed], 63 (19 March 1912), 2.
80 Cf. Andrzej Meissner, Prywatne seminaria nauczycielskie żeńskie w Galicji doby autonomicznej 1896–1914. Powstanie działalność i kadra nauczycielska [Private Female Teachers' Training Seminars in Galicia in the Period of Autonomy 1896–1914. The Creation of Activities and Teaching Staff], in: Kazimierz Z. Sowa (ed.), Galicja i jej dziedzictwo [Galicia and Its Heritage], vol. 6, Nauczyciele galicyjscy. Udział polskich nauczyciele galicyjskich w rozwoju teorii pedagogicznej i badań naukowuch 1860–1918 [Galician Teachers. The Contribution of Polish Teachers in Galicia

quite popular with the parish clergy. Priests' daughters made up about a third of the students.[81]

Some state *gymnasiums* (grammar schools), which were only for boys, opened their doors to girls for secondary education, but this option was not very common among priestly families, who did not appreciate coeducation and could not afford the high fees. Therefore, private schools again became an alternative. The Greek Catholic Church played an important role in establishing Ukrainian secondary schools for girls. After all, in terms of property status, it was almost the main Ukrainian institution that could ensure the functioning of such educational institutions. At the same time, the "Language Law" of 22 June 1867 gave the Church, as the founder of a private school, the right to determine the language of instruction. This ensured the Ukrainian character of the school.[82] The first Ukrainian private girls' *gymnasium* was established in L'viv in 1906 under the auspices of the Basilian Sisters.[83] The example of this educational institution clearly shows the development of the standards of girls' education, particularly in the eyes of the clergy. Education at a *gymnasium* lasted eight years and provided a thorough classical training. It offered a free, friendly atmosphere and a comprehensive approach to youth development. The directorate paid considerable attention to the intellectual, moral, national-patriotic and physical education of girls. *Gymnasiums* had a number of clubs that allowed students to develop their scientific and literary skills. They also studied gender issues. For instance, in their reports and essays, the members of the Lesia Ukrainka Club[84] repeatedly addressed the role of women in history and literature.[85] It was not surprising that the *gymnasium* gained considerable popularity among Ukrainians. Between 1906 and 1913, the number of female students increased by 4.6 times (from 35 to 164).[86] Among them, a significant number of these

---

to the Development of Pedagogical Theory and Scientific Research 1860–1918], Rzeszów 1996, 152–155.

81 For example, at the private pedagogical seminary in L'viv, in the first year of its existence, the daughters of priests accounted for 54% of the students, but after one year their share fell to 30%, cf. Звіт дирекції приватної жіночої гімназії СС Василиянок у Львові з руською викладовою мовою за шкільний рік 1913/14 [Report of the Directorate of the SS St. Basil Private Girls' Gymnasium in L'viv with Ruthenian as the Language of Instruction for the School Year 1913/14], L'viv 1914, 46.
82 Cf. Zbiór ustaw i rozporządzeń odnoszących się do szkół średn. w Galicyi [A Collection of Laws and Regulations Regarding Secondary Schools in Galicia] I, Lwów 1914, 275.
83 Cf. Bohachevsky-Chomiak, Feminists, see note 22, 69.
84 Lesia Ukrainka was the pseudonym of a famous Ukrainian poet (1871–1913), her original name was Larysa Petrivna Kosach.
85 Cf. Звіт дирекції приватної жіночої гімназії СС Василиянок у Львові з руською викладовою мовою за шкільний рік 1913/14 [Report of the Directorate of the SS Basilian Private Girls' Gymnasium in L'viv with Ruthenian as the Language of Instruction for the School Year 1913/14], L'viv 1914, 41–43.
86 Cf. Звіт Дирекції приватної женьскої гімназії СС Василиянок у Львові з руским викладовим язиком за шкільний рік 1906/7 [Report of the Directorate of the SS Basilian Private Girls' Gymnasium in L'viv with Ruthenian as the Language of Instruction for the School Year 1906/7],

were girls from Greek Catholic clergy families, who accounted for more than 50 per cent of the total before the First World War. Later, this proportion decreased as the daughters of peasants, teachers, civil servants, etc. also joined the *gymnasium*.

Academic year	Total number of female students (persons)	Number of female students from intelligentsia families (persons)	Number of female students from priestly families (persons)	Share of priests' daughters among female students from intelligentsia families, %
1906/1907	35	35	24	69
1907/1908	64	53	32	60
1908/1909	103	91	56	61
1913/1914	164	139	72	52
1916/1917	159	123	57	46

Table 1: The number of daughters of Greek Catholic priests at the Gymnasium of the Basilian Sisters in L'viv[87]

Lyceums, six-year educational institutions designed to provide vocational training for women, were not a very popular option for secondary education among Ukrainian girls.[88] One of the main reasons for this was that only one lyceum, the Ruthenian Institute for Girls in Przemyśl (*Руський інститут для дівчат в Перемишлі*)[89], had Ukrainian as the language of instruction.[90] It is noteworthy that the development of this educational institution was personally supervised by the Greek Catholic bishop of Przemyśl, Konstantyn Chehovych (1847–1915), and a number of representatives of the diocesan clergy.[91] Most of the students at the Przemyśl Lyceum were girls from priestly families.

L'viv 1907, 26; Звіт Дирекції приватної женьської гімназиї СС Василиянок у Львові з руским викладовим язиком за шкільний рік 1908/9 [Report of the Directorate of the SS Basilian Private Girls' Gymnasium in L'viv with Ruthenian as the Language of Instruction for the School Year 1908/9], L'viv 1909, 70; Звіт дирекції 1913/14, see note 85, 51.

87 Calculated for: Звіт дирекції, 1907, see note 86, 26; Звіт дирекції, 1909, see note 86, 71; Звіт дирекції, 1914, see note 85, 53; Звіт дирекції приватної дівочої гімназії СС Василиянок у Львові з українською викладовою мовою за шкільний рік 1916/17 [Report of the Directorate of the SS Basilian Private Girls' Gymnasium in L'viv with Ukrainian as the Language of Instruction for the School Year 1916/17], L'viv 1917, 25.

88 For example, in the 1910/11 academic year, 252 Ukrainian girls (16.25%) and 1060 (80.8%) Polish girls studied in schools of this type in Galicia, cf. Sprawozdanie c.k. Rady szkolnej krajowej o stanie wychowania publicznego w roku szkolnym 1910/11 [Report of the i.r. Provincial School Council on the State of Public Education in the School Year 1910/11], Lwów 1912, 75.

89 Cf. Bohachevsky-Chomiak, Feminists, see note 22, 65–69.

90 Cf. Sprawozdanie, see note 88, 7.

91 Cf. XXXII Звіт виділу товариства Руский інститут для дівчат в Перемишлї за рік 1913 [XXXII Report of the Society Board of the Ruthenian Institute for Girls in Przemyśl for the Year 1913], Przemyśl 1913, 4.

Academic year	Total number of female students (persons)	Number of female students from priestly families (persons)	Share of priests' daughters in the total number of female students, %
1904/1905	105	79	75
1908/1909	233	161	69
1910/1911	215	132	61
1911/1912	220	121	55

Table 2: The number of daughters of Greek Catholic priests at the Przemyśl Lyceum[92]

A certain positive dynamic of higher education for priests' daughters can be observed at the turn of the nineteenth and twentieth centuries. Until 1897, girls in the Austro-Hungarian Empire could only study at foreign universities. For material reasons, the daughters of priests had no such prospect.[93] At the end of the nineteenth century, only one such example was known – Sofia Okunevs'ka (Morachevs'ka), who graduated from the medical faculty of the University of Zurich (1894). This was possible thanks to the fact that her father, Atanasiy Okunevs'kyi (1838–?), who, after the death of his wife, received a dispensation from pastoral service from the metropolitan and obtained the degree of a medical doctor. He opened a surgery as a district doctor in Bukovyna, which allowed him to pay for his daughter's education abroad.[94]

The granting of women's right to study at the universities of the Austro-Hungarian Empire in 1897[95] opened up greater opportunities for the daughters of priests to obtain higher education, and families increasingly tried to take advantage of this. Thus, while in the academic year 1900/1901 there was only one daughter of a priest studying at the Faculty of Philosophy of L'viv University, Natalia Budzynovs'ka, (1881–?)[96] in 1910/

---

92 Calculated for: Звіт дирекциї ліцея Руского інституту для дївчат в Перемишли за рік шк. 1904/1905 [Report of the Directorate of the Lyceum of the Ruthenian Institute for Girls in Przemyśl for the School Year 1904/1905], Przemyśl 1905, 39; VI Звіт дирекциї ліцея Руского інституту для дївчат в Перемишли з правами державних шкіл за рік шкільний 1908/1909 [VI Report of the Directorate of the Lyceum of the Ruthenian Institute for Girls in Przemyśl with the Laws of Public Schools for the School Year 1908/1909], Przemyśl 1909, 43; VIII Звіт дирекциї ліцея Руского інституту для дївчат в Перемишли з правами державних шкіл за рік шкільний 1910/11 [VIII Report of the Directorate of the Lyceum of the Ruthenian Institute for Girls in Przemyśl with the Laws of Public Schools for the School Year 1910/1911], Przemyśl 1911, 49; IX Звіт дирекциї ліцея Руского інституту для дївчат в Перемишли з правами державних шкіл за рік шкільний 1911/12 [IX Report of the Directorate of the Lyceum of the Ruthenian Institute for Girls in Przemyśl with the Laws of Public Schools for the School Year 1911/12], 1912, 43.
93 Cf. Bohachevsky-Chomiak, Feminists, see note 22, 64.
94 Sofia Okunevs'ka was the only Ukrainian female medical doctor in Galicia. At the same time, she took an active part in the women's movement. Cf. Скорейко, Феномен Окуневських, see note 19, 8–11.
95 Cf. Женщини на унїверситетах в Австриї [Women at Universities in Austria], in: Руслан [Ruslan], 223 (14 October 1897), 2.
96 Calculated for: Державний архів Львівської області [State Archive of the L'viv Region; hereafter DALO], f. 26, des. 15, ang. 603, 3, 69, 74, 78.

1911 there were already eight such girls (33 per cent of the total number of Ukrainian female students),[97] and in 1913/1914 eleven (28 per cent).[98] Ukrainian women rarely chose to study medicine. In the academic year 1910/1911, only two Ukrainian women studied there, one of them Natalia Turkevych (1890–?), the daughter of a priest.[99] After three years, there were already three daughters of parish priests (60 per cent of the total number of Ukrainian female students).[100]

Rethinking women's issues in Ukrainian society was largely initiated by women themselves.[101] And the daughters of priests played an important role. Despite the girls' desire to get a good education and thus greater opportunities for self-realisation, many of them found themselves in a situation where they had to give up their dream. The reason for this was that in priestly families the education of sons was given priority. Although the family usually tried to compensate for their daughters' schooling with a good home education, women still faced discrimination.[102] This led women to unite in the fight for their rights, to formulate the demands and aspirations and to communicate them to society.

The first such public "voice" of Ukrainian women was the feminist almanac "The First Wreath" (*Перший вінок*, 1887), co-edited by the above-mentioned daughter and wife of a priest, Nataliia Kobryns'ka. Her articles were both a public manifesto for women and a kind of action programme in the struggle for equal rights and opportunities with men[103]. Her views were often at odds with the principles put forward in public discourse by representatives of the clergy. For example, she criticised the significant influence of the clergy on women's educational institutions as a factor that slowed down their progressive development, and rejected the exclusive role of parents in determining the content of their daughters' lectures.[104] Natalia Kobryns'ka also categorically rejected the assumption of physiological and cognitive differences between the sexes as the basis for the distribution of social roles. Following the example of women's movements in Europe, she called on women to take an active social position, to break with the view of women as children,[105] to speak boldly about their problems, to strive for higher education and to ensure their financial independence.[106] Only in this way

---

97 Calculated for: DALO, f. 26, des. 15, ang. 625, 1–729; ang. 628, 1–350.
98 Calculated for: DALO, f. 26, des. 15, ang. 642, 1–479; ang. 643, 1–321; ang. 645, 1–442.
99 Cf. DALO, f. 26, des. 15, ang. 835, 1–437.
100 Cf. DALO, f. 26, des. 15, ang. 840, 534, 604, 696, 725, 726.
101 Cf. Bohachevsky-Chomiak, Feminists, see note 22, 62.
102 For example, cf. Бобикевич-Нижанківська, Спомини, see note 16, 153.
103 Cf. Bohachevsky-Chomiak, Feminists, see note 22, 71; Маланчук-Рибак, Ідеологія, see note 4, 201–204.
104 Cf. Кобринська, Руське жіноцтво, see note 53, 90.
105 Cf. Наталія Кобринська, Передне слово [Preface], in: Перший вінок. Жіночий альманах [Nataliia Kobryns'ka The First Wreath. Women's Almanac], L'viv 1887, 1.
106 Cf. Кобринська, Руське жіноцтво, see note 53, 96; Наталія Кобринська, Про первісну ціль Товариства руських жінок в Станіславові завязаного 1884 [Nataliia Kobryns'ka, About the

would women eventually be able to move from the position of servants to that of partners in the family and society.[107]

To put these ideas into practice, Kobryns'ka founded the Society of Ruthenian Women (*Товариство руських жінок*) in Stanislaviv in 1884,[108] the principles of which reflected the development of the views of Ukrainian women (and particularly women from priestly families) about their role and opportunities in society. For example, while the first Ukrainian women's society, the Society of Ruthenian Ladies (*Общество руських дам*)[109], founded in 1878 in the L'viv Church of Assumption of the Holy Virgin, held more conservative views on the role of women and emphasised educational and charitable activities, the organisation founded by Kobryns'ka aimed to promote the intellectual development and all-round social fulfilment of women.[110]

At the end of the nineteenth century, the Ukrainian women's movement in Galicia gained momentum. This is evidenced by the fact that at the beginning of the First World War, there were already 19 Ukrainian women's societies in the region. By their very nature, they covered a wide range of activities – from clerical to a combination of feminist, educational, charitable, nationalist and entrepreneurial. Active members of many of these societies were women from priestly families (in the Society of Ruthenian Women, for example, they made up 45 per cent – 36 out of 80 members).[111] Before the beginning of the First World War, the Women's Community became the largest and most influential of the Ukrainian women's societies. Its mission was to unite women in cultural, educational, charitable and commercial activities. This was achieved by organising lectures, meetings, cultural and educational events, distributing literature and periodicals for women, caring for orphans and the poor, organising nursery schools and boarding schools for students, establishing educational centres and carrying out economic and entrepreneurial activities.[112] It is worth noting that the society also fought for women's political rights. The activity of the Women's Community society became an important stage in the organisation of the Ukrainian women's movement in Galicia

---

Original Purpose of the Society of Ruthenian Women in Stanislaviv, Established in 1884], in: Перший вінок, 457–462, 457.
107 Cf. Наталія Кобринська, Про рух жіночий в новійших часах [Nataliia Kobryns'ka, About the Women's Movement in Recent Times], in: Перший вінок, 5–23.
108 Cf. Bohachevsky-Chomiak, Feminists, see note 22, 75.
109 Cf. Bohachevsky-Chomiak, Feminists, see note 22, 55, 87–91.
110 Cf. Pacholkiv, Emanzipation, see note 7, 277.
111 Cf. Спис перших членів "Товариства Руських Женщин" у Станіславові, заснованого 7 жовтня 1884 р. [List of the First Members of the "Society of Ruthenian Women" in Stanislaviv, founded on 7 October 1884], in: Наше життя [Our Life], 7 (1950), 5. Calculated by the authors of the article. The affiliation of women to priestly families was established on the basis of memoirs, the press of the late nineteenth and early twentieth centuries, diagrams and the website "Rodovid" [Knowing One's Ancestry]: A Multilingual Genealogical Tree, at: https://uk.rodovid.org, access: 15 January 2024.
112 Cf. Ілюстрований календар товариства "Просвіта" на 1910 р. [Illustrated Calendar of the Society "Enlightenment" for 1910], L'viv 1910, 69.

and was continued in the interwar period by the Ukrainian Women's Union society (*Союз українок*) (1917–1939), which included most of the pre-war organisations, and the Society of Women with Higher Education (*Товариство жінок з вищою освітою*, 1924–1928), the Union of Ukrainian Working Women 'Women's Community' (*Союз українських працюючих жінок 'Жіноча громада'*, 1931–1939), and the Entourage of Ol'ha Knyahynya (Дружина княгині Ольги, 1938–1939).[113] Daughters of priests played an active role in all these societies. It is extremely difficult to calculate their number in the Ukrainian Women's Union because the organisation had more than 60,000 members.[114] But it is quite possible to determine the share in other organisations. For example, by 1925, priests' daughters made up 48 per cent of the leadership and most active members of the Society of Women with Higher Education (11 out of 23 people).[115]

5. Conclusion

The Ukrainian women's movement in Galicia at the end of the nineteenth century was marked by the leading role that daughters of Greek Catholic priests played in its organisation and popularisation as one of the influential forces in the social and political life of the region. The public activity of women from priestly families was a consequence of the dichotomy in the interpretation of gender roles by the clergy, as well as the significance of the national element in the development of the Ukrainian women's movement. On the one hand, a conservative attitude towards women prevailed in the priestly community as in Ukrainian society in general: the sphere of their social competence was seen as the duties of a wife, mother and assistant to their husband/ father in his public work. On the other hand, in the conditions of the intensified struggle of Ukrainians for national rights, the clergy saw the exceptional role of women in the educational activities among the peasants and in the formation of their national self-awareness. This led priests to change their approach to raising their daughters. More often, the clergy tried to give their daughters a good education and sometimes to promote their professional self-realisation. It was the family that often became the cradle of the formation of progressive views of priests' daughters, where they had access to newspapers and the latest literature, participated in the discussion of current social

---

113 Cf. Bohachevsky-Chomiak, Feminists, see note 22, 94–102; Pacholkiv, Emanzipation, see note 7, 284–285.
114 Cf. Руслана Попелюк, Союзниці України. Історія найбільшої жіночої організації XX століття [Ruslana Popeliuk, Allies of Ukraine. The History of the Largest Women's Organisation of the Twentieth Century], in: Локальна історія [Local History], (18 March 2021), at: https://localhistory.org.ua/texts/statti/soiuznitsi-ukrayini-istoriia-naibilshoyi-zhinochoyi-organizatsiyi-khkh-stolittia/, access: 15 January 2024.
115 Cf. DALO, f. 119, des. 1, ang. 2, 1–3; ang. 3, 2–32.

and political problems, and developed their national identity and clear civic position. The expansion of women's educational opportunities and their access to higher education contributed to the strengthening of the social activity of women from priestly families. They played an important role in the organisation of the Ukrainian women's movement in Galicia, founding societies that became a public platform for women's struggle for educational rights, professional self-realisation and financial independence. Priests' daughters developed remarkable activities in various spheres of social life and became quite influential in them, were active participants in the women's movement, dared to break established gender stereotypes, entered traditionally male spheres of activity and achieved significant successes there.

Viktoriia Ivashchenko and Yulia Kiselyova

"I Am Stronger Now, I Know I Can Do So Much". Women Academics in Conditions of Forced Migration during the Russian-Ukrainian War[*]

The Russian invasion of Ukraine has shaken the world. The European community has extended a helping hand to millions of Ukrainian citizens suffering from the war. Among other things, many European academic institutions are involved in the unprecedented effort to help preserve Ukraine's scientific and educational potential. Interestingly, as men of military age cannot leave the country, it is Ukrainian women who benefit most from this support, particularly through long-term resident fellowships that give them the opportunity to cultivate academic contacts and gain a firsthand experience of European research practices.

We believe that this experience will have an impact on the gender configuration of the Ukrainian academic community in the future, as it affects the self-identity of women scholars. Self-identity continuously shapes one's self-assessment of one's competence in career-relevant tasks and is of key importance for the reproduction of the gender order in the academic milieu.[1]

Over the past 30 years, the number of female researchers in Ukraine has gradually increased. In 2018, the share of women engaged in research was 65.8 per cent in the social sciences and 60.3 per cent in the humanities. However, this dynamic has been due less to the influx of women and more to the outflow of men from Ukrainian academia as an unremunerative sphere of activity.[2] Furthermore, the feminisation of the profession is only weakly related to the improvement in women's academic qualifications. Men continue to dominate the academic hierarchy, occupying more positions of authority and defending more doctoral dissertations. In general, the rule is that

---

[*] The authors of this article have contributed to it in equal parts. The project has been kindly supported by the Max Planck Institute for the History of Science (1 October 2022–31 March 2023).
[1] Cf. Shelley J. Correll, Constraints into Preferences: Gender, Status, and Emerging Career Aspirations, in: American Sociological Review, 69, 1 (2004), 93–113.
[2] Cf. Hanna H. Petruchenia and Margaryta I. Vorovka, Gender Issues of Ukrainian Higher Education, in: Chemistry. Bulgarian Journal of Science Education, 23, 5 (2014), 655–664, 659.

the higher the status of a group of scholars, the fewer women there are in it, and this remains the case in all post-Soviet countries.[3]

This state of affairs is explained by power structures and the unequal distribution of labour, when the position of women in academia reflects their status in society and the need to combine the demands of a professional career with caring for family and children. As a result, women take slightly longer than men to reach the next career level.[4]

In trying to explain the gender order in post-Soviet academia, researchers also pay special attention to the socio-psychological values shared by women and the characteristics of their gender self-identity. Discussions of aspects such as women academics' acceptance of the status quo[5] or their insufficient research activity[6] may tend towards 'victim-blaming'. Women academics themselves often deny the existence of gender discrimination in the profession. For example, in a study conducted by the Institute of Sociology of the Belarusian Academy of Sciences, many respondents admitted in theory that a woman's domestic work could negatively affect her academic career. However, citing their own experience, they argued that this factor has a minimal impact if a woman is career-oriented and knows how to manage her time effectively.[7] Such optimistic views seem to testify to the internalisation of gender stereotypes and the inhibited development of women academics' gender self-identity in the post-Soviet world.

The systematic study of the life strategies and values of female academics in the post-Soviet world and the influence of historical, cultural and gender factors on the development of their social identity is still in its infancy. Such work, based on the study of

---

3 Cf. Віра Троян, Жінка і наука в Україні. До 25-річчя заснування громадської організації "Жінки в науці" [Vira Troian, Woman and Science in Ukraine. On the Occasion of the 25th Anniversary of the Founding of the Public Organisation Women in Science], in: Світогляд [Worldview], 92, 6 (2021), 1–11.

4 Cf. Jolanta Kolbuszewska, Academic Emancipation of Women. Scholarly Careers of Polish Female Historians (Nineteenth and Twentieth Century) – Case Study, in: Journal of Humanities and Social Sciences, 15, 2 (2020), 56–69, 68.

5 Cf. Наталья Пушкарева, "Выдумки обиженных женщин" или "дополнительная помощь не вредна": нужна ли женщинам-ученым социальная защита? [Natalia Pushkareva, "Offended Women's Fancies" or "More Help Won't Hurt": Do Women Scientists Need Social Security?], in: Журнал исследований социальной политики [Journal of Social Policy Research], 12, 1 (2014), 39–60, 49.

6 Cf. Віра Троян, Наталія Таран, Проблема гендерної рівності в науці: досягнення та виклики [Vira Troian and Natalia Taran, The Problem of Gender Equality in Science: Achievements and Challenges], in: Наукові записки Національного університету "Острозька академія". Серія. Гендерні дослідження [Research Briefs of the National University 'Ostroh Academy'. Series. Gender Studies], 2 (2016), 98–106, 105.

7 Cf. Татьяна Антонова, Женщины в составе исследователей Республики Беларусь: статистический анализ по итогам 2013 года [Tatiana Antonova, Women Among the Researchers of the Republic of Belarus: Statistical Analysis for 2013], in: Социология науки и технологии [Sociology of Science and Technology], 5, 4 (2014), 117–125, 124.

ego-documents and in-depth (autobiographical) interviews, was pioneered by the Russian researcher Natalia Pushkareva and by Irina Chikalova from Belarus.[8] However, there has been no specialised research on this issue in Ukrainian historiography. An interesting phenomenon occurred during the work on the oral history project "Images of University Science: Kharkiv University in the Mid-20th to Early 21st Centuries": all interviewees, regardless of gender and age, denied any impact of gender inequality on building an academic career,[9] while during public events at the university marking the International Women's Day, this issue became the subject of heated discussions.[10] The new phase of the Russian-Ukrainian War has brought into sharp relief the presence and visibility of women in all spheres of social life and their active role in determining Ukraine's future, and made the problem of gender imbalance even more urgent.[11] The study of women's experiences is thus essential for understanding the impact of the war on Ukrainian society and, in particular, on the transformation of the gender order in Ukrainian academia.[12] Furthermore, the specifics of the wave of Ukrainian forced migration provoked by the full-scale war lie in the fact that it is overwhelmingly female;

---

8 Cf. Наталья Л. Пушкарева, Общая линия жизни и репрезентация успешности в автобиографиях и автобиографических интервью женщин-ученых, в [Natalia L. Pushkareva, The Overall Life Path and Representation of Success in Autobiographies and Autobiographical Interviews of Women Scientists], in: Tractus Aevorum, 1, 1 (2014), 15–27; Ирина Р. Чикалова, "Я и так слишком много делаю для себя – занимаюсь наукой …" Социальные идентичности женщин-ученых в современной Беларуси [Iryna R. Chikalova, "I'm Doing Too Much for Myself as It Is – I Do Science …" Social Identity of Women Scientists in Modern Belarus], in : Е. Ярская-Смирнова и П. Романов (ред.) Профессии. doc. Социальные трансформации профессионализма: взгляды снаружи, взгляды изнутри, [Ye. Yarskaya-Smirnova and P. Romanov (eds.), Professions.doc. Social Transformations of Professionalism. Views from the Outside, Views from the Inside], Moscow 2007, 133–151.

9 Cf. Ольга Красько, Джерела мемуарного характеру другої половини ХХ ст. – початку ХХІ ст. з історії Харківського університету [Olha Krasko, Memoir Sources of the Second Half of the Twentieth and Early Twenty-First Centuries for the History of Kharkiv University], дис. … канд. іст. наук [dissertation for the degree of Candidate of Sciences], Dnipro 2017, 172.

10 Cf. Засідання Клубу університетських історій Музею історії Харківського університету [Meeting of the Club of University Stories Kharkiv University History Museum] 2021, at: https://www.facebook.com/permalink.php?story_fbid=pfbid0ZU6mPEmt6gEz9nsTZ7MJVBVWN3QELQSTFvzQxDCNFKtMf6sFh2PSfbBEDynArGjal&id=1466588730242138, access: 10 August 2023.

11 Cf. Перезавантаження науки після війни: Біла книга. Проєкт "Наука в небезпеці" [Reloading Science after the War. The White Book. Project "Science at Risk"] 2022, 16, at: scienceatrisk.org. access: 28 August 2023.

12 Cf. Оксана Кісь, Жіночі досвіди війни. Літо 2022 року [Oksana Kis, Women's Experiences of War], in: Гендер в деталях [Gender in Detail], 29, 7 (2022), at: https://genderindetail.org.ua/season-topic/dosvidy-viyny/zhinochi-dosvidy-viyny-lito-2022.html?fbclid=IwAR0-e4VCpM_b76OQJELNKqabfXFR4f9tTFEoib7wmFRune6Lbwn5t76XQfI#_ftn4, access: 10 January 2023, paragraph 71. For an example of a popular media project focusing on women academics' experience of the war, cf. Women in Science: Stories of Ukrainian Women in Science during the Full-Scale Russian-Ukraine War, at: https://inscience.io/en/women-in-science/, access: 10 February 2023.

as it unfolds, the "self-consciousness of forced migrants creates a mass situational context, it triggers a social process that changes women".[13]

In this paper, we aim to identify points of growth in the self-perception of Ukrainian women academics under conditions of forced migration as a result of the Russian-Ukrainian War, with regard to their professional activities and their social and personal lives. Our analysis is based on interviews collected for the oral-history project "'Moving West': Ukrainian Academics in Conditions of Forced Migration", which explores strategies of survival and career-building among the Ukrainian humanities scholars of the first (2014) and second (2022) waves of migration caused by the Russian-Ukrainian War. To date, 28 interviews with Ukrainian academics (including 26 women) have been conducted, as well as 14 interviews with representatives of host countries (Poland, Germany, Czech Republic, Switzerland, France). 27 interviews have been transcribed.

In our interviews, we deliberately refrain from asking questions about gender relations. We assume that the interviewees will touch on this issue in the course of answering other questions. Thus, gender themes appear in the form of free autobiographical narration. Interviewees prioritise as they see fit and talk about what they think is important.

Our research combines narrative and contextual approaches. We see each account of migration experience (biographical structure) as a meaningful whole (narrative structure) that exists in the form of a complete story. At the same time, we accept that biographical constructions are not only cognitive or linguistic processes but complex actions; therefore, first, the construction of a biography is the product of social interaction and, second, it occurs in specific conditions and spatio-temporal contexts and has consequences that also have a material basis.[14]

We will attempt to trace the progress of women academics' self-identity at three levels. The first level is the practices of self-identification – individualised, collective or professional; they register both the existing gender order and deviations from it, on which reflection may remain incomplete. The second is the autobiographical construction of gender in the structure of interpersonal relationships and conflicts that influence the redefinition of gender roles. Finally, the third level of analysis involves the study of the construction of the authorial 'I' by the narrative subject in the context of intrapersonal conflicts. At this level, in the course of 'rewriting' autobiography, moments of everyday experience are combined with new forms of emancipatory action;[15] the subject consciously develops a position of her own in the course of living through dramatic, and to some extent traumatic, experiences.

---

13 Josephine Andrews et al., Feminized forced migration: Ukrainian war refugees, in: Women's Studies International Forum, 99 (2023), 1–11, 8.
14 Cf. Bettina Dausien, Biographie und Geschlecht. Zur biographischen Konstruktion sozialer Wirklichkeit in Frauenlebensgeschichten, Bremen 1996, 575, 573.
15 Cf. Dausien, Biographie, see note 14, 590.

1. Self-identification as a marker of gender order

Gender self-identification not only reflects gender associations and stereotypes that exist in a society. It is also a vivid manifestation of the value system, lifestyle, role precepts and interpersonal relationships characteristic of a particular community. In analysing the narratives of female migrant scholars, we will focus particularly on such forms of self-identification as the use of feminitives/masculinitives, narration in the first person singular or plural (I/We), and the definition of one's status as object/subject through the concepts of refugee/scholar.

The most obvious marker of gender order is self-identification using feminitives/masculinitives. Researchers note the long tradition of using feminitives in Ukrainian, but at the same time stress that the feminisation of the Ukrainian lexicon accelerated at the beginning of the twenty-first century,[16] which is reflected in the latest version of the Ukrainian orthography (2019).[17] Discussions about the factors, means and consequences of forming feminitives have gone beyond the purely academic and have created in the media space (and more broadly in society) a 'politically irritating' issue of the "forced feminisation of the Ukrainian women's lexicon",[18] which has both supporters and opponents.[19]

This undoubtedly affects the practices of self-identification among Ukrainian women academics. Several interviewees, when talking about their professional status, traditionally identify themselves as "historians", "employees" and so forth. Only one interviewee exclusively uses feminitives,[20] which can be explained both by her belonging to the younger generation of historians and by the specifics of the professional milieu of the Kyiv-Mohyla Academy, which shaped her as a researcher. This particular aspect, related to the active promotion of feminitives, has been commented on by another student of the academy: "During my studies in Mohylianka, I noticed a rather powerful wave of protest and a positively 'Game-of-Thrones' struggle for the introduction of feminitives wherever and whenever."[21]

---

16 Cf. Алла Архангельська, Femina cognita. Українська жінка у слові й словнику [Alla Arkhanhelska, Femina Cognita. The Ukrainian Woman in Word and Dictionary], Kyiv 2019, 444.
17 Note that unlike in German, where the feminine ending -in is introduced to feminise professions, in Ukrainian suffixes are used for this purpose, most often -k, -its, or -in.
18 Архангельська, Femina cognita, see note 16, 376.
19 Cf. Людмила Смоляр, Три причини, чому варто вживати фемінітиви [Ludmula Smoliar, Three Reasons to Use Feminitives], at: https://life.pravda.com.ua/columns/2017/10/28/227141/, access: 7 February 2023.
20 Cf. ZUMK, 8 Sept. 2022. The names of the interviewees are encoded as follows: form of recording, surname code, place of residence abroad and in Ukraine, date of interview. All interviews are deposited at the Museum of History of V. N. Karazin Kharkiv National University (Ф. 7. Оп. 21).
21 Юлія Гордійченко, Кураторка, менеджерка, директорка: що думають жінки про фемінітиви [Yulia Gordiychenko, Curator, Manager, Director. What Do Women Think about Femininity], at: https://hmarochos.kiev.ua/2017/11/21/ kuratorka-menedzherka-direktorka-shho -dumayut-zhinki-pro-feminitivi/, access: 10 February 2023.

However, most interviews exhibit a transitional pattern of designating female characters, when both feminitives and masculinitives are used in the same text: historian/historienne, woman archivist, directress;[22] "a woman scholar or more of an administrator",[23] and so forth. The unfinished nature of the feminisation of the lexicon is most evident in the interview with a researcher whose scholarly interests include gender. She introduces herself as a "historian, or historienne, as they say now [laughs] … that's what it's called".[24] Another interviewee talks about her colleague in a similar way: "She is … an ethnologist, an oral historian … oral historienne [smiles]."[25] In the latter case, the context of the remark is quite interesting. The interviewee is discussing the volunteer work of Ukrainian women academics at the beginning of the war and notes that this work quickly took the form of looking for research ideas, primarily in the field of gender history:

> "All those who came together were like, well, friends and colleagues, and so this is a sort of scholarly society… because we discussed there, let's say … that, in all this aid there is a huge emphasis on FEMALE[26], and we all noted that there were, for example, hygiene products, diapers for a child, that is, that=that all this humanitarian aid was primarily organised by WOMEN, that is, some such in such, volunteer academic society they, well, some such opportunities were born collectively scholarly ideas …"[27]

Thus, the use of feminitives does not seem accidental; it is clear evidence of the growth of gender sensitivity in the Ukrainian academic milieu, manifesting women scholars' reflection on their gender identity, which is directly related to their professional activities.

A less obvious but important marker of gender order is the construction of the narrative in the first person singular or plural. While our interviewees often narrate in the first person singular, constructing the narrative in the first person plural also sheds important light on the configuration of the gender order.

When talking about the early days of the war, most married interviewees speak on behalf of their families: "[…] we made sure that we had enough food, we started doing something about the windows", "[…] we started looking for information with=with

---

22 Cf. ZHBK, 2 Oct. 2022.
23 ZKRK, 5 Oct. 2022.
24 ZRBK, 29 Oct. 2022.
25 ZPBL, 15 Aug. 2022.
26 In order to bring the spoken and written language as close together as possible, our transcription marks all exclamations and hesitations by the interviewee, short (comma) and long (full stop and ellipsis) pauses, emphasis on certain words and phrases (capital letters), quick combinations of words (equals sign), stumbles (fragment of a word followed by a hyphen, for instance si- sit), illegible fragments that cannot be deciphered and abbreviations (ellipsis in square brackets). The interviewee's behaviour and reactions to the questions (laughter, excitement, embarrassment, etc.) are also commented on.
27 ZPBL, 15 Aug. 2022.

the terrible question, 'How to survive?'"[28]; "We, [...] already EXPECTED that there would be war."[29] Unmarried interviewees, on the other hand, mostly used the first person singular, even if they did not live alone.[30] Only occasionally do we find the 'We-image' at the beginning of such narratives, referring to relatives, colleagues or the territorial community. A turning point comes with the departure from the country. At this point, almost all women become the main characters of their stories, even those who left with children and parents. A pronounced familial 'We-image' is present in the story of one interviewee who overcame all the difficulties of moving West with her fiancé (a citizen of another country), whom she married while already abroad. Therefore, throughout the interview she almost always speaks on behalf of the new family: we, my fiancé and I, husband and I.[31] Another interviewee continued to build most of the subplots around 'us', which represents the creative team formed at her place of work in Ukraine. Along with the description of her work on new projects during her stay abroad, she symbolically joins initiatives realised only in Ukraine, presenting her memories through the 'We-image': "[...] we began to collect unique specimens"; "[...] we were able, found an opportunity, visited this woman"; "[...] we record recollections everywhere".[32]

However, the 'We-image' does not disappear, but rather surfaces episodically and becomes more diverse: along with the family and colleagues, 'we' occurs as friends, the migrant community, academic migrants or academics in general, as well as Ukrainians and, more broadly, Europeans: "[...] THE SAME [smiles]. We are the SAME, we think the same, we are ... we have the same values. We ... European countries, we value freedom, yes, we are proud, we will not allow ourselves, there, to be oppressed. We=we are fighting for our dignity, in this we are the same."[33]

A couple of interesting points can be noted regarding the use of 'We-images'. First, they are not always homogeneous. For example, the image of 'We-nation/Ukrainians' breaks down in situations of conflict between compatriots, or when one distinguishes oneself from migrants from eastern Ukraine, who, according to one interviewee, had a more traumatic experience.[34] Second, even in conflict situations, some communities are so important to women academics that they continue to identify with them even after the official connection has been severed (for example, 'we are the university').[35]

In constructing their narrative of the migration experience, Ukrainian academics consistently create an 'I-image', demonstrating a conscious responsibility for their own

---

28 PEMK, 22 Aug. 2022.
29 ZPBL, 15 Aug. 2022.
30 Cf. ZHBK, 2 Oct. 2022.
31 Cf. ZKRK, 5 Oct. 2022.
32 ZRGK, 20 June 2022.
33 ZMLM, 31 Oct. 2022.
34 Cf. ZUMK, 8 Sept. 2022.
35 Cf. ZMLM, 31 Oct. 2022.

actions, both in their personal and professional lives. At the same time, 'We-images' only serve in some cases to express shared responsibility; in all other cases they also reflect women academics' proactive attitude both in searching for their own identity and in building various communities, making these women agents of change. This is also evidenced by our interviewees' self-identification using the terms 'refugee' or 'academic'. It is in this case that the question of self-identification, both on an individual and a collective level, is most acutely raised, as well as the questions of choosing a specific strategy of behaviour and reflecting on the academics' mission in the extreme conditions of war.

It is noteworthy that a large number of interviewees directly refused to describe themselves as 'refugees', stressing that they were abroad at the invitation of European academic institutions and intended to continue their professional activities: "Well, you know, I still refuse, as far as I am concerned ... the definition of a forced expatriate or forced migrant or refugee, because after all I was leaving Ukraine for a project ... And I am well aware that I have a scholarship, when my scholarship ends, I'm going back to Ukraine."[36]

Openly referring to themselves as 'refugees' is most characteristic of those academics who left in the early days of the war or came from the temporarily occupied territories, but even they see any subsequent receipt of a grant as a change in status: "And I just received this scholarship that I had applied for and I'm ... no longer here as, as a REFUGEE, you know, but as a scholar who is doing research, and this, this status, it's very important to me."[37]

Furthermore, most of the interviewees consistently emphasise their desire to solve any "challenges" they face independently, thus demonstrating that their behaviour is different from that of war refugees. The awareness of the uniqueness of one's own migration experience is reflected both in actions (refusing to apply for papers confirming their status or for various types of refugee assistance) and in the naming of different groups of refugees. In some interviews we find self-identification by distinguishing oneself from other categories of refugees ("they", "Ukrainians").[38] Even in cases where the interviewees acknowledge help from colleagues or local residents, they stress their independence: they mark their status not only as objects but also as subjects of aid, donating part of the money they receive to charitable initiatives or the Ukrainian army.

Overall, the various, sometimes contradictory, forms of self-identification used by Ukrainian women academics abroad testify both to a willingness to change the existing gender order and to the often unconscious nature of the gender adjustments that are taking place in Ukrainian academia. However, changes that are just beginning to be

---

36 ZSRO, 31 Aug. 2022.
37 ZVML, 11 Sept. 2022.
38 Cf. PKWK, 5 Aug. 2022.

understood at the level of self-identification are already well underway at the level of familial, professional and social practices and relationships, as will be seen below.

2. Gender consciousness in the structure of interpersonal relations of migrant academics

The biographical construction of gender takes place in the everyday interaction between women and men and through the interaction with images of men and women and structures of requirements and judgments in specific milieus.[39] Therefore, it is important to pay attention to 'images of others' in the autobiographical narratives of Ukrainian women academics.

Several key female character types stand out in our narratives. The first one is a *friend* who accompanied and helped the narrator on the journey[40] or welcomed the narrator abroad, providing not only a place to stay but also important psychological support.[41] The image of a *volunteer* is important: these characters often exhibit sensitivity, understanding of the situation and the ability to help effectively.[42] In some cases, *colleagues* from European academic institutions, where narrators find temporary employment or scholarships, are represented as quite effective. Beyond professional support, they try to integrate the migrants into the local environment and help with relocation and housing.[43] For many interviewees, these relationships turn into true friendships.[44]

Finally, narratives often feature *women refugees*. They come to the fore when their fate causes the interviewee to feel compassion[45] or offer help.[46] However, sometimes we encounter negative images of refugees associated with conflict situations at the border. In describing such conflicts, gender serves to amplify the condemnation of wrongdoing:

> "There is neither a HUSBAND nor a SON-IN-LAW with you. You, just women and children. And that this is how women behave towards OTHERS, CHILDREN first of all, towards other WOMEN. That is, FOR THEM THEIR SUITCASES, BAGS were MORE IMPORTANT than the fact that a child was standing in front of them ... how scary it is when you find yourself in a crowd where people do not unders=just do not have a culture of upbringing and there is no respect for other people."[47]

---

39 Cf. Dausien, Biographie, see note 14, 587.
40 Cf. PILK, 18 April 2022; ZMLM, 31 Oct. 2022.
41 Cf. ZKPC, 27 July 2022.
42 Cf. PPEK, 28 June 2022.
43 Cf. ZHBK, 2 Oct. 2022; ZUMK, 8 Sept. 2022.
44 Cf. ZKRK, 5 Oct. 2022.
45 Cf. ZKRK, 4 Aug. 2022.
46 Cf. ZKRK, 5 Oct. 2022.
47 PKKD, 18 June 2022.

This kind of ethical conflict indicates the persistence of the gender stereotypes that assign women the role of guardians of honour and social values, making them more culpable for violations of moral and social norms.

Our interviewees also react sharply to the behavioural conflicts that arise at the point of collision between behavioural styles of different categories of migrants. The interviewees distinguish themselves from other migrant women, condemning their inaction and refusal to take responsibility for solving their own problems: "[…] people si- sit for 3–4 months and do nothing, they just sleep, I'm sorry, they JUST SLEEP MORNING TO NIGHT, well, I don't get it, […] and other, WORSE stories, even WORSE STORIES … We had a TOTALLY DIFFERENT, a different vision of our stay here."[48]

Such stories testify to the narrators' refusal to accept the role of the victim, with all its negative and personally destructive consequences.[49] Women academics do not want to feel helpless; they stress their desire to take full responsibility for their own lives and professional development. These ethical conflicts controvert received gender stereotypes. They point to the variability of women's behaviour and at the same time show that different behavioural styles were determined by the professional habitus, which in extreme cases reinforced women's role as academics.

This, in turn, influenced the construction of the image of the 'Ukrainian women academics' that our interviewees encountered in European institutions. The interviewees mention colleagues with whom they have worked on research projects, but they almost never describe this cooperation. Sometimes they even voice criticism of their female colleagues.[50] Thus, while the experience of extreme events gave rise to numerous practices of female solidarity, the return to normal professional life gave rise to practices of competition and rivalry. The emergence of these conflicts was to some extent caused by institutional conditions. For example, obtaining long-term grants at German and French academic institutions was only possible through the mediation of universities and other academic organisations and depended directly on the help of European colleagues. As true competition of achievement was not possible during the initial short-term fellowships, when issues of legalisation and adaptation were the priority for the Ukrainian academics, it was the growth of professional self-awareness and claims to professionalism that determined both specific strategies of professional behaviour and critical attitudes towards the behaviour of others. "[…] they were constantly asking if … if I NEEDED anything […] I had requests like, here take a look at my text, and I want to present it, and could I […] consult with you."[51]

---

48 ZRGK, 20 June 2022.
49 Cf. Renos K. Papadopoulos, Involuntary Dislocation. Home, Trauma, Resilience, and Adversity-Activated Development, London/New York 2021, 35, 172.
50 Cf. PEMK, 22 Aug. 2022; PPMK, 19 Aug. 2022.
51 PEMK, 22 Aug. 2022.

It is interesting to note that some of the interviewees explicitly stated that they consciously refused to apply the term "refugee" to themselves, preferring to describe their experience as "academic mobility".[52]

Images of relatives and loved ones deserve special attention. In the interviews, the family circle of the interviewees included people with whom they had a caring relationship: first and foremost children whom the interviewees tried to save by fleeing abroad, elderly parents without whose help the interviewees could not have continued working, and elderly parents who remained in Ukraine and whose care fell to the husbands. For a number of interviewees, the main characters of their stories are their older daughters. On the one hand, the daughters are *children*; the need to protect them is the main factor in making and justifying the decision to leave Ukraine. On the other hand, in the narratives of three interviewees, the daughters are characters who successfully take on complex tasks. The mothers relate these stories with pride and perceive their daughters' actions as a continuation of their own: the daughters become their partners in constructing the meaning of the experience of forced migration as a spur to professional and personal development. Besides, as the daughters matured in emigration, the burden of maternal care began to ease:

"[…] my daughter has decided NOT to return to Ukraine in the near future. She has started to learn Polish, she has, she has rented a place of her own, she got a job, that is … she has become an adult […] she has untied my hands, that is, now I have to, I have the opportunity to think first of me and my, about m-, well, of my husband and of … my professional career."[53]

Conversely, the narratives of younger and middle-aged interviewees who left the country with their mothers are full of intergenerational conflict, including over such fundamental issues as the decision to leave.[54] Stories of conflict often illustrate the struggle for power within the family, for the right to make decisions. The daughters fought for this right because they were prepared to take on "responsibility" and had important resources – their foreign colleagues who were willing to welcome and help them, including in obtaining academic fellowships.[55]

In order to characterise the changes in the relationship system, it is also important to look at the images of men. Most of them are positive. First and foremost is the image of the *loving husband*, as seen in the 'heart-breaking' scenes of men saying goodbye to their families.[56] There are also the images of a *gentleman* giving up his seat to a child in an overcrowded bomb shelter,[57] and of a *helper* coming to the aid of the interviewee's

---

52 ZSRO, 31 Aug. 2022; ZTLK, 10 June 2023.
53 ZRGK, 20 June 2022. The daughter in question is 18 years old.
54 Cf. PKLK, 16 April 2022; PPEK, 28 June 2022.
55 ZKRK, 4 Aug. 2022; PPEK, 28 June 2022.
56 Cf. PILK, 18 April 2022.
57 Cf. ZKPC, 27 July 2022.

relatives left behind in Ukraine.⁵⁸ Finally, there are the *defenders* – military servicemen whose confidence gives the interviewee optimism as the world around her collapses:

> "I saw military vehicles, I saw rescue vehicles, I saw the coordinated work of our defenders, and for these four hours while I was walking on the roadside, I saw that … there is going to be resistance, it will be serious resistance, because, there were a lot of people in military uniform, who knew EXACTLY what they had to do. And I was, well, so reassured, inspired by this observation […]."⁵⁹

However, there are also negative images that are viewed as an anomaly. These are the men who try to take advantage of the situation for personal gain⁶⁰ or break the rules – for example by jumping the queue at the border. In such situations, the male world is perceived as hostile and threatening.

At European academic institutions, many of the interviewees also worked with male colleagues. Our interviewees find it necessary to talk in detail about the support they received from these men, but in most cases they want to stress the professional nature of the relationship; stories of friendship are very rare. Interestingly, colleagues who remained in Ukraine are also rarely mentioned, even though our questionnaire touches on the interviewees' circle of interaction and the functioning of their home institutions during the war. In response to such questions, interviewees only mention that they keep in touch with their colleagues. Exceptions include academic supervisors, with whom three interviewees maintain close personal contact.⁶¹

The most important male figures are, of course, family members. Our interviewees stress their role and support in the difficult decision to leave the country, seeing it as a sign of marital partnership⁶² and genuine care for the family.⁶³ However, sometimes such support was perceived as pressure, which provoked an internal conflict at the intersection of patriotic feelings, understanding of professional duty and familial love. In one case, the decision to leave, taken under pressure, led to the woman's temporary return to Ukraine. Another respondent recalls with humour her behaviour at the border: "When there was no such clear motivation to leave, I still wanted to stay, so … well, what does a sensible, mature woman do, she calls her husband and shouts, 'It's you, it's you who cooked up all this, it's you who forced me to leave […].'"⁶⁴

However, for all respondents it was a watershed moment when they had to move from joint decision-making to full responsibility for their own lives and the lives of their families. In fact, the husbands' attitudes were only one factor in the decision to leave. In the vast majority of interviews, the interviewees stress the independence of this step. In

---

58 Cf. ZKRK, 4 Aug. 2022.
59 ZRBK, 29 Oct. 2022.
60 Cf. ZKRK, 5 Oct. 2022; ZVML, 11 Sept. 2022.
61 Cf. ZUMK, 8 Sept. 2022; PPEK, 28 June 2022; PKLK, 16 April 2022.
62 Cf. PPMK, 19 Aug. 2022.
63 Cf. ZSRO, 31 Aug. 2022; PKKD, 18 June 2022.
64 PEMK, 22 Aug. 2022.

some cases, this is evidenced by the refusal to mention the husband's opinion when describing the decision-making process,[65] in others by directly stating the difference in outlook: "In him, unlike me, the war did not awaken a sense of mobility."[66] The independence of making the fateful decision is underscored by the interviewees' intentions not just to flee from the war but also to look for opportunities to continue working and be useful: "And ... then, then I just made a decision for myself that if I were to leave, I would not just go anywhere, but I would work. That is, do what I can, because this is also important and relevant."[67] In one dramatic case, the husband was against his wife's departure, and the woman bore the full burden of the decision from the outset, which subsequently led to a deepening of the internal and familial conflict.[68]

Another example concerns a conflict between a daughter and a father. It must be said that the image of the 'father' has positive connotations in the stories of female interviewees, especially younger ones, for whom the effective support of their fathers[69] in a crisis determined the vector of their actions.[70] However, in one case, when faced with the choice between her father's will and that of her fiancé, the interviewee chose the latter; this decision provoked an acute feeling of guilt and an emotional crisis, which the interviewee is tackling with the help of a therapist.[71]

Overall, the challenges of migration led our interviewees to reconsider the importance of family relationships and to recognise their priority over material[72] or professional interests.[73] In some cases, interviewees noted a conflict between professional and family responsibilities in situations where a promising academic fellowship was available to them, but they were unable to fully live up to their own expectations of professional conduct because they needed to care for their loved ones.[74] As has been observed with regard to Ukrainian forced migrants, it is generally family ties that act as an anchor, determining both strategies of integration and the refugees' decision to return home.[75] In relation to our interviewees, it should be noted that factors concerning the family situation and the adaptability of each individual family member have a significant impact on strategies of professional behaviour, including cases of refusal to continue promising fellowships.

---

65 Cf. PKLK, 16 April 2022.
66 PPMK, 19 Aug. 2022.
67 ZSRO, 31 Aug. 2022.
68 Cf. PKMK, 22 Aug. 2022.
69 We should remember that all interviews describe long-distance relationships, as men aged 18 to 60 are prohibited from leaving Ukraine.
70 Cf. ZKRK, 4 Aug. 2022; ZUMK, 8 Sept. 2022.
71 Cf. ZKRK, 5 Oct. 2022.
72 Cf. ZKRK, 4 Aug. 2022.
73 Cf. PILK, 18 April 2022.
74 Cf. PPEK, 28 June 2022; PKMK, 22 Aug. 2022.
75 Cf. Jakub Isański and Marek Nowak, Autobiographies of Ukrainian war refugees. From forced migration to anchoring, in: Studia Politologiczne, 68 (2023), 220.

Overall, sociological surveys of the needs of Ukrainian academics during the war found that women academics with at least one minor child are in greater need of most types of support than men with at least one minor child.[76] This reflects women's traditionally greater involvement in childcare, which was reinforced by the war. Migration, in turn, added new challenges to women's 'normal' duties. For several of our interviewees, this was the first experience of driving a car long distance and legalising the family's stay in a European country. Sometimes the woman became the sole breadwinner in the family.[77] Such vicissitudes boosted women's belief in their own strength. One interviewee, when asked about the meaning of her migration experience, began by saying: "I know that I can do a lot."[78]

It is important to note that the experience of migration affected not only our interviewees, but also the men close to them. Today, researchers are moving away from the view of migrant women as active agents whose gender awareness is transformed while the gender awareness of those at home remains frozen in time.[79] For example, an interviewee whose husband was against her and their child going abroad noticed signs of change in his gender awareness: "He understands more and more that, well, somehow we have survived here for six months, so maybe I will find a way here to continue to survive, and yes we will keep waiting, that for the sake of the children he now sees that, well, it was really worth it here for the sake of the children."[80]

Nevertheless, the question remains as to how these shifts in gender awareness will affect gender roles in the families of Ukrainian academics in the future. Studies of the labour migration of Ukrainian women testify that, in the post-migration period, most women return to their pre-migration gendered family roles, losing the status of the family breadwinner.[81]

Thus, on the one hand, coping with the hardships of war allowed women to gain valuable experience of female cooperation and actualise the role of the female comrade. On the other hand, migration provoked power struggles in women's world, particularly intergenerational family conflicts and identity conflicts among migrants. Once in European academic institutions, Ukrainian academics develop practices not only of mutual support and cooperation but also of competition. The advantages of long-term

---

76 Cf. Anastasiia Lutsenko, Nataliia Harashchenko, Lidiia Hladchenko, Nadiia Korytnikova, Ruslana Moskotin and Oleksandra Pravdyvaya, The Results of The Survey on The Needs of Ukrainian Scientists (First Wave Report) in: Max Planck Institute for Innovation & Competition (Hg.), Research Paper No. 23–03 (19 January 2023), 39.
77 Cf. PKLK, 16 April 2022.
78 ZKPC, 27 July 2022.
79 Cf. Olena Fedyuk, The Gender Perspective in Ukrainian Migration, in: Olena Fedyuk and Marta Kindler (eds.), Ukrainian Migration to the European Union, Glasgow/Warsaw 2016, 80.
80 PKMK, 22 Aug. 2022.
81 Cf. Вікторія Володко, Вплив трудової міграції на сімейні ролі сучасних українських жінок [Viktoriya Volodko, The Influence of Labour Migration on the Family Roles of Modern Ukrainian Women], dissertation report, Kyiv 2011.

scholarships and fellowships for women, in comparison with the working conditions of Ukrainian male academics, who are unable to leave the country, give women new authority and a new kind of symbolic equality, but at the same time ignore the overall unequal conditions of their work. War and forced migration particularly exacerbate the latter, placing the entire burden of family care on women. This, in turn, has led to a redefinition of gender roles within the families of our interviewees. The long-term sustainability of these shifts will depend both on the prospects for remuneration for academic work in Ukraine and on the depth of women academics' reassessment of their values, which will be discussed below.

3. The 'I-image' and the transformation of the gender order

A considerable part of our questionnaire is devoted to specific events, interpersonal relationships and reflections on contemporary social developments; yet the main character of our interviewees' narratives remains their authorial 'I'. One interviewee, summing up the interview experience, noted her reluctance to reflect, but stressed her desire to talk about her experiences.[82] In fact, most of the interviews are replete with self-reflection on the emotional state of the interviewees and the choices these women were forced to make ("social construction"[83]), while also showing a degree of confusion due to the unfinished nature of the events and the impossibility of making 'final' decisions. We can therefore speak primarily of *intentions* in constructing the meaning of biographical experience. We will focus on internal conflicts and strategies for overcoming them, highlighting points of tension at the level of the 'individual self', which, together with interpersonal relations, contribute to the transformation of the gender order.

Internal conflicts are most often characterised by emotional terms with negative connotations: fear (shock), guilt, apathy, weakness. The feeling of fear dominates the description of the first days of the war; it is also present in stories about the early period of adaptation in a new country. In the latter case, emotional hardship was complicated by other problems of adaptation, such as difficulties in organising professional activities (lack of equipment and access to the Internet) or health problems. Fear often went hand in hand with apathy, and this emotional current is defined by our interviewees as 'weakness': "My nerves held out for two weeks. I am probably weak in this regard … I, I don't know, for me the people who stayed in Mykolaiv, in Kharkiv, in Zaporizhzhia and where the bombs are falling, they are just such living heroes for me … I am not that STRONG, probably, not so brave."[84]

---

82 Cf. ZPBL, 15 Aug. 2022.
83 Dausien, Biographie, see note 14, 582–583.
84 ZMLM, 31 Oct. 2022.

However, the prevalent emotion in the stories of women academics abroad is the sense of guilt. To some extent, this feeling is gendered, specifically associated with women's responsibilities and opportunities. Some of our interviewees feel guilty towards their relatives who remain in Ukraine, and almost all of them felt guilty towards their people and their country. Sometimes the interviewees express regret that they do not know how to fight,[85] but would like to "contribute physically to this war".[86] The women are unanimous in saying that they did not intend to leave and describe this event as a difficult moral choice. In one characteristic story, the interviewee had only planned to accompany her children to the border and then return home. It was only after seeing the chaos at the border in the early days of the war and the helplessness of her eldest daughter that she decided to continue the journey. It is interesting that only three interviewees mention the condemnation of their actions by other people, but almost all of them look for arguments that would justify their decision. This is particularly true for women from the 'safer' areas – western and central Ukraine. They often explain their decision by the proximity of their homes to military facilities.[87]

Despite the destructive impact of these emotions, for many interviewees they were the drivers of internal change that allowed them to turn their own 'weakness' into 'strength': "And how I was just ... well ... I was MAD at myself, I HATED myself, why am I so FRAIL, why am I so WEAK, THIS IS NOT RIGHT, I must ACT! ENOUGH! COME ON, LET'S WORK."[88]

Awareness of one's own strength comes through hard inner work, which the interviewees describe as "rethinking oneself",[89] "a shock that, in general, basically, COMPLETELY changes you",[90] "a new phase",[91] "getting totally out of the comfort zone",[92] new resourcefulness[93] and, in the end, full acceptance of one's experience: "[…] we have already been through this and we already have this experience and there is no more of this fear."[94] Of course, the traumatic experience is not fully overcome, but the internal transformation mentioned by many interviewees makes it possible to take full responsibility for one's life:

"[…] and so I AM DIFFERENT because we have become, you know, our values have probably changed ... We have become more independent, so, I never thought that I would

---

85 Cf. PPMK, 19 Aug. 2022.
86 ZMLM, 31 Oct. 2022.
87 Cf. PKMK, 22 Aug. 2022; ZPBL, 15 Aug. 2022.
88 PEMK, 22 Aug. 2022.
89 PEMK, 22 Aug. 2022.
90 PILK, 18 April 2022.
91 ZRBK, 29 Oct. 2022.
92 ZUMK, 8 Sept. 2022.
93 Cf. PKWK, 5 Aug. 2022.
94 ZPBL, 15 Aug. 2022.

have to find somewhere, well, not knowing the language, um, reserves, and actually inner reserves, and although I want to say that ... there are times when I feel very lost [...]."[95]

All of the narratives not only mention the internal transformation but also speculate on its possible trajectories, resulting from a rethinking of moral obligations in response to external challenges and internal conflicts. In fact, stories of social and professional self-mobilisation become a justification, a way of overcoming feelings of guilt. Early in the war, some interviewees became involved in voluntary and aid work, which allowed them to stabilise their inner state. For one of them, this was a turning point: she admitted that in the future she wanted to "move towards volunteer work".[96] Other interviewees returned to their professional work, but many of them combined it with social activism, viewing their work as a special "informational front": "I can only add one thing, that, everyone must do everything on their own front, so that we win as soon as possible. And-and I believe that our work, and for us it is information work, that this informational front plays a very important role [...]."[97]

In the end, it is in the professional sphere that the interviewees say they will be able to realise themselves most fully. There are several strategies that Ukrainian migrant academics use to project their professional trajectories, both for the duration of the war and after its end. While in the case of forced migration, interviewees speak of professional self-development (learning languages, mastering new teaching and research practices), new opportunities to work on projects started before the war and participation in new international projects, which in turn means seeking funding opportunities and taking part in academic and other events. They see the integration of Ukrainian researchers into the European academic community as an important goal of such work, and, more broadly, speak of a special mission – "to do our utmost now so that the world hears us, sees us, understands who Ukrainians are".[98]

Despite the traumatic nature of everything future-related, most of the interviewees have also decided on the direction of their careers after the end of the war. Almost all said they planned to return to Ukraine; two respondents have already done so. Even those who lost their jobs due to going abroad are confident they will continue their academic careers: "But I decided 'No! I still want to stay in my country'. And now my decision is the same. That is, as soon as the war ends, well, my fellowship ends, I'm going to Ukraine. Even if I don't have a job, I'm sure I'll find something."[99]

Some of the interviewees speak of restructuring their careers: changing or adjusting the research interests, increasing academic mobility, establishing closer ties with foreign

---

95 PKKD, 18 June 2022.
96 PDLR, 17 June 2022.
97 ZMLM, 31 Oct. 2022.
98 ZRGK, 20 June 2022.
99 ZKRK, 4 Aug. 2022.

scholars or intensifying social activism.[100] The latter point is particularly striking. Most interviewees identify systemic problems in the organisation of Ukrainian academia and have wide-ranging views on reforms in this area, especially in the field of human resources. Older interviewees tend to be more pessimistic about the future of their profession after the war, but many see themselves as agents of change. They see their role as educating a new generation of students,[101] incorporating the experience they have gained abroad into the educational process,[102] participating in the work of international organisations and popularising the Ukrainian educational product.[103] As one interviewee observes, "we still don't know what peace will be like after the war, and that's up to us, too".[104]

The interviewees were more reluctant to discuss their personal needs. However, if during the first months abroad most women denied themselves even basic needs, two strategies took shape over time. Some women strictly control their free time, allowing themselves only 'small pleasures' such as walks and visits to museums,[105] while others somewhat extend the boundaries of what is 'allowed', including, for instance, travelling.[106] Whenever the subject is raised, however, the interviewees reject the idea of really taking time off, stressing that "if I'm HERE already, then I will do my UTMOST here … for my country, for my family, and for myself"[107]; "I will do the best I can with what … God is giving me in my life right now."[108] Interestingly, they view this lifestyle as temporary and specifically mention that they will reconsider their lifestyle when they return home – for example, giving up additional work in favour of research and proper recreation: "[…] to work as a researcher, to work as a teacher, but not five jobs … as it used to be, yes, in Kharkiv, but just one, to have time for the family, to have time for some other aspects of life […]".[109]

In this way, Ukrainian academic migrants, in constructing their 'I-images', first and foremost highlight the points of tension which will later allow them to move on to the construction of a new identity, in which 'weakness' becomes 'strength'. This process includes becoming aware of the new reality in which women academics are not victims of circumstance but agents of change, and mapping out possible directions of this change. The focus is on the professional sphere, while the rethinking of personal needs, although recognised as an important component of the future life scenario, is postponed until the end of the war.

---

100 Cf. PKWK, 5 Aug. 2022; PEMK, 22 Aug. 2022.
101 Cf. PKKD, 18 June 2022.
102 Cf. ZUMK, 8 Sept. 2022.
103 Cf. PEMK, 22 Aug. 2022.
104 PEMK, 22 Aug. 2022.
105 Cf. ZVML, 11 Sept. 2022; ZPBL, 15 Aug. 2022.
106 Cf. PEMK, 22 Aug. 2022; ZRBK, 29 Oct. 2022.
107 ZSRO, 31 Aug. 2022.
108 PPEK, 28 June 2022.
109 PPEK, 28 June 2022.

4. Conclusion

Overall, the study of the transformation of the gender order under extraordinary conditions, as almost tectonic shifts unfold in all spheres of Ukrainian social life, clearly shows the growth of women's self-awareness at all levels, although not always with the same intensity. The narratives we have analysed record a variety of interpersonal and intrapersonal conflicts (points of tension), both at the level of interpersonal relations and at the level of the professional self-perception of the female researchers. An interesting disproportion may be observed: although intra-family conflicts are sometimes the most traumatic, the growth of gender consciousness at the family level is not linear. On the one hand, in most cases it is the need to save loved ones that becomes a push factor for migration, and the experience of facing the challenges of migration reinforces the personality. On the other hand, family ties remain anchors that define the limits of women's real freedom, compelling them to correlate individual prospects with the needs of others. It is also fair to assume that family ties sometimes serve as an excuse for unrealised professional potential during the time abroad and as a justification for a possible return to traditional gender roles in Ukrainian society in the future, during the post-war reconstruction.

In these conditions, it is the transformations that take place at the level of professional academic self-consciousness that may be able to guarantee the irreversibility of change in the definition of gender roles. Interestingly, the analysed interviews demonstrate that the question of satisfying personal needs is less prominent for Ukrainian academic migrants. On the contrary, all interviewees have a new vision of their professional development, which not only includes their academic career but also social activism. This phenomenon can only be explained in terms of the contexts and values from which these narratives have emerged. The new opportunities for professional fulfilment and growth, on the one hand, intensify the sense of guilt of women academics and, on the other hand, form and sharpen their understanding of their duty as intellectuals to serve as society's critical consciousness. The resulting internal crisis, aggravated by a number of other factors (the rupture of the existing social ties, sometimes the loss of one's position in academia, uncertainty about one's professional future, conflict between one's civic attitude and family obligations, etc.), can be overcome by forming a clear idea of one's mission. This mission, seen as a kind of professional battleground, both allows one to write migration into the autobiographical narrative and serves as a manifestation of group identity, which indicates shifts in the existing gender order, reflected both in specific actions and in the creation of a specific narrative language.

Finally, it is important to stress that gender identity, like any identity, is a process of 'being' or 'becoming' rather than of 'declaring'. Undoubtedly, women's academic and social activity in the context of migration, their willingness to shoulder full responsibility for their loved ones and their reflection on changing gender identity in response to internal value conflicts are all part of this process of 'becoming'. But the real test of the sustainability of the transformation in gender consciousness will come with a change of context – in this case, the return of the women academics to Ukraine. It seems to us that the case of the Ukrainian academics will be able to shed important light on the relationship between the context that causes the growth of gender consciousness, the values it shapes and the potential for these values to participate in the formation of a new context – specific structures and relations within the academic community of post-war Ukraine. In our view, the success of the project will depend to a great extent on the unity of the gender discourses that are being formed inside and outside Ukraine.

Tetiana Isaieva

Das Gendermuseum in Charkiv. Ein Dialog über Geschlechtergleichheit und Menschenrechte – 15 Jahre informelle Bildung

In den Jahren 2008/09 wurde das erste interaktive Museum zum Thema Gender in der postsowjetischen Ukraine in meiner Heimatstadt Charkiv gegründet, das gleichzeitig auch das erste Gendermuseum im östlichen Europa darstellt.[1] Die Idee zu einem Museum für Frauen- und Geschlechtergeschichte entstand bereits 2006 in Schweden und wurde dann von einigen Frauen, die für Fragen der Geschlechterverhältnisse sensibilisiert waren, in die Tat umgesetzt. Zunächst engagierten sich neben mir auch einige Menschen aus Charkiv, nämlich Marija Čorna, Ljudmyla Stefanova, Inna Lazaruk, Ol'ha Karas'ova und Dmytro Martynenko für die Durchführung des Projekts. Sie meinten: „Wir wissen nicht, ob und wie es funktionieren kann, aber wir unterstützen Dich!" Auch in Kyïv haben mehrere Frauen (Olesja Bondar, Olena Suslova und Larysa Kobelyans'ka) das Vorhaben mitgetragen, woran ich mich gerne erinnere, denn Unterstützung ist gerade in solchen Dingen so wichtig. Das Museumsprojekt ist Teil der NGO Centre of Gender Culture (*Centr hendernoï kul'tury*) und wird von mehreren Organisationen gefördert: dem Ukrainischen Frauenfonds (*Ukraïnc'kyj žinočyj fond*) im Rahmen des Programms für Gleichbehandlung und Frauenrechte in der Ukraine, der Abteilung für Familie und Jugend der Regionalverwaltung Charkiv und dem US-amerikanischen Global Fund for Women[2], der finanzielle Mittel für Frauenprojekte und -initiativen bereitstellt. Partnerorganisationen des Museums sind nationale und internationale NGOs, die sich für Geschlechtergleichheit und das *Empowerment* von Frauen einsetzen, so zum Beispiel die 2007 in Meran gegründete International Association of Women's Museums[3]. Dem Vorstand gehört auch Stefania Pitscheider Soraperra an, seit 2009 Leiterin des Frauenmuseums Hittisau in Österreich[4].

Zu den Hauptaktivitäten des Museums zählen geschlechterorientierte Bildungsarbeit und Informationskampagnen; die zentralen Ziele bestehen im Ausbau von kul-

---
1 Siehe die Website des Museums, unter: https://gender.at.ua/publ/5-1-0-293, Zugriff: 9.1.24.
2 Siehe https://www.globalfundforwomen.org/, Zugriff: 9.1.24.
3 Siehe https://iawm.international/, Zugriff: 9.1.24.
4 Zum Frauenmuseum Hittisau vgl. Stefania Pitscheider, Das Frauenmuseum Hittisau – ein Ort der Vielstimmigkeit und Inklusion, in: L'Homme. Z. F. G., 34, 1 (2023): Kinder in Heimen, hg. von Anelia Kassabova und Sandra Maß, 127–134.

turellen Beziehungen zwischen der Ukraine und anderen Ländern, der Stärkung der Frauenbewegung und der Lancierung von Wissen über Geschlechtergeschichte und Geschlechterthemen in die journalistische und allgemeine Öffentlichkeit.

Das Museum sammelt Objekte, die den Konstruktionscharakter von Geschlecht und die damit verbundenen Positionierungen in der Gesellschaft illustrieren, um deutlich zu machen, dass diese nicht nur Frauen betreffen. Die Ausstellungen zeigen, dass trotz aller positiven Veränderungen in der Ukraine (die Entscheidung für einen demokratischen Weg und die Entwicklung einer Zivilgesellschaft, die das politische Handeln positiv beeinflusst) Frauen wie Männer unter Diskriminierung leiden. Mehr als 4.000 Ausstellungsstücke verdeutlichen, dass die Frauenbewegung in der Ukraine und auch international kein temporäres Phänomen, sondern einen natürlichen und regulären Prozess darstellt, der seit mehreren hundert Jahren in der Menschheitsgeschichte voranschreitet. Dies wurde uns umso klarer, je genauer wir uns mit der Geschichte der Frauen, deren Stellung und Aktivitäten in der Ukraine beschäftigten (vor allem in der Zeit bis 1917, als die Bolschewiki an die Macht kamen).

Die Ausstellungen umfassen ein breites Spektrum an für die Frauen- und Geschlechtergeschichte relevanten Themen, unter anderem Geschlechterstereotypen, Sexismus, häusliche Gewalt und Männlichkeit. Viele Menschen in der Ukraine wissen nicht, dass sich die Geschlechterforschung nicht nur mit Frauen befasst, sondern sich auch mit der Stellung der Männer in der Gesellschaft beschäftigt. Ich denke, dass Geschlechterstereotype in der Familie und im Bildungssystem am einschneidensten sind. Um auch Männer zu erreichen, sprechen wir ihre niedrige Lebenserwartung an, die in der Ukraine nur 60 bis 62 Jahre beträgt.

Das Museum präsentiert einige seiner Ausstellungen auch online, so etwa „Something about Gender", „HERstory of the War", „Women in Defense of Peace and Security", „Inventions and Innovations from Sweden", „About Sexism" und „The Truth about March 8th" (alle Ausstellungen sind auf Ukrainisch und Englisch auf der Website des Museums[5] zugänglich).

1. HERstory of the War

„HERstory of the War" ist ein Projekt über die Erfahrungen von Frauen, in deren Leben der Krieg eindrang. Die Ereignisse Ende Februar 2022 unterteilten das Leben aller Menschen in der Ukraine und auch weit jenseits der Landesgrenzen in ein Vorher und ein Nachher. Um Quellen zum Geschehen der ersten Tage, Wochen und Monate des Überfalls Russlands auf die Ukraine zu bewahren, bat das Team des Gendermuseums eine Reihe von Frauen, ihre Geschichte zu erzählen. Viele antworteten und gaben uns Einblick in ihre Tagebücher, Fotos, Zeichnungen, Gedichte, Chroniken,

---

5 Siehe www.gendermuseum.com, Zugriff: 9.1.2024.

Erzählungen und Geschichten. Die Art und Weise, wie sie sich beteiligten und in welchem Umfang sie berichteten, blieb den Zeitzeuginnen überlassen. „HERstory of the War" wurde mit Hilfe des Ukrainischen Frauenfonds umgesetzt und zielt darauf ab, eine Online-Anthologie von Geschichten von Frauen über den russisch-ukrainischen Krieg für das Gendermuseum aufzubauen. Mehr als 100 schriftliche und mündliche Geschichten wurden gesammelt und auf Ukrainisch sowie Englisch auf der Internetseite des Museums zugänglich gemacht.

Am 22. August 2022 (dem Unabhängigkeitstag der Ukraine) erfolgte im Haus der Geschichte Österreich die Eröffnung der Ausstellung „My Voice Means Something. Ukrainian Women About War (Mij holos maje značennja: ukraïns'ki žinky pro vijnu)"[6]. Ermöglicht wurde diese Ausstellung, die zwölf Erzählungen aus der virtuellen Ausstellung „HERstory of the War" präsentierte,[7] durch die fruchtbare Kooperation zwischen dem Gendermuseum Charkiv und dem Haus der Geschichte. Einige Texte von „HERstory of the War" wurden auch in anderen Ländern gezeigt, so in der Ausstellung „Women of Ukraine. Stories of Life and War (Žinky Ukraïny. Istoriï žyttja ta vijny)", die am 3. März 2023 im Heilig-Geist-Haus in Nürnberg eröffnet wurde. Sie wurde vom Online-Museum „Frauenkultur Regional-International" (Verein „Frauen in der Einen Welt") in Kooperation mit dem Gendermuseum Charkiv organisiert. Darüber hinaus wanderte das Projekt auch nach Taiwan, wo im National Museum of Human Rights (Taiwan) ab 21. April 2023 die zweisprachige Ausstellung (englisch und chinesisch) „When Temporary Becomes the Ordinary" lief.

2. Ausblick: das Konzept der Ausstellung „Die Unglaublichen (Nejmovirni)"

2024 feiert die ukrainische Frauenbewegung ihren 140. Jahrestag. Am 8. Dezember 1884 gründete Natalja Kobryn'ska, eine ukrainische Schriftstellerin und Feministin, den Verein ruthenischer Frauen in Stanislau (*Tovarystvo ruskich zhenshchin v Stanislavovi*; heute Ivano-Frankivs'k). Ziel dieses Vereins war es, gebildete Frauen für Literatur zu interessieren und neue soziale Ideen publik zu machen.

Über Frauengeschichte wird bis heute in der Ukraine im Alltag kaum gesprochen, da sie als zweitrangig und unbedeutend gilt. Vieles ist noch unbekannt. Aber die Frauengeschichte wird immer sichtbarer, und die Gesellschaft ist täglich mit ihrem Erbe konfrontiert. Trotz dieser Entwicklung schenken die ukrainischen Medien und die Politik Frauenangelegenheiten meist nur am 8. März verstärkte Aufmerksamkeit. Wir hoffen daher, dass die Aktivitäten, die dem Jahrestag gewidmet sind, Frauenge-

---

6 Siehe https://hdgoe.at/my_voice_means_something, Zugriff: 9.1.2024.
7 Im Anschluss an diesen Text werden exemplarisch vier Beiträge von Frauen, die sich an dem HERstory of the War-Projekt beteiligt haben, präsentiert [Anm. der Herausgeberinnen].

schichte einer breiteren Öffentlichkeit zugänglich machen. Der Kampf für ein ‚normales Leben', das jede Person unabhängig von ihrem Geschlecht verdient, geht auch heute weiter. Aber was wir schon erreicht haben, ermutigt uns, trotz der Schwierigkeiten auf diesem Weg fortzufahren. Mehr als nur ein Buch wäre nötig, um den Kampf zu beschreiben. Doch gerade die Bezugnahme auf die Vergangenheit ist wichtig, um zu verstehen, was heute passiert. Dies ist auch die Leitidee der Ausstellung „Die Unglaublichen", die uns die Geschichte der ukrainischen Frauen erzählt. Sie soll einem internationalen Publikum Ukrainerinnen in Öffentlichkeit, Kultur, Wissenschaft und Sport präsentieren und deren Einfluss auf die Entwicklung aller Sphären der ukrainischen Gesellschaft sowie auf die europäische und globale Geschichte während der 140 Jahre der ukrainischen Frauenbewegung (1884–2024) veranschaulichen. Die Ausstellung soll 70 Kunstprojekte zeigen: Werke von ukrainischen Künstlerinnen, in vielfältigen Techniken, etwa Fotos und Videos, wobei die Kunstprojekte von biografischen Informationen über die Künstlerinnen, ihre Rolle und Erfolge begleitet werden.

Aus dem Englischen von Dietlind Hüchtker

„HERstory of the War". Der Krieg gegen die Ukraine in Erfahrungsberichten ukrainischer Frauen

Das Gendermuseum in Charkiv hatte nach dem Überfall der Russischen Föderation auf die Ukraine im Februar 2022 einen Aufruf gestartet, der Frauen dazu einlud, über ihre durch den Krieg völlig veränderten Lebenssituationen zu berichten. Die Resonanz auf diesen Aufruf war groß und sehr viele Frauen aus allen Teilen der Ukraine schilderten Auswirkungen des Krieges, beschrieben private und berufliche Herausforderungen sowie Erfahrungen mit Kriegsgewalt und Heimatverlust. Das Haus der Geschichte Österreich (HdGÖ) hatte in Kooperation mit dem Gendermuseum Charkiv von August bis Oktober 2022 Ausschnitte aus den Selbstzeugnissen von zwölf Frauen im Rahmen der Ausstellung „My Voice Means Something – Ukrainische Frauen über den Krieg" in deutscher und englischer Übersetzung präsentiert. Für die vorliegende L'Homme-Ausgabe haben wir vier Texte ausgewählt, die bis auf den Text von Alina Sarnatska nicht in der Auswahl des HdGÖ vertreten waren, und sie ins Deutsche übertragen. In diesen sehr anschaulichen Erfahrungsberichten aus ganz unterschiedlichen Perspektiven wird der Krieg gegen die Ukraine als radikaler Einschnitt in die jeweilige Lebenswelt lesbar.

Valentyna Andrejeva, 56-jährige Geschichtslehrerin und Direktorin des Lyzeums in Kam'jana Jaruha, im Gebiet Charkiv

Mein Mann und ich wachen normalerweise früh auf, so gegen 4 Uhr morgens. Während mein Mann frisch gemahlenen Kaffee kocht, mache ich meinen Plan für den Tag oder passe ihn an. Dann schauen wir die Nachrichten, frühstücken und fangen an zu arbeiten, jeder an einem anderen Ort … Ich komme gerne so gegen 7 Uhr in die Schule. Ich mag es, den Schulhof und die sauberen Klassenzimmer zu bewundern, in eine noch schlafende Schule zu kommen, wenn die Hausmeister mit ihrer Arbeit fertig sind und die Kantinenarbeiter anfangen zu kochen.

So war es auch am 24. Februar 2022. Aber an diesem Morgen wollte ich keine Pläne machen. Ich wusste, dass wir am Samstag, den 26. Februar, am Abend unser Klassentreffen veranstalten wollten. In der Ukraine ist es Tradition, am letzten Wochenende im Februar ehemalige Klassenkameraden zu treffen. Aus diesem Grund fasse ich in diesen Tagen immer mein Leben zusammen. Ich wurde in Charkiv geboren, besuchte dort die Schule Nr. 25, dann das Polytechnische Institut und arbeitete dort in der Abteilung für Kunststoffe. Meine Familie baute ein geräumiges Haus. Als ich über vierzig war, „landete" ich dann in der Schule. Und das Leben änderte sich schnell. Zunächst unterrichtete ich Geschichte, später wurde ich Schulleiterin. Ich machte einen zweiten Abschluss in Pädagogik. Ich kenne mich mit Imkerei aus, schreibe Gedichte und kürzlich widmete man mir einen Eintrag in einem Almanach. Meine erste Liebe war die einzige meines Lebens. Mein Mann und ich sind seit 37 Jahren zusammen. Ich habe einen gutaussehenden Sohn, er ist Lehrer und in seinem Job wirklich ein Profi. Mein Enkel Leo ist ein Jahr und zwei Monate alt. Eine Sache, die mir Sorge bereitet, ist, dass das Privatleben meines Sohnes nicht geregelt ist. Er ist derzeit alleinerziehender Vater. Vor sechs Monaten kam er mit einem Kind im Arm nach Hause. Aber das ist wirklich nicht schlimm, alles wird gut. Er wird sein Glück finden.

Während mein Mann Kaffee kochte, stöberte ich in einem Online-Shop nach neuen Sachen. Ein wunderschönes Kleid und schicke Stöckelschuhe auf einer britischen Website gefielen mir sehr. Hier ist mein Kaffee: köstlich, wohlriechend, inspirierend, belebend. Was habe ich in diesem Moment gedacht? Ich dachte, wie gut es war, dass die Kleidung der 1980er Jahre (die Jahre meiner Jugend) wieder in Mode war. Ich dachte, dass ich jetzt noch eine Handtasche für die ausgewählte Kleidung bräuchte. Welche sollte es sein: die kleine oder die große? Ich entschied mich für die kleine Ledertasche in der Farbe der Schuhe. Plötzlich wurde mir klar, dass ich für dieses Outfit ein Parfüm brauchte, um das Bild abzurunden. Ich kramte in meiner Parfümsammlung und sah, dass nichts passte. Der Duft sollte an den Frühling erinnern, voller Leben, Energie und Frische sein. Dann erinnerte ich mich an den Duft meiner Jugend, „Eden" von Cacharel. Das war's, den wollte ich kaufen.

Plötzlich hörte ich ein Rumpeln. Wir wohnen zwischen Charkiv und Čuhuïv[1] und sind das Dröhnen von Flugzeugen und Hubschraubern gewohnt. Aber es war ein bedrohliches Rumpeln, das alles in mir ergriff. Dann begannen schreckliche Explosionen. Ein Lichtschein brach durch das Fenster. Weit weg, in Charkiv, erzitterte mein geliebtes Saltivka[2], wo ich meine Jugend verbracht hatte, vor Schmerz. Dann eine weitere entsetzliche Explosion. Ich rannte zum Ostfenster. Eine schwarze Rauchsäule erschien über Čuhuïv. Was war das? Mein Herz sagte es mir: KRIEG!!! Der Verstand weigerte sich zu begreifen … Vor meinen Augen wurden die Geschichten meiner Großmutter über den Krieg, der vor 77 Jahren geendet hatte, lebendig. Das sehnsüchtige Warten auf einen Brief ihres Mannes, stattdessen die Beerdigung, das Leben

---

1 Hauptort des gleichnamigen Rajon im Gebiet Charkiv.
2 Stadtviertel von Charkiv.

unter Besatzung, die Begegnung mit Erich Koch[3], die sie wie durch ein Wunder überlebte, und die Freude über den Sieg.

Und das Chaos begann. Jemand rief an, stellte törichte Fragen, ich gab (meistens dumme) Antworten. Besonders ärgerten mich die Frage der Lehrer, die meinten, die Eltern würden sich erkundigen, ob ihre Kinder zur Schule gehen müssten. Ich antwortete, dass sie die Kinder bei starkem Regen nicht zur Schule gehen lassen und dass es etwas überraschend sei, dass sie das nun fragten. Wie sehr ich mich jetzt für diese Wut und Grausamkeit schäme.

Dann „klebte" die ganze Familie vor dem Fernseher. Wir saugten jedes Wort der Sprecher auf. Es war klar, dass unsere zerbrechliche Welt aus den Fugen geraten war und eine schreckliche Tortur auf mein geliebtes Heimatland wartete.

Der Tag verging wie im Halbschlaf. Die Nacht näherte sich und hüllte alle in eine zähe Umarmung, die Angst und Ungewissheit mit sich brachte.

Ich ging in mein Zimmer. Auf dem Schreibtisch stand eine Tasse mit einem Rest Kaffee und auf dem Computerbildschirm eine kleine Ledertasche. Das war alles im vergangenen Leben.

Dann versteckten wir uns im Keller des Hauses und lauschten auf jedes laute Geräusch. Tage und Nächte verschwammen. Ich arbeitete, weil ich die Schule am Leben erhalten musste, aber ohne Kalender konnte ich mich weder an das Datum noch an den Wochentag erinnern. Ich zählte nur die Tage seit Beginn des Krieges. Kriege sind grausam und sinnlos.

Ein paar Tage später begannen die Familien das Dorf zu verlassen. Die Menschen ließen alles zurück, auch die weinenden Fenster ihrer Häuser. In meiner Familie stellte sich die Frage der Evakuierung erst gar nicht. Hinter jedem Mitglied meiner Familie stehen die Schicksale vieler Menschen. Wir sind hier zu Hause! Wir sind in unserem Land! Wir müssen hier nützlich sein! WIR BLEIBEN!

Ich habe das Richtige getan. Von der gesamten Schulbelegschaft, 40 Personen, gingen nur zwei fort. Alle anderen haben gearbeitet und arbeiten weiter, jeder an seinem Platz.

Jeden Tag begann ich damit, meine Lehrerinnen und Lehrer in unserer Viber-Gruppe zu begrüßen. Es war ziemlich schwierig für mich, Worte der Unterstützung zu finden, weil es – wie ich dachte – eben nur Worte waren. Ich wusste, dass es unsagbar schwierig für die Menschen war. Etwa einen Monat nach Kriegsbeginn war ich durch meine eigenen Probleme so abgelenkt, dass ich vergaß, meine Kollegen zu begrüßen. Um 9 Uhr morgens rief mich ein Kollege an: „Valentyna Hryhorjevna, geht es dir gut? Warum schreibst du uns nicht? Wir sind besorgt!" Ich rannte zum Computer, begrüßte alle und weinte zum ersten Mal seit Beginn des Krieges. Ich dankte Gott für alles, was

---

3 Der Nationalsozialist Erich Koch (1896–1986) war von 1941 bis 1944 Leiter des Reichskommissariats Ukraine. In den dortigen Gebieten der westlichen und zentralen Ukraine etablierten die Nationalsozialisten eine grausame Besatzungsherrschaft.

mir widerfahren war. Und besonders für die Menschen um mich herum, die mich unterstützen, beschützen und inspirieren: mein Ehemann, mein Sohn, mein Enkel.

Heute ist Freitag, der 13. Mai, der 79. Tag des Krieges, der 133. Tag des Jahres. Wir sind am Leben. Wir haben gelernt, uns an die neuen Bedingungen anzupassen, unter diesen neuen Bedingungen zu arbeiten.

Ich kann nun köstliches selbstgemachtes Brot backen, ich kann einen ausgehenden Beschuss von einem eingehenden unterscheiden. Ich habe gelernt, Babynahrung für meinen Enkel zu „jagen", die wir in unserem Dorf nicht mehr kaufen können. Ich werde nicht müde, den Menschen zu danken, die unter Einsatz ihres Lebens Waren für die Kinder bringen. Ich habe gelernt, bei Nacht wie Scarlett O'Hara einzuschlafen und alle Gedanken zu verdrängen.

Die Schule ist bald zu Ende. Alle Kinder haben die Möglichkeit zu lernen, wenn auch von zuhause aus. Unsere Schule hat 28 Flüchtlingskinder aufgenommen. Ich plane schon für das nächste Schuljahr. Das didaktische Programm und der Lehrplan sind schon ausgearbeitet und die vorläufigen Gehälter für die Lehrerinnen und Lehrer festgelegt. Der Schulhof ist nach dem Winter in Ordnung gebracht, sogar Blumen wurden gepflanzt.

Mir wird klar, dass man einem friedlichen Leben näherkommen kann, wenn man seine Arbeit gewissenhaft erledigt! Und trotzdem habe ich meinen Duft „Eden" von Cacharel bestellt …

Das Leben geht weiter!

Maria Tverdochlibova, 36-jährige Bäuerin aus dem Dorf Alisivka (im Rajon Derhači, Gebiet Charkiv), am 8. Mai 2022

Unser Bauernhof lag im Rajon Derhači, im Gebiet Charkiv, zwei Kilometer von der russischen Grenze entfernt. Unser kleines Dorf mit 30 Häusern ist fast seit Beginn des Krieges besetzt. Im Moment ist die Frontlinie sehr nahe, und die Besatzer haben fast direkt unter unserem Haus Schützengräben ausgehoben. Mein Mann und ich hatten beschlossen, bis zum Sieg der Ukraine auf dem Hof zu bleiben. Wir sind es gewohnt, mit den Geräuschen des Krieges zu leben, haben gelernt, die verschiedenen Arten von Granaten zu unterscheiden. Ich wollte nicht einmal daran denken, unsere Tiere zu verlassen. Aber nur bis zu dem Tag, an dem ein russischer Soldat mit einer Gruppe von Gleichgesinnten auf die Idee kam, meinen Mann zu foltern. Durch das Fenster sah ich, wie er eine Schaufel tragend unter den Läufen von Maschinengewehren in den Wald gebracht wurde. Eugene musste sein eigenes Grab schaufeln, aber er nutzte einen passenden Moment und floh mit Hilfe eines mitfühlenden Soldaten.

Ich saß im Haus und betete, flehte darum, dass mein Mann am Leben blieb, und war bereit, mit ihm zu fliehen, sogar zu Fuß. Das nenne ich eine Umwertung von Werten. Was sollte ich mit all meinen Tieren, wenn wir getötet würden? Wir haben die ganze Nacht nicht geschlafen, wir haben unsere Sachen zusammengepackt. Am Morgen wechselte mein Mann zwei zerstochene Reifen an unserem Auto – das Werk des Henkers, der aus Rache unsere Flucht verhindern wollte. Gott sei Dank hatten wir genau zwei Ersatzräder …

Wir sind mit fünf Ziegen, ihren drei Zicklein und unserem Norwich-Hund Bilka losgefahren. Das waren alle Tiere, die wir in einem Auto mit Anhänger evakuieren konnten. Den Rest der Ziegen, 18 ausgewachsene und 15 drei Monate alte Tiere, haben wir auf der Weide zurückgelassen. Wir befestigten die Stalltür so, dass die Ziegen allein in den Stall konnten. Dann füllten wir Wasser in alle verfügbaren Behälter: in die großen Becken, die sich auf dem Hof und in der Käserei befanden. Unsere großen Hofhunde und unsere Katze blieben ebenfalls auf dem Hof. Das war die schwerste Entscheidung, die wir je in unserem Leben getroffen haben – alles zu verlassen und ins Ungewisse zu gehen. Die evakuierten Ziegen leben jetzt auf dem Hof unserer Freunde. Und ich träume davon, dass unser Dorf von den Russen befreit wird und wir alle verbliebenen Tiere in sicheres Gebiet zurückbringen können.

Alina Sarnatska, „Aeneas Club", Vorstandsmitglied einer NGO, früher Kyïv, dann 207. Einheit der regionalen Verteidigung, Streitkräfte der Ukraine

Als ich am 24. Februar um 05:30 Uhr in meiner Küche Kaffee kochte, hörte ich eine Explosion.

Als Nächstes saß ich im Hauptquartier der Landesverteidigung auf dem Boden und sah zu, wie ein Maschinengewehr vor mir zerlegt wurde. Ich schrieb meinen Namen auf den Aufnahmeantrag. Ich las: „Hiermit beantrage ich die Aufnahme in die Streitkräfte der Ukraine." Und in diesem Moment verstand ich, dass die Regionalverteidigung ein Teil der Armeedivisionen war, nicht einfach nur eine Freiwilligenabteilung. Ich trat also tatsächlich in die Armee ein. Dann fragte mich jemand: „Werden Sie den Antrag einreichen?" Ich antwortete: „Natürlich werde ich das." Ich füllte das Formular mit krakeliger Schrift fertig aus, weil meine Hände vor Panik zitterten.

Am nächsten Tag gab es nachmittags Artilleriebeschuss und ein feindlicher Quadcopter flog im Tiefflug, fast über meinem Kopf. Ich sah ihn, und sein Pilot sah mich. Zum ersten Mal verstand ich, dass es sich nicht um irgendwelche abstrakten „Orks"[4] aus einer Fantasiewelt handelte. Es wurde mir klar, dass es Menschen waren, die uns töten wollten.

---

4 In der Ukraine werden die russischen Truppen u. a. als „Orks" bezeichnet in Anlehnung an die Fantasiewelt von J.R.R. Tolkien und seinen „Der Herr der Ringe", wo sie angeblich aus Mordor, einer Brutstätte des Bösen, kommen.

Ich hatte meine Munition verloren, als unsere Einheit umzog. Als ich wieder etwas Munition fand, habe ich alle meine Sachen mit einem schwarzen Marker gekennzeichnet.

Später e-mailte mir jemand, dass, während andere ihre Arbeit verloren hätten, ich schlauerweise zur Armee gegangen sei und es mir dort gut gehen lasse. Ich las das um 5 Uhr morgens, und es war sehr kalt draußen. Ich bereute es, meine Finger aus dem Handschuh gezogen zu haben, nur um diesen Mist zu lesen. Ich suchte nach der Thermoskanne in meiner Tasche, aber es stellte sich heraus, dass ich keinen heißen Tee mehr hatte.

Der Feind hatte unsere Schützengräben entdeckt und sie beschossen, also sprangen wir in die Straßengräben. Offenbar hatte eine andere Einheit ganz in der Nähe einen Stapel Kisten mit Kanonenmunition zurückgelassen, der so hoch war wie ich selbst.

Wir entkamen dem Beschuss, indem wir uns in den Wald flüchteten. Ich lief zusammen mit einem Mann, der gestern noch Zivilist gewesen war, genau wie ich. Es kam mir vor, als wären nur zehn Minuten vergangen, aber in Wirklichkeit waren es zwei Stunden.

Jedes Mal, wenn wir telefonierten, fragten mich meine Verwandten, warum ich in die Armee eingetreten sei, und diese Gespräche endeten immer damit, dass sie weinten. Ich schämte mich und wusste nicht, was ich ihnen sagen sollte. Wir hatten mehrere Wochen lang solche Telefongespräche.

Einmal wurde mir in einer persönlichen Nachricht in einem sozialen Netzwerk mitgeteilt, dass ich nur Soldatin spielen würde, aber keine echte sei. Dort stand auch, dass es viele solche Leute gebe, die nur Fotos mit Maschinengewehren und in Militäruniform machten. Und, dass es an meiner Stelle Profis geben sollte.

Ich wusste nicht, ob ich eine echte Soldatin war, wahrscheinlich nicht. Und ja, es sollten definitiv Profis an meiner Stelle sein, doch es gibt keine. Aber ich bin hier.

Ich stehe am Rande der Grube bei der Kirche in Buča,[5] und die Grube ist voller Leichen. Es ist kalt und es regnet. Eine Leiche ist in ein Bettlaken mit Blumen gewickelt.

Früher wusste ich nicht, wer ich sein wollte, wenn ich groß bin. Aber jetzt weiß ich es. Ich möchte jeden Tag Verwandte sehen, viel schlafen, in einem warmen Zimmer mit Fenstern wohnen und mich umarmen. Ich möchte einfach so durch die Straßen laufen. Ich möchte jeden Tag andere Klamotten tragen.

Klamotten in leuchtenden Farben.

---

5 Buča ist ein Vorort von Kyïv, in dem die russischen Invasionstruppen im Frühjahr 2022 bei dem Versuch, die Hauptstadt der Ukraine einzunehmen, über 400 ukrainische Zivilist*innen ermordeten.

Nataliia Čermošentseva, NGO-Aktivistin, zunächst Cherson, dann Kyïv

Die ersten Worte, die ich am Morgen des 24. Februar hörte, waren: „Steh auf, Liebes, es hat angefangen. Wir müssen die Badewanne mit Wasser füllen." Dann riefen wir meine Schwester, meine Mutter und Freunde an. Alle schliefen noch. Natürlich schliefen sie, das tun Menschen normalerweise um 5 Uhr morgens, da sie nicht auf eine Bombardierung warten.

In den ersten Tagen empfand ich Angst und Verwirrung. Ich konnte nicht glauben, dass ein umfassender Krieg ausgebrochen war. Wie kann so etwas im 21. Jahrhundert möglich sein?

Man sagt, dass jeder Mensch Stress auf seine eigene Weise erlebt: durch Erstarren, Rennen oder durch Schläge. Ich habe alles gleichzeitig gespürt. Und dann nacheinander.

Erstarren: Ich konnte nicht essen, nicht richtig funktionieren und nur mit Beruhigungsmitteln schlafen, die nur für vier Stunden wirkten, wie es in der Beschreibung stand. Und Angst. Daran erinnere ich mich genau. Ich saß auf dem Boden im Flur, hörte die Sirenen und Explosionen und hatte schreckliche Angst.

Rennen: Am ersten Tag suchten wir nach Luftschutzbunkern, einer Apotheke, einem Lebensmittelgeschäft und einer regionalen Verteidigungseinheit in der Nähe unseres Hauses. Sie haben uns nicht aufgenommen.

Am Abend kamen unsere Freunde zu uns, mit denen wir dann drei Monate verbrachten und später gemeinsam aufbrachen. Als wir draußen Maschinengewehrsalven hörten (später fanden wir heraus, dass es unsere Jungs waren, die in der Nähe unseres Hauses feindliche Aufklärer zerschlugen), fassten wir den Entschluss, sofort zu gehen. Wir nahmen unsere wertvollsten Habseligkeiten mit: die Katze, Dokumente und Geld. Wenn ich später Jeans trug, erinnerte ich mich oft an meinen Freund aus Donezk, der einmal während einer Kaffeepause bei einer Schulung in Jeans und Pullover aufstand und sagte: „Das ist alles, was ich habe." Das ist eine Frage des Ressourcenzugangs, mit der ich mich aufgrund meiner Arbeit gut auskenne und über die ich bei meinen Schulungen sprach. Alles funktionierte auf diese Weise. Und es war sehr beängstigend. Wir hatten kein Auto, und wenn uns nicht Freunde mitgenommen hätten, wären wir einfach gelaufen, um dem Beschuss zu entgehen, genau wie die Menschen, die wir unterwegs trafen.

Ich habe noch nie so viel geflucht wie in den ersten drei Wochen des Krieges. Und das war damals auch wirklich nötig. „Russisches Kriegsschiff, fick dich!"[6]

---

6 Mit diesem Funkspruch hatte ein ukrainischer Soldat bei Kriegsbeginn im Februar 2022 während der Verteidigung der im Schwarzen Meer vor der ukrainischen Küste gelegenen Schlangeninsel auf die Aufforderung der russischen Invasionstruppen sich zu ergeben reagiert. Er steht seitdem für die Widerstandskraft der Ukraine.

Wir fanden uns in Frankivs'k[7] wieder. Das Erste, woran ich mich erinnere, war ein warmes Mittagessen mit den Eltern von Freunden und eine Frau im Laden, die uns einen Rabatt gab, als sie erfuhr, dass wir nicht von hier waren. Das war sehr rührend und schön. Und dann folgte ich dem klassischen Schema: Ich fühlte mich schuldig, das nannte sich „die Schuld der Überlebenden", wie wir alle später erfuhren; ich hatte den Eindruck, dass ich sehr wenig getan hatte, und die Erwartung, dass das alles schnell zu Ende gehen sollte …

Schläge: Der Krieg ist wie das Wahrheitsserum, nach dem so viele suchen. Man sieht sich so, wie man ist, selbst wenn man vorher die Möglichkeit hatte, sich zu verstecken. Mir wurde klar, dass ich nicht zur Waffe greifen konnte. Ich kann es noch immer nicht. Und das war eine sehr schmerzhafte Erkenntnis für mich. Um nicht verrückt zu werden, steckte ich meine ganze Kraft in die Freiwilligenarbeit. Meine Freunde und ich gründeten ein Freiwilligenzentrum, um Frauen und Kinder von Binnenvertriebenen, die in kleine Gemeinden gezogen sind, mit Hygieneartikeln zu versorgen. Wir helfen auch mit Medikamenten, kaufen Produkte von örtlichen Bauern und liefern sie in die vorübergehend besetzten Gebiete von Cherson und Zaporižja. Dabei geht es nicht so sehr um die notwendigen Arzneimittel, sondern vielmehr um Aufmerksamkeit, darum, dass wir uns an sie erinnern, sie lieben, für sie kämpfen und sie so gut wie möglich unterstützen. Manche meiner Verwandten haben Cherson verlassen, einige sind während des Beschusses gegangen. Es ist schwer zu erklären, was man fühlt, wenn man auf eine kurze SMS wartet, die bestätigt, dass sie die russischen Kontrollpunkte erfolgreich passiert haben. Einige Menschen, die mir sehr wichtig sind, bleiben in den besetzten Gebieten. Es ist bereits eine Woche ohne Kommunikation vergangen. Ich hasse die Raschisten[8].

Unsere alten Netzwerke, die durch gemeinsame Werte verbunden sind, haben von den ersten Tagen an zu 100 Prozent funktioniert. In jeder Region gibt es Frauen und Männer, die ich anrufe und um Hilfe bitte, welche ich immer bekomme. Denn unsere Werte Freiheit, Gleichheit und Schwesterlichkeit sind nicht nur Worte. Hier sind sie! Ich kann sie anfassen! Ich kenne ihre Namen! Die Menschen sind der größte Schatz.

Wir nähern uns unserem Sieg. Wir werden definitiv gewinnen! Das denke ich nicht nur, weil ich Ukrainerin bin, sondern weil ich die Sache wie eine Historikerin betrachte. Die Geschichte bringt immer alles an seinen Platz. Alles und immer.

Ich werde Folgendes nicht vergessen: die Stimme meines Patenkindes aus Cherson, das sagte, dass es riesige Angst habe, weil es so viel „Bumm" gemacht habe, meine eigene überwältigende Angst, die enorme Unterstützung meiner Bekannten und Menschen, die ich nie zuvor getroffen habe, die Tränen bei der Rückkehr nach Kyïv, die Hilflo-

---

7 Ivano-Frankivs'k ist die Hauptstadt der gleichnamigen Oblast in der Westukraine.
8 Weit verbreiteter Ausdruck für die russischen Invasoren: Mischung aus „Raschja", wie Russland auf Englisch ausgesprochen wird, und Faschist.

sigkeit, wenn man seine Verwandten nicht anrufen kann, um zu erfahren, wie es ihnen geht.

Jeden Tag schreibe ich in unseren Team-Chat: „Hi, meine beste Mannschaft, wünsche allen einen friedlichen (wenn das überhaupt möglich ist) und warmen Tag." Das ist mein tägliches Ritual.

Und mir ist klar geworden, dass wir alle jetzt so unterschiedliche Erfahrungen machen, dass man diese gar nicht vergleichen, sondern nur akzeptieren kann. Diejenigen, die nicht unter Besatzung gelebt haben, werden nicht in der Lage sein, diejenigen zu verstehen, die dort gewesen sind. Diejenigen, die zu Binnenvertriebenen geworden sind, werden nicht in der Lage sein, diejenigen vollständig zu verstehen, die geblieben sind, um die Schrecken des Krieges in ihrer Heimat zu durchleben. Diejenigen, die einen Ort haben, an den sie zurückkehren können, werden nicht in der Lage sein, diejenigen zu verstehen, die alles verloren haben ... Wir sind vielleicht nicht in der Lage, alles zu verstehen, aber wir fühlen alles wie ein großes Herz.

Aus dem Englischen (und mit Anmerkungen versehen) von Claudia Kraft

Susanna Burghartz

„Die Vergangenheit ist unendlich reizvoll und bisweilen sogar eine Quelle der Hoffnung."[1] Nachruf auf Natalie Zemon Davis (1928–2023)

Natalie Zemon Davis, eine der führenden Vertreterinnen der Frauen- und Geschlechtergeschichte und eine der bedeutendsten HistorikerInnen des frühneuzeitlichen Europas, starb am 21. Oktober 2023 im Alter von 94 Jahren in Toronto. Mit großer intellektueller Kreativität und Unerschrockenheit überschritt sie scheinbar fixe disziplinäre Grenzen und erweiterte mit ihrem unerschöpflichen Interesse für die einfachen Leute, die Frauen und Randfiguren in der Geschichte und mit ihren innovativen Forschungsmethoden die Möglichkeiten der Geschichtsschreibung entscheidend. Als feministische Historikerin war sie für Generationen von HistorikerInnen ein Vorbild und als faszinierende Erzählerin hat sie ein breiteres Publikum für sich gewonnen.

Natalie Zemon Davis wurde 1928 in eine jüdische Mittelschichtfamilie in Detroit geboren. Ihr Studium in den späten 1940er Jahren absolvierte sie zunächst am Smith College und anschließend am Radcliffe College, die beide zu den führenden Frauencolleges der Seven Sisters gehörten. Sie war schon früh politisch aktiv in marxistischen Diskussionsgruppen und engagierte sich in Kampagnen gegen Rassendiskriminierung. 1959 promovierte sie an der University of Michigan zur Sozial- und Kulturgeschichte des 16. Jahrhunderts mit einer Arbeit über „Protestantism and the Printing Workers of Lyon. A Study in Religion and Social Class". Methodisch wurde sie durch ihre Recherchen in den Archiven von Lyon, wo sie nach Handwerkern, Druckern, Händlern, Frauen und Randständigen suchte, genauso geprägt wie durch die Lektüre der von ebendiesen Druckern hergestellten Bücher, die sie in den Rare-Book-Abteilungen amerikanischer Bibliotheken las. Das brachte sie dazu, die Bedeutung der Klassentheorie für den historischen Wandel zu überdenken und – neu – Kultur als wesentlichen Faktor für historische Veränderungen zu begreifen. Gemeinsam mit Edward P. Thompson und einigen anderen wurde sie zur (Mit-)Begründerin der „New Cultural History". Auch in den folgenden Jahrzehnten sollte sie in vielerlei Hinsicht eine Vorreiterin für die Geschichtswissenschaft bleiben.

---

1 Natalie Zemon Davis, Ad me ipsum, in: dies., Lebensgänge. Glikl, Zwi Hirsch, Leone Modena, Martin Guerre. Aus dem Amerikanischen von Wolfgang Kaiser, Berlin 1998, 75–104.

Ihre akademische Laufbahn begann Natalie Zemon Davis 1959 an der Brown University. 1963 wurde sie Professorin an der University of Toronto. Dort und an der University of California at Berkely, an die sie 1971 berufen wurde, setzte sich die Mutter von drei Kindern für eine bessere Kinderbetreuung und Frauenförderung ein und initiierte die ersten Kurse in Frauengeschichte. In Berkeley und an der Princeton University, an die sie 1978 berufen wurde, spielte die Inhaberin der Henry Charles Lea Professur und Leiterin des Shelby Cullom Davis Center for Historical Studies eine zentrale Rolle bei der Einrichtung von Womens-Studies-Programmen. Von 1975 bis 1985 war sie im Editorial Board von „SIGNS. Journal of Women in Culture and Society". 1987 wurde Natalie Zemon Davis zur Präsidentin der American Historical Association gewählt und war damit erst die zweite Frau in diesem Amt. Neben zahlreichen anderen Ehrungen erhielt sie 2010 den Holberg International Memorial Prize und wurde im Jahr 2012 zum Companion of the Order of Canada ernannt und vom amerikanischen Präsidenten Barak Obama mit der National Humanities Medal ausgezeichnet.[2]

1975 erschien der Band „Society and Culture in Early Modern France"[3], der ihre wichtigsten Arbeiten aus dieser Zeit vereinte. Damit gelang ihr ein erster großer Wurf. Indem sie auf neue Art und Weise Fragen der Sozialgeschichte und der Ethnologie verband, wurde sie zu einer wichtigen Protagonistin der neu aufkommenden Historischen Anthropologie. Das Interesse an Konzepten aus der Ethnologie griff Davis später in ihrem Buch über Geschenke in der Frühen Neuzeit als Formen nichtmarktförmiger Austauschbeziehungen wieder auf.[4] Nur ein Jahr später, 1976, erschien ihr grundlegender Artikel „Women's History in Transition", in dem die damals bereits national wie international bekannte Historikerin ausgehend vom Forschungsstand zur europäischen Frauengeschichte argumentierte, dass Frauengeschichte immer im Zusammenhang mit Geschlechtergeschichte entwickelt werden müsse und daher nicht nur Frauen und Weiblichkeitskonstruktionen, sondern auch Männer und Männlichkeit untersucht werden müssten.[5]

1983 wurde Natalie Zemon Davis einem breiteren Publikum mit ihrem Buch „The Return of Martin Guerre"[6] bekannt, das im Anschluss an die Verfilmung einer Skandalgeschichte aus dem 16. Jahrhundert mit Gérard Depardieu erschien, welche sie

---

2 Vgl. Beth Wenger, Natalie Zemon Davis, November 8, 1928–October 2, 2023, last updated October 23, 2023, unter: https://jwa.org/encyclopedia/article/davis-natalie-zemon, Zugriff: 8.1.2024.
3 Natalie Zemon Davis, Society and Culture in Early Modern France. Eight Essays, Stanford 1975 (deutsche Übersetzung: Narrenherrschaft und die Riten der Gewalt. Gesellschaft und Kultur im frühneuzeitlichen Frankreich, Frankfurt am Main 1987).
4 Natalie Zemon Davis, The Gift in Sixteenth-Century France, Oxford 2000 (deutsche Übersetzung: Die schenkende Gesellschaft. Zur Kultur der französischen Renaissance, München 2002).
5 Natalie Zemon Davis, „Women's History" in Transition: The European Case, in: Feminist Studies, 3, 3/4 (Spring/Summer 1976), 83–103.
6 Natalie Zemon Davis, The Return of Martin Guerre, Cambridge, MA 1983 (deutsche Übersetzung: Die wahrhaftige Geschichte von der Wiederkehr des Martin Guerre, München 1984).

als historische Beraterin begleitet hatte. Ins Zentrum ihrer Geschichte stellte sie Bertrande de Rols, die den Hochstapler Arnaud du Tilh als ihren falschen Ehemann Martin Guerre jahrelang gedeckt hatte. Ihr nächstes Buch „Fiction in the Archives"[7] ging der Frage nach, welche Erzählstrategien sich einfache Leute in ihren Gnadengesuchen an den französischen König zunutze machten. Hier wie in ihren weiteren Büchern ließ Natalie Zemon Davis sich auch von literaturwissenschaftlichen Fragestellungen inspirieren, um die Möglichkeiten ihres historiografischen Erzählens zu reflektieren und zu erproben.

Seit den 1990er Jahren standen Randfiguren und GrenzgängerInnen zwischen den Welten im Zentrum ihrer Aufmerksamkeit. In ihrem Buch „Women on the Margins" (Drei Frauenleben) setzte sie sich mit den Lebensentwürfen von drei außergewöhnlichen Frauen im 17. Jahrhundert auseinander: mit der jüdischen Kauffrau Glückl von Hameln, mit der nach Surinam reisenden Malerin und Naturforscherin Maria Sibylla Merian und mit Marie de L'Incarnation, einer französischen Nonne, die in Québec die erste Mädchenschule Nordamerikas gründete und sich in der Mission engagierte.[8] Das Buch war ein Meilenstein für die Frauengeschichte, begriff die Geschichte von Jüdinnen und Juden als Teil der „allgemeinen" Geschichte und war ein erster Beitrag zur *braided history* (verflochtene Geschichte), die Davis auch künftig ein Anliegen bleiben sollte. Das zeigte sich exemplarisch in ihrem 2006 erschienen Buch „Trickster Travels"[9] über den Grenzgänger zwischen den Kulturen al-Hasan ibn Muhammad al-Wazzan al Fasi alias Leo Africanus. Der um 1490 in Granada geborene Diplomat, Rechtsgelehrte und Reiseschriftsteller aus Marokko wurde, von Piraten gefangen, 1518 in Rom vom Papst auf den Namen Giovanni Leone de' Medici getauft.

In den letzten Jahren arbeitete Natalie Zemon Davis intensiv an einer Monografie über AfrikanerInnen, Juden und Jüdinnen, ChristInnen, SklavInnen und SklavenhalterInnen in Surinam.[10] Sie analysierte die Wechselwirkungen von Religion, Kultur, *race* und Macht am Beispiel von David Nassy, einem ehemaligen Konvertiten und Sklavenbesitzer aus dem 17. Jahrhundert. Und sie veröffentlichte mit der Biografie des jüdisch-rumänisch-französischen Linguisten und Rabelais-Experten Lazare Sainéan[11]

---

7 Natalie Zemon Davis, Fiction in the Archives. Pardon Tales and their Tellers in Sixteenth-Century France, Stanford 1987 (deutsche Übersetzung: Der Kopf in der Schlinge. Gnadengesuche und ihre Erzähler, Berlin 1988).
8 Natalie Zemon Davis, Women on the Margins. Three Seventeenth-Century Lives, Cambridge, MA 1995 (deutsche Übersetzung: Drei Frauenleben. Glikl, Marie de l'Incarnation, Maria Sibylla Merian, Berlin 1996).
9 Natalie Zemon Davis, Trickster Travels. A Sixteenth-Century Muslim between Worlds, New York 2006 (deutsche Übersetzung: Leo Africanus. Ein Reisender zwischen Orient und Okzident, Berlin 2008).
10 Vgl. dazu u. a. Natalie Zemon Davis, Decentering History: Local stories and cultural crossings in a global world, in: History and Theory, 50 (May 2011), 188–202.
11 Natalie Zemon Davis, Listening to the Languages of the People. Lazare Sainéan on Romanian, Yiddish, and French, Budapest 2022.

ein letztes Buch, das ihr Interesse an Sprache, kultureller Übersetzung und dem französischen 16. Jahrhundert mit einer Reflexion über jüdische Identität und Intellektualität im 20. Jahrhundert verband.

Natalie Zemon Davis war eine Historikerin des Dialogs: im Gespräch mit Studierenden und anderen Forschenden ebenso wie in ihrer Auseinandersetzung mit der Vergangenheit.[12] Sie suchte und fand im Archiv die Stimmen der Anderen. Im konzeptuell informierten und zugleich immer mit der Evidenz der Quellen verknüpften Nachdenken über Geschichte erschloss sie sich und uns die Möglichkeit, die Gegenwart engagierter, reflektierter und zugleich auch mit größerer Distanz zu betrachten.

---

12 Vgl. Genderview Natalie Zemon Davis, „History through Natalie Zemon Davis' eyes: The pleasure of discovery and the pleasure of telling about it", in: Historica, 39, 1 (2016), 29–34.

Oksana Kis, **Survival as Victory**. Ukrainian Women in the GULAG (= Harvard Series in Ukrainian Studies 79), Cambridge, MA: Harvard University Press 2021, 652 S., ca. EUR 78,–, ISBN 9780674258280.

2021 erschien im Verlag Harvard University Press das Buch „Survival as Victory. The Ukranian Women in the Gulag", verfasst von der Anthropologin und Historikerin Oksana Kis. Anhand von autobiografischen Texten und Interviews widmet sich die Autorin vertiefend den Erfahrungen und Überlebensstrategien ukrainischer Frauen im Gulag. Dabei fragt sie nach der Rolle der ethnischen beziehungsweise nationalen Solidarität im Überlebenskampf der Lagerinsassinnen sowie generell nach den sozialen Handlungsmöglichkeiten von Frauen im Gulag.[1]

Kis nimmt in ihrer Studie auf Erinnerungen weiblicher Gulag-Häftlinge Bezug. Deren Menge ist beeindruckend: Insgesamt fließen ca. 150 Selbstzeugnisse in die Untersuchung ein (S. 26).

Grundsätzlich geht es der Autorin zum einen darum, die ukrainischen Insassinnen des Gulags, die in der Forschung bislang kaum berücksichtigt wurden, sichtbar zu machen. Zum anderen widmet sich Kis detailliert den beschriebenen Anpassungs-, Überlebens- und Widerstandspraktiken von Frauen im Lager, die es ihnen ermöglichten, „den zerstörerischen Auswirkungen des Systems zu widerstehen und unter Bedingungen zu überleben, die Chancen, Rechte und Ressourcen extrem einschränkten".[2]

Das Buch gliedert sich in sieben Kapitel und wird durch visuelles Material aus den Archiven und Museen ergänzt. Gezeigt werden mehrere Fotografien, Briefe, selbstgemachte Grußkarten, aber beispielsweise auch Stickereien.

Zu Beginn skizziert Kis die historiografische Entwicklung innerhalb der Gulag-Forschung, wobei ihr besonderes Interesse den Werken gilt, die Frauenerfahrungen im Lager behandeln. Hier macht sie eine doppelte Leerstelle aus. Erstens wurde und wird in der ukrainischen Historiografie kaum auf die Geschlechtergeschichte fokussiert. Die Gulag-Forschung bildet dabei keine Ausnahme (S. 14). Zweitens werden in den jetzt schon existierenden wissenschaftlichen Arbeiten die Zeugnisse ukrainischer Frauen vernachlässigt. Diese historiografische Lücke möchte das vorliegende Buch schließen.

Im ersten Kapitel analysiert die Autorin die Möglichkeiten und Grenzen von Gulag-Memoiren und zeichnet ein grobes Bild der Verfasserinnen. Die Einbeziehung der Ukrainerinnen in die Analyse der Gulag-Literatur zeige, so Kis, dass die bislang ent-

---

1 Die Grundlage für die englische Fassung des Buchs bildete die ukrainische Monografie, die 2017 in erster Auflage erschien und 2020 neu aufgelegt wurde: Oksana Kis, Ukrajinky v Hulagu. Vyzhyty znachyt peremohty [Ukrainerinnen im Gulag. Überleben heißt gewinnen], Drohobych ²2020.
2 Im englischen Original: „[...] to resist the destructive impact of the system and survive under conditions where opportunities, rights, and resources were limited in the extreme", in: Oksana Kis, Survival as Victory. Ukrainian Women in the GULAG, Cambridge, MA 2021, 35.

wickelten Kategorien für schreibende Frauen im Lager[3] nicht ausreichen (S. 58). So zum Beispiel lassen sich die aus den ländlichen Gebieten stammenden Frauen, die aufgrund ihrer Tätigkeit im nationalistischen Untergrund verhaftet wurden und später Erinnerungen hinterließen, keiner Kategorie zuordnen.

Im zweiten Kapitel werden autobiografische Berichte über die Lebensbedingungen im Lager in den Blick genommen. Die dichte Beschreibung des Eingeschlossenseins in unbeheizten Baracken, dem die stets unterkühlten, kranken und ausgehungerten Frauen ausgesetzt waren, macht diesen Buchabschnitt besonders eindringlich und emotional. Die Leser*innenschaft folgt den Frauen durch ihren riskanten, mühseligen Arbeitstag, mit minimalen Pausen, in denen der Hunger ihnen die letzten Kräfte raubt, bis hin zur Nacht in der ewig kalten Baracke.

Wie man unter solchen Bedingungen überleben kann, wie man die Kraft findet, morgens aufzustehen, und wie man schließlich auf die Zukunft hoffen kann, schildert Oksana Kis in den darauffolgenden drei Kapiteln. Sie befassen sich vor allem mit der Bedeutung des nationalen Zusammenschlusses, der kreativen Tätigkeit und der Frauensolidarität für das Überleben im sowjetischen Lager. Der Zusammenschluss in verschiedenen Gruppen (nach Sprache, Religion, aber auch nach politischen Ansichten) half den Frauen schneller Eingang in ein Unterstützungsnetzwerk zu finden und so ihre Überlebenschancen zu erhöhen. Gebete, aber auch Poesie, Gesang, Geschichtserzählungen und Stricken schufen eine Insel der Freiheit, eine Art parallele Realität, in der die Frauen sich an ihr Leben vor dem Lager erinnern und Kraft für das Heute und Morgen schöpfen konnten.

Kapitel sechs befasst sich mit Körperlichkeit, Sexualität und intimen Beziehungen im Lager. Die weiblichen Häftlinge waren massiven sexuellen Übergriffen und körperlichen Demütigungen ausgesetzt. Die Autorin schildert verschiedene Formen sexueller Gewalt (Zwangsprostitution, Vergewaltigung), verweist hier allerdings auf die Notwendigkeit weiterer Forschungen zur geschlechtsspezifischen Gewalt gegen ukrainische Frauen im Gulag (S. 435).

Im abschießenden Kapitel werden Fallbeispiele aufgegriffen, die die Mutterschaft im Lager thematisieren. Einerseits werden die schmerzlichen Erfahrungen von Müttern beschrieben, die ihre Kinder kaum sahen und schließlich von ihnen getrennt wurden; andererseits integriert Kis auch die Erinnerungen von Frauen, die in Kinderstationen arbeiteten, und schildert so den Alltag von Gulag-Kindern.

In der Untersuchung von Oksana Kis treten die Frauen als aktiv handelnde Personen auf. Um zu überleben, mussten sie immer wieder aufs Neue tätig werden. „Überleben heißt gewinnen" lautet der ukrainischsprachige Titel des Buches, der

---

3 Oksana Kis zitiert hier Veronika Schapovalova, die Kategorien entwickelt hat, die auf den Bildungsgrad der Schreiberinnen, ihre politische Einstellung und die Beweggründe für ihr autobiografisches Schreiben Bezug nehmen. Vgl. dazu Veronika Schapovalova, Lager kak obraz zhizni. Zhenskie lagernye memuary [Lager als Lebensform. Lagermemoiren von Frauen], Moskau 2003.

gleichzeitig einen Motor des Handelns bildete, ein Mantra zum Weitermachen, nicht zuletzt, um die Erinnerungen derer zu bewahren, die ihre Erfahrungen nie wieder selbst aufschreiben werden können.

Die Untersuchung stützt sich auf eine sehr große Anzahl von Memoiren. Auf einige davon wird mehrfach Bezug genommen. Zur besseren Orientierung wäre es wünschenswert gewesen, biografische Skizzen der Verfasserinnen jener Memoiren zur Verfügung zu stellen, aus denen am häufigsten zitiert wird. Dadurch ließen sich die Quellen einer interessierten Leser*innenschaft besser zugänglich machen.

Generell leistet die Studie einen wertvollen Beitrag zur Erforschung der Erfahrungen von Frauen im Gulag. Mit der Veröffentlichung dieses Werkes auch in englischer Sprache hat die Autorin bisher kaum berücksichtigte Selbstzeugnisse in die aktuelle Forschungsliteratur integriert. Gleichzeitig dient das Buch der Würdigung weiblicher Gulag-Häftlinge, deren Stimmen lange ungehört blieben und deren Geschichten teilweise noch immer darauf warten, erzählt zu werden.

Olena Petrenko, Bochum

Jessica Zychowicz, **Superfluous Women. Art, Feminism, and Revolution in Twenty-First-Century Ukraine**, Toronto/Buffalo/London: University of Toronto Press 2020, 424 S., 66 Abb., ca. EUR 73,–, ISBN 978148501686.

In „Superfluous Women" analysiert Jessica Zychowicz feministische künstlerische Protestaktionen zwischen der Orangen Revolution 2004/05 und dem sogenannten Euromaidan 2013/14. Der Titel spielt auf ironische Weise auf den literarischen Topos des 19. Jahrhunderts, des *lishnii chelovek* (überflüssigen Mannes), an. Dieser von Iwan Turgenjew geprägte Begriff beschrieb ursprünglich ranghohe Männer der 1830er Jahre, deren Beitrag zur Gesellschaft als gering eingeschätzt wurde; später stand besagter Terminus für eine ganze verlorene Generation. Mit dieser Anspielung adressiert Zychowicz die anfänglich ablehnende Haltung gegenüber Feministinnen der 2000er Jahre, die ebenfalls als überflüssige Generation, die lediglich um des Protestes willen protestiere, betrachtet wurde.

Ihre Analyse ukrainischer feministischer künstlerischer und aktivistischer Bewegungen fokussiert einerseits den weiblichen Körper als Symbol und Schauplatz für politische Forderungen. Andererseits nimmt sie besonders jene politischen und künstlerischen Aktivismen, revolutionären Gruppen und *communities* in den Blick, die sich kollektiv und kritisch mit Formen, Phänomenen und Problemen des Alltäglichen, Profanen und Gewöhnlichen auseinandersetzten. Im Zuge dessen zeigt Zychowicz, dass diese unterschätzten und marginalisierten Performerinnen, Künstlerinnen und Aktivistinnen als eine (feministische) Avantgarde zu betrachten sind, deren richtungsweisender und nachhaltiger Einfluss auf die ukrainischen politischen Diskurse weit über ihr eigentliches Wirken hinausgeht.

Anhand von Interviews, Fotografien, Literatur, Manifesten und anderen Materialien zeigt Zychowicz, wie feministische Kollektive in den 2000er Jahren Menschenrechte für Frauen* forderten, indem sie Geschlecht und Sexualität ins Zentrum ihrer Kunst und ihres Aktivismus rückten. Die Themen und Forderungen, welche die Feministinnen basierend auf den lokalen Bedingungen aufwarfen, dekonstruierten nicht nur sowjetische, sondern auch westliche Vorstellungen von Feminismus. Durch verschiedene Techniken und Medien erschufen sie eine neue Ästhetik, die den weiblichen Körper als Medium des Widerstandes einsetzte und neu mit Bedeutung versah. Dabei arbeiteten sie sich sowohl an Repräsentationsschemata vergangener kanonischer Werke der slawischen und sowjetischen Literatur, Malerei und Fotografie des 19. und 20. Jahrhunderts als auch an westlichen feministischen Traditionen ab. Die international bekannteste dieser Gruppen ist sicher Femen und deren sogenannter Nacktprotest. Zychowicz lässt sich weder von den heroisierenden noch von den marginalisierenden Analysen von Femen mitreißen, sondern nimmt sie als künstlerische und aktivistische Gruppe mit *agency* innerhalb des ukrainischen Kontextes ernst. Diese historische und lokale Verortung von Femen und anderen feministischen Kollektiven verdeutlicht, dass deren Feminismen im Spannungsverhältnis zwischen pro-westlichen und pro-russischen Diskursen, zwischen Sowjetnostalgie und der Ablehnung dieses Erbes entstanden und auf diese reagierten. Zychowicz betont auch, dass Femen ein diverses Kollektiv war, das zumindest anfangs auch einen entschieden antirassistischen Fokus hatte, nicht zuletzt durch die angolanisch-ukrainische Aktivistin Angelina Diash. 2011 verließ diese jedoch die Gruppe, unter anderem, weil sie von der (internationalen) Presse zunehmend als „Token", also als angeblicher Beweis für Vielfältigkeit, in den Mittelpunkt gestellt wurde.

Die zentrale Frage, die Zychowicz in „Superfluous Women" zu beantworten sucht, ist, wie Protest besonders dort bedeutsam wird, wo Ästhetiken zwischen Aktivistinnen und dem Publikum zirkulieren, die den Körper rhetorisch als einen ideologischen Spielort der öffentlichen Rede benennen.

Zychowicz kombiniert Ansätze der Geschichtswissenschaft, Anthropologie, Literaturwissenschaft sowie der Kunst- und Kulturwissenschaft, um den Zusammenhang von Versammlung in öffentlichen Arenen, feministischer Politik, weiblichen Körpern und Ästhetik zu entschlüsseln. Im Kontext des postsowjetischen Raums, der Feminismus als eine Art rotes Tuch betrachtet und in dem patriarchale Strukturen dominieren, die Frauen generell und Feministinnen im Besonderen abwerten, zeigt sie, wie Künstlerinnen und Aktivistinnen um ihren Platz in der Gesellschaft kämpfen.

Dabei bezieht Zychowicz nicht nur das Spannungsverhältnis zwischen pro-europäischen und anti-europäischen/pro-russischen Politiken ein, sondern vermittelt auch zwischen unterschiedlichen Verständnissen von „westlich" und „östlich" orientierten Perspektiven, beispielsweise in Hinblick auf unterschiedliche Verständnisse von

Menschenrechten, ziviler Partizipation oder revolutionären Kämpfen. Zychowicz versucht die komplizierten Verortungen und das komplexe Verhältnis von Feministinnen und linken AktivistInnen, das von der Forschung bislang selten bis gar nicht thematisiert wurde, in seiner Vielschichtigkeit darzustellen. Sie versteht Postkommunismus als eine nicht-klassische Form der Postkolonialität und geht von der Koexistenz von nationaler Autonomie und Feminismus aus. Während in Mainstreamdiskursen die unterschiedlichen nationalen Identitäten oft vereinheitlicht und deren Unterschiede negiert werden, würden feministische Diskurse die divergierenden nationalen Identitäten zusammenführen und in einen produktiven Dialog bringen, so Zychowicz. Sie verortet die Protesttexte, Kunst und Artefakte ihrer Studie historisch demzufolge nicht nur „nach" der Orangen Revolution, sondern auch „nach" dem Postkommunismus, Postkolonialismus, Postmodernismus. Begründet wurde dieser Ansatz durch Vitaly Chernetsky, der betonte, dass die Ukraine der 1990er Jahre durch ein postmodernes postkoloniales Bewusstsein geprägt war.[1] Obwohl bereits die Einleitung des vorliegenden Werks Postkolonialismus als kritische Perspektive festlegt und an zahlreichen Stellen wiederholt wird, dass Homophobie, Antifeminismus und der Aufstieg der extremen Rechten in der Ukraine an der Schnittstelle verschiedener Formen von Kolonialismus und der regressiven Wirkung von Nationalismus entstehen (etwa auf S. 186), bleibt letztlich unklar, was genau diese verschiedenen Formen des Kolonialismus ausmacht und von welchen Machtzentren sie ausgehen.

Trotz dieses Defizits ist „Superfluous Women" eine wichtige Studie, die viele aufschlussreiche Beobachtungen zu den ukrainischen Feminismen der 2000er Jahre und deren Verhandlung von sowjetischem Erbe und westlichem Einfluss enthält. Besonders überzeugend ist Kapitel 3, das unter anderem die feministischen Straßenproteste der Gruppe Ofenzywa in Auseinandersetzungen mit den lokalen traditionellen Gedenkfeiern zum Internationalen Frauentag untersucht. Zychowicz veranschaulicht, wie die Gruppe an die friedlichen Zusammenkünfte der Orangen Revolution anschloss, indem sie mit feministischen Parolen durch die Straßen Kyivs marschierte. Während und nach der Orangen Revolution war die Straße jener Ort, an dem das Nationale und Ideen zum Ukrainischen Volk (hiermit sind vermutlich nicht Staatsbürger*innen, sondern ethnische Ukrainer*innen gemeint) als Einheit mit demokratischem Ethos entworfen wurden; daran anschließend muss Ofenzywas Versuch der Repolitisierung des 8. März ebenfalls als Verhandlung des Nationalen gesehen werden. Ofenzywas Proteste und Kritik am Ausschluss von Frauen aus dem öffentlichen Raum und an der Feminisierung des Privaten waren wichtige Aspekte, die unter anderen auch zum Euromaidan im Jahr 2014 führten. Diese Erkenntnis korrigiert die in der westlichen Welt vorherrschenden Sichtweisen, die den Euromaidan ausschließlich auf das EU-Assoziierungsabkommen bezogen. Wie genau die Gruppe Ofenzywa feministische

---

[1] Vgl. Vitaly Chernetsky, Mapping Postcommunist Cultures. Russia and Ukraine in the Context of Globalization, Montreal 2007.

Themen zum Gegenstand öffentlicher Debatten machte und was im Fokus der Auseinandersetzung stand, zeigt Zychowicz unter anderem an den fotografischen Arbeiten von Yevgenia Belorusets. Deren Fotoserien „32 Gogol St." und „A Room of One's Own" nehmen das Leben von Frauen an den Rändern der Gesellschaft in Armut und Arbeitslosigkeit sowie das alltägliche (Über-)leben von LGBTIQ-Paaren und deren Privatsphären in den Blick. Durch beide Projekte, so Zychowicz, verschiebt Belorusets den öffentlichen Blick darauf, was als „Geografien des Widerstandes" gelten kann. Anhand dieser Beispiele versucht sie auch anglophone Konzepte wie *queer time* oder *queer space* neu zu deuten. Sie zeigt beispielsweise, wie sich Frauen* und LGBTIQ-Personen im Kontext des damals schon russisch-besetzten Donbas private und semiprivate Freiräume schufen. Diese kritische Neudeutung veranschaulicht, wie queeres tägliches Leben gänzlich außerhalb der Ökonomie der (öffentlichen) Repräsentation und jenseits der Produktion von ukrainischer StaatsbürgerInnenschaft gelebt wird. Die öffentliche Präsentation solcher privaten Bilder stört die binäre Unterscheidung von öffentlich/privat und die darin eingeschriebenen Geschlechterbinaritäten. Zychowicz versteht die Veröffentlichung der Zeugnisse des beharrlichen queeren Lebens, der queeren Liebe und Erfüllung trotz Repression und Gewalt als Forderung eines Zugangs von ausgeschlossenen Minderheiten zu öffentlichen Räumen und der öffentlichen Arena. Obwohl diese Analyse sehr überzeugend ist, stellt sich beim Lesen die ethische Frage, welche negativen Konsequenzen die plötzliche Hypervisibilität für die marginalisierten, im Verborgenen lebenden queeren Menschen hatte beziehungsweise haben könnte.

Katharina Wiedlack, Wien

Maryna Shevtsova, **LGBTI Politics and Value Change in Ukraine and Turkey. Exporting Europe?**, London/New York: Routledge 2023, 196 S., ca. EUR 50,–, ISBN 978-0367676421.

Maryna Shevtsova widmet sich in ihrer schlanken Monografie einer kritischen Phase der europäischen Politik. Mit dem Beginn der 2000er bis zu den späten 2010er Jahren beleuchtet sie eine Zeit, in der sich das Fortschrittsdenken der Europäischen Union langsam in ein Stagnationsempfinden und eine Ratlosigkeit in den europäischen Gesellschaften wandelte. Nach der Wirtschaftskrise von 2008 kam es im darauffolgenden Jahrzehnt zur sogenannten „Flüchtlingskrise" sowie durch die Aggression Russlands zum Krieg in der Ostukraine. Die politischen Vorzeichen, die noch zu Beginn des 21. Jahrhunderts so klar schienen, formten sich um; aus den Krisen resultierten in vielen europäischen Staaten ein Hinterfragen des Fortschrittnarrativs und ein Erstarken konservativer oder reaktionärer Kräfte. Den progressiven Kräften wird eine sitten- und traditionslose Gesellschaftsvision vorgeworfen, wobei neben der Migrationsthematik als Herzstücke dieser Argumentation die Begriffe „Gender" und „LGBTI" fungieren, die für die Bedrohung der traditionellen Familien- und Geschlechterordnung stehen. Die Fronten verhärteten sich vor knapp zehn Jahren zunehmend, verstärkt durch die Verbreitung der partizipativen und damit oft ungefilterten sozialen Medien.

Shevtsova stellt sich im vorliegenden Buch die Frage, welche Rolle die LGBTI-Politik in den transnationalen Dynamiken zwischen der EU und deren Nachbarstaaten tatsächlich spielt. Darüber hinaus erörtert sie, ob die EU-Politik mit ihrem nachdrücklichen Engagement für die Rechte von LGBTI-Personen für konservative, ja teilweise reaktionäre *Backlashes* verantwortlich gemacht werden kann. An der im Buch verhandelten Frage nach der Gleichstellung von geschlechtlicher und sexueller Vielfalt lassen sich auch die allgemeinen Tendenzen der Abschottung und Repression von Andersartigkeit nachverfolgen und mitdenken; denn die von Shevtsova vorgelegte Studie zur Ukraine und der Türkei als potenzielle Kandidatinnen für den EU-Beitritt hat auch Bedeutung für die EU-Mitgliedstaaten selbst, in denen sich teilweise ähnliche Dynamiken beobachten lassen. Die Monografie behandelt somit eine Problematik der europäischen Politik und Gesellschaftsentwicklung, die für das Verständnis heutiger Konfliktlinien erhellend ist.

Die Autorin untersucht und evaluiert die Instrumente der Konditionalität (*conditionality*), Überzeugungsarbeit (*persuasion*) und Hilfe zur Selbsthilfe (*capacity building*). Diese werden von der EU in Drittstaaten auf der Ebene nationaler Regierungen und/oder NGOs eingesetzt, um LGBTI-Rechte zu fördern. Shevtsova zeigt anhand der beiden „Pufferstaaten" Türkei und Ukraine auf, wie die Bemühungen der EU je nach (außen)politischem Kontext und lokalen Gegebenheiten unterschiedlich konturiert und fruchtbar waren. Die Autorin problematisiert das Drängen der EU auf die gesellschaftliche Normdiffusion einer LGBTI-freundlichen Politik: Die Forderungen der EU gegenüber Drittstaaten stünden teilweise im Widerspruch zu den eigenen politischen Aktivitäten der EU. Dieser Umstand wurde von opponierenden Kräften auf unterschiedliche Weise ausgenutzt.

Im Anschluss an die Skizzierung der Auslegeordnung ihrer Studie im ersten Kapitel historisiert Shevtsova im zweiten Kapitel den Fokus der EU auf die Rechte von LGBTI-Personen. Zentral ist hierbei vor allem die Entwicklung von einer wirtschaftsorientierten Struktur hin zu einer werteorientierten „Agenda", mit der die EU zunehmend nach außen auftritt und die in der EU-Osterweiterung zum politischen Kriterium wurde. Einen weiteren Punkt, den Shevtsova anspricht, ist die explizite Nennung von sexueller Orientierung und Geschlechtsidentität als Diskriminierungsgrund, auf den die EU im Rahmen der Einhaltung der allgemeinen Menschenrechte hinweist.

In der Auseinandersetzung mit der Situation in der Türkei zeichnet die Autorin im dritten Kapitel zunächst die Bestrebungen zur Demokratisierung und „Europäisierung" nach, die jedoch aus türkischer Sicht von der benachteiligenden Behandlung der Türkei durch die EU während ihrer Beitrittsverhandlungen in den 1990er Jahren behindert und im Zuge der EU-Osterweiterung ausgebremst wurden. Innen- und außenpolitische sowie wirtschaftliche Entwicklungen führten ebenso wie die „Flüchtlingskrise" 2015 zu einer Verschiebung im diplomatischen Machtgefüge und einer Emanzipation der Türkei von den Forderungen der EU. Wie Shevtsova im vierten Kapitel klarmacht, hat dies ebenso wie die parteipolitischen Kämpfe innerhalb der Türkei direkte negative Auswirkungen auf die Möglichkeiten einer LGBTI-freundlichen Politik. Nach einer verstärkten Sichtbarkeit 2015/2016 im Zusammenhang mit den Gezi-Protesten und den darauffolgenden Wahlen sind die Anliegen von LGBTI-Aktivist*innen vermehrt Repressionen und einem immer offensichtlicheren, von höchster politischer Ebene ausgehenden *Backlash* ausgesetzt; die Interventionen der EU in dieser Angelegenheit zeigen angesichts des neuen Selbstbewusstseins der Türkei nur eine sehr beschränkte oder gar konträre Wirkung.

Im fünften und sechsten Kapitel geht Shevtsova auf die Situation in der Ukraine ein, wobei sie besonders auf deren geopolitische Lage zwischen der EU und Russland verweist. Diese erweise sich als Dilemma der Ukraine und im Spezifischen der ukrainischen LGBTI-Anliegen. Die Autorin verknüpft hier die Diskussionen über einen möglichen Beitritt der Ukraine zur EU respektive die Verhandlungen über die Abschaffung der Visumspflicht direkt mit den Entwicklungen in der LGBTI-Szene und -Politik, was etwas unübersichtlich wirkt. Die beiden Kapitel sind unterteilt in die Entwicklungen vor sowie nach den Euromaidan-Protesten von 2013 bis 2014 und der Zuspitzung des Konflikts mit Russland. Anders als im Fall der Türkei sieht Shevtsova die EU-Politik gegenüber der Ukraine als stärker mitverantwortlich für die Bredouille der ukrainischen LGBTI-Politik, die zwischen den pro-EU-, den pro-russischen und den nationalistischen Kräften gleichsam zerrieben wurde. Zugleich konstatiert die Autorin aber, dass der Druck der EU eine LGBTI-Politik und gewisse Allianzen überhaupt erst möglich gemacht habe. Detaillierter als am Beispiel der Türkei schildert Shevtsova die sich in der Ukraine herausbildende Szene von LGBTI-Aktivist*innen und verweist konkreter auf Anti-LGBTI-Strömungen und deren Argumente sowie kritisch auf die Herausbildung eines „homopatriotischen" Diskurses im Zusammenhang mit dem Krieg in der Ostukraine seit 2014 (S. 146).

Einen vergleichenden Blick auf die Ukraine und die Türkei wirft Shevtsova im siebten Kapitel. Der politische Druck der EU in Bezug auf LGBTI-Rechte und ein sichtbarer lokaler LGBTI-Aktivismus hätten sich in der Ukraine zehn Jahre später als in der Türkei, dafür aber umso rasanter herausgebildet. Sie geht hier auf die strategischen Entscheidungen der EU in Bezug auf die LGBTI-Politik kritisch ein und fasst die Beschränkungen einer Politik der Konditionalität zusammen. Wenn nämlich die EU Bedingungen stellt, die Drittstaaten im Hinblick auf einen EU-Beitritt erfüllen müssen – also beispielsweise den Schutz von Minderheiten gesetzlich zu verankern –, können diese Bedingungen im Umkehrschluss als Argument gegen die EU und für eine traditionalistisch-nationalistische Schließung der betreffenden Gesellschaft dienen. Die Wirksamkeit von Bedingungen verkehrt sich so in ihr Gegenteil. Dabei stellt Shevtsova fest, dass besonders ein direkter Kontakt mit der lokalen Bevölkerung oder lokalen

Politiker*innen fehle, da die Positionen der EU stets durch die vorherrschenden Medien, die oft eng mit den regierenden Kräften verbunden sind, in den lokalen Diskurs einfließen und dabei meist stark verzerrt würden. Die Überzeugungsarbeit der EU erreiche insbesondere jene Kräfte nicht, die eine LGBTI-freundliche Politik ablehnen oder dieser ambivalent gegenüberstehen. Zugleich sei die Thematik der LGBTI-Rechte zwar zentral in der Diskussion über eine Annäherung an die EU und überhaupt über das Selbstbild der jeweiligen Staaten geworden, müsse aber als Austragungsort eigentlich ganz anderer – geopolitischer, machtstrategischer und wirtschaftsinteressengeleiteter – Kämpfe herhalten, die nun auf dem Rücken der Moralpolitik ausgetragen würden.

Obwohl Shevtsova explizit die Rolle der EU in der Förderung LGBTI-freundlicher Politiken untersucht und damit in das politische Diskursfeld der von der Ukraine und der Türkei mehrheitlich angestrebten „Europäisierung" gerät, wäre ein etwas kritischerer Umgang mit den Begrifflichkeiten der „Europäisierung" und „Verwestlichung" (*Westernization*) wünschenswert gewesen. Eine ausschließliche Betrachtung antidiskriminatorischer Politiken, verbunden mit einer binären Sicht auf „Europa" und „(Noch-)nicht-Europa" ist der Förderung einer LGBTI-freundlichen Politik nicht zwingend dienlich, sondern reiht sich in ein wenig konstruktives Zuspitzungs- und Frontenschema ein, das Shevtsova auf den letzten Seiten kurz anspricht. Eine eingehendere Analyse der Aussagen von Aktivist*innen und Politiker*innen wäre in Bezug auf machtpolitische Instrumentalisierungen dieses Diskurses aufschlussreich gewesen. Damit wäre es vielleicht gelungen, die Problematik eines „importierten" LGBTI-Aktivismus noch stärker in den lokalen Gegebenheiten zu verorten und eine hierarchisierende Ost-West-Dichotomie zu umgehen. Eine detaillierte Diskursanalyse liegt jedoch außerhalb des Rahmens dieses kurzen, informativen und mehrheitlich auf die außenpolitischen Interferenzen der LGBTI-Politik fokussierenden Buchs.

Nina Seiler, Zürich

Emmanuelle Santinelli-Foltz, **Couples et conjugalité au haut Moyen Âge (VIe–XIIe siècles)** (= Collection Haut Moyen Âge 43), Turnhout: Brepols 2022, 414 S., EUR 95,00, ISBN 978-2503595030.

Mit der 2022 veröffentlichten Studie von Emanuelle Santinelli-Foltz (Université Polytechnique des Hauts-de-France) „Couples et Conjugalité au haut Moyen Âge" ist das Forschungsfeld der mittelalterlichen Ehe durch einen innovativen Beitrag bereichert worden. Die Monografie, die eine eindrückliche Studie (west-)fränkischer Paarbeziehungen zwischen dem 6. und 12. Jahrhundert angeht, ist besonders deshalb eine willkommene Ergänzung zur aktuellen Forschung, weil sie dezidiert nicht nur nach der Institution Ehe und nach Ehepaaren fragt, sondern von einem Paarbegriff ausgeht, der sich nicht über die kirchliche Vermählung definiert. Damit knüpft Santinelli-Foltz an den Ansatz jüngerer Forschungen an, mit einem offeneren Verständnis des Ehebegriffs auf mittelalterliche Beziehungen zu blicken. Wie die Autorin in der Einleitung hervorhebt, geht es ihr darum, eine umfassendere Darstellung von Paarbeziehungen zu erreichen, die über institutionell geschlossene Ehen hinausreicht und vielfältige Beziehungen zwischen Männern und Frauen einschließt, die unter anderem durch Emotionen, sexuelle Aktivität und Kohabitation sowie gemeinsame Kinder miteinander verbunden waren (S. 11). Da sich die entsprechende Forschung notgedrungen zu einem beträchtlichen Teil auf Material stützt, das aus einem klerikalen Umfeld stammt und einen starken Fokus auf durch kirchliche Trauung formalisierte Ehen und Monogamie aufweist, wird diese Vielfalt jedoch häufig nur im Zuge einer sehr sorgfältigen Quellenlektüre sichtbar. Diese Schwierigkeit navigiert Santinelli-Foltz souverän mit einer überaus reflektierten Analyse ihres Quellenkorpus', der sowohl narrative, historiografische und hagiografische Quellen als auch Rechtsquellen, unter anderem karolingische Polyptyche oder Hufenverzeichnisse, sowie die reichhaltigen Urkunden der Abtei Cluny umfasst. Stärken der Studie sind vor allem die Offenheit, mit der die Autorin sich der Komplexität ihrer Fragestellung widmet, und die Präzision, mit der sie die Möglichkeiten und Grenzen des ihr zur Verfügung stehenden Quellenmaterials aufzeigt.

Die Autorin betont, dass es speziell für den von ihr untersuchten Zeitraum nicht zielführend sei, von verheirateten Personen zu sprechen, da die institutionalisierte Ehe noch nicht in allen Schichten die Norm war und man, um die Gesamtheit der Paarbeziehungen fassen zu können, auch unverheiratete und polygam lebende Personen einbeziehen müsse. Dazu zählen zum Beispiel die vielen Kleriker, die trotz der Verpflichtung zum Zölibat weiterhin im Konkubinat lebten, aber auch die große Anzahl an Paaren, für die Heirat einen Luxus bedeutete, der eher den Oberschichten vorbehalten war. Darüber hinaus geht Santinelli-Foltz davon aus, dass die Polygamie in Adelskreisen sehr viel verbreiteter war, als dies in den Quellen deutlich wird, erkennt gleichzeitig aber auch innerhalb polygamer Beziehungen Paarbeziehungen, die eine ähnliche Stabilität aufwiesen wie monogame Beziehungen, die die Mehrheit aus-machten. Ziel der Monografie ist aber nicht bloß, diese Beziehungsformen zu analysieren. Vielmehr wird mit dem Begriff der *conjugalité* das Zusammenleben als Paar und die Wahrnehmung von Paarbeziehungen in der Gesellschaft in den Mittelpunkt gerückt (üblicherweise würde man auf Deutsch wohl von ‚Ehelichkeit' oder ‚Eheleben' sprechen, wenn damit nicht die von der Autorin betonte Alltäglichkeit der nichtehelichen Lebensform negiert würde).

Der Frage nach diesem Zusammenleben und dessen Stellenwert in der Gesellschaft, die bereits im einführenden Kapitel aufgeworfen wird, geht Santinelli-Foltz in drei weiteren Hauptkapiteln nach. Im ersten dieser Kapitel fragt sie nach der Gestalt von Paaren im untersuchten Zeitraum, nach den unterschiedlichen bezeugten Formen des Zusammenlebens und danach, welche Art der Zweierbeziehung als legitim oder illegitim betrachtet wurde. Als Zeichen der gesellschaftlichen Akzeptanz eines Paares eruiert sie drei hauptsächlich in den Quellen nachweisbare Faktoren: die Identifikation über die gemeinsamen Kinder, die Gedächtnispflege und die Anerkennung innerhalb des Verwandtschaftsnetzes. Im zweiten Kapitel thematisiert sie die Wahrnehmung des Paares in der Gesellschaft und die Art und Weise, wie sich Paare präsentierten und repräsentiert wurden. Das letzte Kapitel versucht schließlich die lebensweltliche Realität des Paarlebens zu umreißen. In welchem Verhältnis standen Ideal und Realität, wie gestaltete sich das Leben zu zweit und was lässt sich überhaupt darüber sagen, wie zwei Individuen im Alltag miteinander ‚funktionierten'. Es folgt ein Anhang von nicht nur beachtlicher Länge, sondern auch großem Wert, der den Leser:innen neben einem ausführlichen Register sowohl Stammtafeln fränkischer Dynastien (S. 345–354) als auch eine Auswahl an Textstellen mit Übersetzung (S. 297–343) bietet und eine äußerst nützliche Liste zum in der Studie verwendeten Vokabular (S. 291–295) zur Verfügung stellt.

Santinelli-Foltz zieht in ihrer Studie einige grundlegende Schlüsse. Die Beobachtung, dass ‚das Paar' in der mittelalterlichen Lebensrealität ein vielförmiges Konstrukt war, überrascht nicht. Dennoch scheint es wichtig, dies erneut herauszustreichen, vor allem in Anbetracht dessen, dass die Autorin speziell ab dem 10. Jahrhundert ein deutliches Bestreben der Kirche ausmacht, Zweierbeziehungen als möglichst gleichförmig und die darin involvierten Personen als legitim verheiratet und monogam lebend darzustellen, wobei sich diese Intention eindeutig in der Mehrheit der überlieferten Quellen abzeichnet. Sowohl die große Anzahl der in einer Paarbeziehung lebenden Kleriker als auch der Laienpaare, die nicht kirchlich verheiratet waren, veranschaulichen, dass nicht allein die seitens der Kirche erwünschte Form der Paarbeziehung in der Gesellschaft akzeptiert wurde. Wichtiger als die kirchlich-rechtliche Legitimation der Ehe war einerseits die Identifizierung als Paar durch die Gesellschaft, andererseits aber auch das Zusammengehörigkeitsgefühl der jeweiligen Individuen, die *nostrité*, wie es Santinelli-Foltz bezeichnet. Erschaffen und bestärkt wurde dieses Zusammengehörigkeitsgefühl durch eben jene Charakteristika, die auch ausschlaggebend dafür waren, dass die Gesellschaft das Paar als solches anerkannte: die Etablierung einer partnerschaftlichen Gemeinschaft durch Zusammenarbeit, Solidarität, Kohabitation und Zuneigung. Die Familie beziehungsweise die gemeinsamen Kinder spielten vor allem in den Eliten aus zukunftsorientierter Sicht eine wesentliche Rolle, aber auch das Totengedenken und die Erinnerungsarbeit stärkten das Bild des Paares in der Gesellschaft. Der Fokus auf diese Gemeinschaft des Paares schien ab dem 10. Jahrhundert deutlich stärker zu werden, textuelle wie auch bildliche Darstellungen der Kernfamilie nahmen zu und das Paar als Elternpaar nahm eine immer sichtbarere Position in der Gesellschaft ein. Dabei stellte, so streicht Santinelli-Foltz heraus, die institutionelle ‚Absegnung' des Paares gar keinen so zentralen Faktor dar, solange die – tendenziell monogam gedachte, wenn auch in der Realität nicht immer praktizierte – Zweierbeziehung in allen anderen Aspekten der Norm entsprach.

Maria Tranter, Basel

Julia Burkhardt und Christina Lutter, **Ich, Helene Kottannerin. Die Kammerfrau, die Ungarns Krone stahl**, Darmstadt: wbg/Theiss 2023, 192 S., EUR 24,70, ISBN 978-3-8062-4567-7.

An den Höfen des spätmittelalterlichen Europa wurde nicht nur viel gelesen, sondern auch viel geschrieben, bedenken wir allein die große Anzahl an Briefen, die auf uns gekommen ist, auch die zahlreichen Frauenbriefe. Dennoch liegt – klammern wir die Berufsschreiberin Christine de Pizan aus, eine veritable Vielschreiberin, – wenig Systematisches zu den Frauen vor, die an den Höfen und für die Höfe in verschiedener Funktion, aber auch zum Zeitvertreib schrieben: Hervor treten Gelegenheitsdichterinnen wie Margarethe von der Mark (gest. 1409), die ihrer kleinen Schwester drei von ihr selbst „gemachte" Liedchen schickte, die sie in ihr Liederbuch eintragen sollte, oder die Hofdamen der Margarethe von Schottland (1424–1445), die mit ihren Gedichten wetteiferten. Wohl ihrerseits zum Zeitvertreib übertrug Elisabeth von Lothringen (gest. 1456) in der Spätphase ihrer Regentschaftszeit mehrere französische Romane in die deutsche Sprache; ob auch Eleonore von Portugal (gest. 1467), die Ehefrau Kaiser Friedrichs III., als Roman-Übersetzerin wirkte, ist hingegen umstritten; mit Sicherheit war sie aber eine wichtige Mittlerfigur zwischen den Hof-Kulturen (Habsburg und Portugal). *Memoiren* waren es, die die Hofdame Eleonor López de Córdoba (gest. 1430) zu schreiben begann, nachdem sie 1412 vom Hof Heinrichs III. von Kastilien und seiner Gemahlin Katharina von Lancaster verbannt worden war; während die Hofdame Alienor von Poitiers (gest. 1509) am Hof der Herzöge von Burgund das Zeremonienbuch weiterführte, das ihre Mutter dereinst zu schreiben begonnen hatte.

In diesen bunten Reigen von Briefen, Gedichten und Memoiren, in dem die Hofdamen als versierte Schreiberinnen hervortreten, reihen sich schließlich auch die „Denkwürdigkeiten" der Helene Kottannerin (gest. um 1470) ein, Hofdame der

Königin Elisabeth (1409–1442), Erbtochter des Kaisers Sigismund von Luxemberg (1397–1439) und Ehefrau des Königs Albrecht II. von Österreich (1397–1439). Der Titel „Denkwürdigkeiten" ist den Aufzeichnungen erst im 19. Jahrhundert verliehen worden, wie damals auch vielen anderen Schriften mit autobiografischen Zügen, die sich keiner Großgattung zuordnen ließen, so auch Eberhart Windeckes (gest. 1440/1441) „Buch von Kaiser Sigmund" in der Edition von Wilhelm Altmann.

Dank Gustav Freytags (1816–1895) „Bilder aus der deutschen Vergangenheit" sind die „Denkwürdigkeiten" der Helene Kottannerin der Forschung seit langem bekannt. Eine kritische Edition des Textes besorgte 1971 der ungarische Germanist Karl Mollay. 1998 übersetzte Maya Bijvoet Williamson die „Denkwürdigkeiten" in die englische Sprache und verlieh ihnen den Titel „Memoirs".

Julia Burkhardt und Christina Lutter kommt mit ihrem knapp 200-seitigen Band nun der große Verdienst zu, den mittelhochdeutschen Text in lebendiges, modernes Deutsch gebracht zu haben (S. 13–58); dazu haben sie einen informativen Kommentar zusammengestellt, der alles enthält, was es zum besseren Verständnis der Ereignisse braucht, von denen die „Denkwürdigkeiten" handeln. Der Kronraub ist nur eines dieser Ereignisse, aber das Ereignis, das in der Forschung am meisten Aufmerksamkeit auf sich zog, wie auch der Untertitel des vorliegenden Bändchens veranschaulicht („Die Kammerfrau, die Ungarns Krone stahl"). Auf dieses politische Schelmenstück, das die Ansprüche des am 22. Februar 1440 in Helenes Anwesenheit geborenen Ladislaus Postumus auf den ungarischen Thron sichern sollte, fokussieren ihre „Denkwürdigkeiten".

Helene Kottannerin erzählt aus der zweifachen Perspektive der Augenzeugin und der Akteurin: Bald verschwindet sie als Erzählerin hinter den Ereignissen, bald berichtet sie in der ersten Person Singular oder Plural und lässt die Leserschaft dadurch erkennen, dass sie nicht nur Beobachterin, sondern an dem Geschehen, das sie beschreibt, auch beteiligt ist. Eine große Verbreitung war dem Text aber nicht beschieden; auf uns gekommen ist eine einzige (wie vermutet wird) Abschrift ihrer Aufzeichnungen. Den Authentizitätsanspruch des Geschilderten steigert die Verfasserin, indem sie Gesprächsfragmente in direkter Rede in den Text einflicht, eine in der spätmittelalterlichen Geschichtsschreibung weit verbreitete Praxis. Die direkte Rede erhöht nicht nur den Authentizitätsanspruch, sondern steigert auch die Dramatik der geschilderten Ereignisse. Besonders deutlich wird dies im Abschnitt, der von der Geburt des Ladislaus Postumus handelt, der Sohn von Elisabeth und Albrecht. Letzterer verstarb kurz vor der Geburt von Ladislaus, was diesem den Beinamen Postumus einbrachte (S. 31 f.). Helene Kottannerin orchestriert das Geschehen: Sie heißt ihre Herrin, sich auszuziehen, sieht an ihrem Körper „etliche Zeichen, an denen ich gut erkannte, dass es bis zur Geburt nicht mehr weit war". Mitten in der Nacht schickt sie nach der Hofmeisterin und nach der Hebamme, die weiterschläft und nicht aufstehen will. Helene ihrzt sowohl die Königin als auch die Hofmeisterin, die Königin wiederum duzt ihre Kammerfrau. Die beiden sind nicht standesgleich und doch stehen sie sich sehr nahe. Aus Dankbarkeit für ihre treuen Dienste wünscht die Königin, dass Helene die Patenschaft des kleinen Ladislaus übernimmt. Helene schlägt bescheiden aus und empfiehlt an ihrer statt die Hofmeisterin zu wählen.

Der Geburt des Sohnes voraus ging der Kronraub. Auch hier präsentiert sich Helene als die Strippenzieherin, die plant und ausführt und sich dabei im Interesse der Sache auch über die Wünsche der Königin hinwegsetzt. Julia Burkhardt und Christina Lutter fassen treffend zusammen: „Diese aufsehenerregende Aktion, die in anderen zeitgenössischen Zeugnissen nur angedeutet wird, und ihr prominenter politischer Hintergrund wären schon Grund genug, die Geschichte wiederzugeben und zu kommentieren. Doch damit nicht genug: Helene gibt die Ereignisse aus ihrer Perspektive wieder: ‚Ich, Helene Kottannerin' ist eine ihrer häufigen Formulierungen. Sie ist zugleich Akteurin, Augenzeugin und Erzählerin der Geschichte."

Der rund einhundert Seiten umfassende Kommentarteil enthält eine kurze Zusammenfassung des Geschehens, eine Vorstellung des am Raub beteiligten Personals und der Schreiberin sowie der Schauplätze des Geschehens. Dazu gesellen sich weiterführende Erläuterungen zur spätmittelalterlichen Herrschaftspraxis, zum religiösen Horizont der Akteure und zum Leben bei Hof, einem Hof, der noch keine Residenz kennt, sondern auf Reisen war und dabei seine Herrschaftsinsignien mitführte. Auf das *Close Reading* des Textes folgt eine umfassende Bibliografie, eine Ortsnamenkonkordanz, da die Schauplätze mehrheitlich im heutigen Ungarn liegen, sowie ein Orts- und Personenregister (S. 156–189). Helene Kottannerin verwendet ausschließlich die deutschen Ortsnamen, deren Benutzung aus politischen Gründen heute nicht mehr opportun ist. Alles in allem sind die zweihundert Seiten eine ebenso unterhaltsame wie lehrreiche Lektüre, die sich durchaus auch als Einleitung in die Welt der spätmittelalterlichen Höfe eignet.

Gabriela Signori, Konstanz

Katrin Keller, **Die Kaiserin. Reich, Ritual und Dynastie**, Wien: Böhlau 2021, 429 S., EUR 55,–, ISBN 978-3205213376.

Die Geschichte des Alten Reichs, seiner Institutionen und Rituale, insbesondere aber die Geschichte der diversen (Habsburger-)Kaiser, die dieses Reich regierten, gehört zu den Kernbeständen der Frühneuzeit-Forschung, und die Historiografie dazu hat selbst schon eine lange Geschichte. Bedauerlicherweise spielten in dieser Historiografie die Kaiserinnen, also die jeweiligen Gattinnen der Kaiser, bislang keine Rolle, wie Katrin Keller in der Einleitung zu ihrer Pionierstudie festhält. Und dies nicht nur, weil die frühneuzeitlichen Quellen dazu wenig hergeben, sondern vor allem, weil die Historiker des 19. und 20. Jahrhunderts überzeugt waren, dass Politik Männersache sei und die

Ehefrauen der Kaiser – wie die Betrachtung von Ehefrauen generell – keinen für die Reichsgeschichtsschreibung relevanten Forschungsgegenstand darstellten.

Man fühlt sich in die Frühzeit der frauen- und geschlechterhistorischen Forschung in den 1970er Jahren zurückversetzt, wenn man den Forschungsüberblick zur (Nicht-)Historiografie über die Kaiserinnen zwischen ca. 1500 und 1800 in der Einleitung der umfangreichen Studie liest – und zollt Katrin Keller, einer Spezialistin für die Geschichte der Habsburger und anerkannten Geschlechterhistorikerin, umso mehr Respekt und Dank dafür, dass sie sich diesem bislang leider völlig vernachlässigten Thema zugewandt hat. In ihrer fast 400 Seiten umfassenden Monografie über „die Kaiserin" stellt sie im Übrigen weniger eine der vielen interessanten Persönlichkeiten in den Mittelpunkt, die neben den zahlreichen Kaisern einen wichtigen Platz im politischen Geschehen im Reich einnahmen. Es geht ihr vielmehr um strukturelle Aspekte der Position der Kaiserin, auch wenn die Kaiserin-Witwe Eleonora Magdalena von Pfalz-Neuburg durch ihre Regentschaft 1697–1705 eine besondere Bedeutung und Sichtbarkeit durch die Auswertung ihrer (auch) diplomatischen Korrespondenz erhält. Die Ergebnisse sind im vierten und letzten Teil der Studie nachzulesen, der die Handlungsfelder der Kaiserinnen thematisiert.

Der Hauptteil der Monografie hingegen ist den klassischen Themen der Reichs- und Institutionengeschichte gewidmet: Es geht zunächst um die verfassungsrechtliche Positionierung der Kaiserin und ihre persönliche Rechtsstellung, die zwischen institutioneller und dynastischer Logik changierte. Dass die Kaiserin einen sichtbaren, wenn auch keinen besonders prominenten Platz in der Reichspublizistik, also in der gelehrten Debatte über Reichsrecht und -verfassung der Frühen Neuzeit, einnahm, ist eine wichtige Feststellung, die auch nochmals unterstreicht, wie sehr die Historiografie des 19. und 20. Jahrhunderts die Thematik gegenüber der frühneuzeitlichen Debatte marginalisiert hat. Dabei zeigt sich, dass die Frage, ob eine Frau tatsächlich „Kaiser" werden, also das Reich in eigenem Recht regieren könne, was in den vorangegangenen Jahrhunderten durchaus der Fall gewesen war, weiterhin als diskussionswürdig erschien, auch wenn die gelehrten Juristen dies nach Abwägung aller Argumente mehrheitlich verneinen.

Den zweiten Themenschwerpunkt bildet die Krönung der Kaiserin mit ihren rituellen Vorgaben und den nicht seltenen Problemen oder gar Konflikten in Bezug auf Zeitpunkt und Vorgehensweise. Trotz aller rituellen Festlegungen gab es doch jeweils Abweichungen und Sonderkonstellationen, die es zu beachten galt. Vor allem wurden längst nicht alle Kaisersgattinnen gekrönt – obgleich, wie Keller zu Bedenken gibt, dieses Zeremoniell eine so zentrale Bedeutung und auch Legitimationsfunktion für die gesamte Dynastie und ihre Herrschaftsansprüche, aber auch für die Reichsstände und -fürsten hatte. Besonders im 18. Jahrhundert wurde die Krönung der Kaiserinnen zunehmend unüblicher, wie überhaupt die Inszenierung kaiserlicher Herrschaft und ihrer Rituale zunehmend unter Druck geriet. In dieser Zeit lösten sich nämlich habsburgische und kaiserliche Aufgaben zusehends voneinander, so dass die Krönungen, die unbedingt auf Reichsterritorium zu erfolgen hatten, häufig auch aus praktischen Erwägungen nicht mehr durchgeführt wurden. Im Prinzip jedoch gehörte die Krönung seit dem 10. Jahrhundert zur Kaiserin, (fast) wie zum Kaiser – und wurde nur umständehalber, etwa während Kriegen oder wegen Krankheit der Kaisersgattin nicht vollzogen, wie Keller resümiert, wobei die Reichsstände und -fürsten jeweils mindestens ebenso sehr ein Interesse an diesem Zeremoniell demonstrierten wie das Kaiserhaus selbst.

Im dritten Teil des Buchs geht es um die Darstellung der Kaiserin in den damaligen Medien, die eine der wichtigsten Ressourcen für Kaiser und Habsburger-Dynastie zur Sicherung und Legitimierung der eigenen Person und Politik bildeten. Dabei spielten die Kaiserinnen vor allem als Mitglieder der kaiserlichen Dynastie eine wichtige Rolle, etwa bei Hochzeiten oder Todesfällen, aber auch hier war vor allem die Krönung der jeweiligen Kaisersgattinnen von großer Bedeutung, was erneut, so Keller im Fazit des Kapitels, von der changierenden Position der Kaiserinnen zwischen in engerem Sinn politisch-verfassungsrechtlichen und familiären Logiken zeugt.

Letzteres zeigt sich auch in den Handlungsfeldern der Kaiserinnen. Hier waren insbesondere vermittelnde – anders gesagt diplomatische – Tätigkeiten zentral, da die Kaiserin aufgrund ihrer Nähe zum Kaiser durchaus effiziente politische Einflussmöglichkeiten besaß. Auch Audienzen gehörten zu den Aufgaben der Kaiserinnen – wobei dabei eine interessante Geschlechterordnung, ja -segregation zu beobachten ist, da die Kaiserin ausschließlich Vertreterinnen fremder Fürsten- oder Diplomatenfamilien in Audienz empfing. Vor allem aber nutzten die Kaiserinnen Korrespondenzen, um (auch politische) Kontakte zu knüpfen oder (etwa zu ihrer Herkunftsfamilie) zu erhalten.

Einen Sonderfall stellt dabei die Regentschaft dar, die die oben erwähnte Kaiserin-Witwe Eleonora-Magdalena von Pfalz-Neuburg einige Jahre nach dem Tod ihres Gatten in Vertretung ihres damals noch unmündigen Sohnes ausübte. Sie hatte damit eine praktisch dem Kaiser gleichgestellte Handlungsmacht und Position, was im Prinzip der verfassungsmäßigen Rahmung der Kaiserwürde widersprach und sich letztlich nur aus der dynastischen Logik heraus erklären lässt. Doch auch für die übrigen Kaiserinnen kann Keller teilweise erhebliche Einflussnahmen auf das politische Tagesgeschäft nachweisen und kommt daher zu dem Schluss, dass die Bedeutung der Kaiserin zu jeder Zeit weit über das rein Familiär-Dynastische und Repräsentative hinausreichte. Wie sehr ihnen das jeweils gelingen konnte, müsste erst noch in Einzelstudien zu den diversen Kaiserinnen der Frühen Neuzeit erforscht und herausgearbeitet werden.

Auch wenn es sich hier um eine im Hinblick auf die Handlungsmöglichkeiten der diversen frühneuzeitlichen Kaiserinnen begrenzte Pionierstudie zur Rolle, Funktion und Bedeutung *der* Kaiserin, der höchsten Frau im Alten Reich, handelt, hat Katrin Keller bereits eine höchst überzeugende Forschungsarbeit dazu vorgelegt. Ihre sehr gut lesbare, klar strukturierte und überzeugend argumentierende Monografie mit der umfangreichen Bibliografie zum Thema kann schon jetzt als „Klassiker" der Historiografie zur Geschlechtergeschichte von Kaisertum und Reich gelten.

Claudia Opitz-Belakhal, Basel/Freiburg

Corinne T. Field und LaKisha Michelle Simmons (Hg.), **The Global History of Black Girlhood**, Urbana/Chicago/Springfield: University of Illinois Press 2022, 312 S., EUR 25,50, ISBN 978-0252086694.

Fatima El-Tayeb beschreibt *race* als eine Technologie des Ausschlusses. Bafta Sarbo argumentiert, dass Rassismus eine soziale Beziehung ist, mitsamt ihrer materiellen Realität.[1] Und natürlich macht die Realität von *race* auch vor Kindheiten nicht halt. Kindheiten von weißen und Schwarzen Mädchen unterscheiden sich also meist signifikant. Welche Rolle spielen Rassifizierungsprozesse, die in Abgrenzung zur weißen ‚Norm' stattfinden, in Schwarzen Kindheiten an unterschiedlichen Orten und zu unterschiedlichen Zeiten? Schwarze (und in nochmals anderer Weise weiße) Jungen werden häufig anders behandelt als Schwarze Mädchen. Wie drückt sich das in der Konstruktion, Imagination und Erfahrung von Kindheiten Schwarzer Mädchen aus? Nicht alle Mädchen werden zu Frauen, nicht alle Frauen hatten eine Kindheit als Mädchen. Wie kann die Geschichte von *girl*hood* queer gelesen werden? Black-Girl-Ästhetik, von *Braids* über *Hoops* bis zu bestimmten Kleidungsstilen, ist schon lange im Mainstream angekommen, wird aber oft verzerrt oder schrill besprochen oder von weißen Personen angeeignet und sogar in Kapital umgemünzt. Die Kommodifizierung und Vermarktung der Black-Girl-Ästhetik, oft durch weiße Personen, existiert parallel zu und teilweise sogar im Zusammenspiel mit dem wachsenden Rechtspopulismus unserer Zeit. Welche Antworten auf Mehrfachdiskriminierung und die Kommerzialisierung Schwarzer Ästhetik haben *Black (queer) girls** historisch und zeitgenössisch selbst formuliert?

„The Global History of Black Girlhood", herausgegeben von Corinne T. Field und LaKisha Michelle Simmons, findet Antworten auf diese zentralen Fragen. In der Einleitung fragen die Herausgeberinnen danach, was es bedeutet ein Mädchen zu sein, wie Mädchen Schwarzsein definieren und wie sie ihre Rolle in einer globalen Afrikanischen Diaspora verstehen. Field und Simmons knüpfen an Hortense Spillers zentralen Gedanken an, dass Schwarzsein eine ‚ungegenderte' Kategorie sei, entstanden durch die Kommodifizierung Schwarzer Körper im Versklavungshandel.[2] Dement-

---

1 Vgl. Against Barriers and Binaries: An Interview With Fatima El-Tayeb, unter: https://criticaldiversity.udk-berlin.de/fatima-el-tayeb/, Zugriff: 18. 9. 2023; Eleonora Roldán Mendívil und Bafta Sarbo (Hg.), Die Diversität der Ausbeutung. Zur Kritik des herrschenden Antirassismus, Berlin 2023.
2 Vgl. Hortense J. Spillers, Mama's Baby, Papa's Maybe. An American Grammar Book, in: Diacritics, 17, 2 (1987), 64–81.

sprechend verdeutlichen sie, dass in Gesellschaften wie den USA, die durch die Arbeit versklavter Personen Reichtum generierten – mit Nachwirkungen bis heute –, Schwarze Kinder sich „out of time" oder „without specific age" wiederfanden, reduziert dazu, Kapital zu generieren (S. 18). Die Herausgeberinnen zeigen, dass es keine einheitliche Definition von Schwarzer *girl*hood* geben kann. Vielmehr sind Kindheiten sozial konstruiert und Alterszuschreibungen haben viel mit Macht, (fehlender) *agency* und Abhängigkeit zu tun: Wer bestimmt, wann und wie eine Kindheit für Mädchen endet? Field und Simmons halten es deswegen für wichtig, Kindheiten als situativ, kontextuell und historisch wandelbar zu verstehen, anstatt sich an einer weißen, vermeintlich allgemeingültigen Norm von Kindheit zu orientieren.

Die Fülle der dargestellten Themen in „The Global History of Black Girlhood" ist groß. Anasa Hicks etwa legt dar, dass auch im unabhängigen Kuba des frühen 20. Jahrhunderts trotz einer egalitären Rechtslage Schwarze Mädchen aus der Arbeiterklasse nicht nur leichter Opfer von Vergewaltigungen und Missbrauch durch weiße Männer wurden, sondern auch im Falle der juristischen Ahndung von den Gerichten kaum ihr Recht zugesprochen bekamen. Jennifer L. Palmer zeigt anhand der Geschichte eines freien *bi-racial* Mädchens namens Marie-Jeanne Fleuriau Mandron, dass deren Schwarzsein im Saint Domingue des 18. Jahrhunderts eine völlig andere Bedeutung und einen deutlich höheren Status hatte als in Frankreich zur selben Zeit. Das erfuhr Marie-Jeanne Fleuriau Mandron, die mit 14 Jahren Saint Domingue verließ und ihrem Vater nach Frankreich folgte, am eigenen Leib. In einem Beitrag zum Aufwachsen Schwarzer Mädchen in fast ausnahmslos weißen Familien während des Nationalsozialismus und im Deutschland der Nachkriegszeit verdeutlicht Vanessa D. Plumly, wie die spezifisch deutsche Konstellation von Rassismus, die eng mit dem ‚Rassenwahn' des Naziregimes verzahnt ist, Kindheiten über Generationen strukturierte. Das Gefühl der Kinder, nicht zugehörig oder sogar in Gefahr zu sein, sowie das Schweigen und teilweise die Scham der Mütter belastete die Beziehung zwischen weißer Mutter und Schwarzer Tochter, verschloss aber nicht die Möglichkeit einer innigen Beziehung zwischen Großmutter und Kind. Nazera Sadiq Wrights Beitrag ist eine transgenerationale Familienbiographie. Wright rekonstruiert eine Generationenabfolge Schwarzer Kindheiten, die beginnend mit der letzten versklavten Generation bis in die ‚relative' Freiheit des späten 19. Jahrhunderts und von South Carolina bis Philadelphia reicht. Dabei nutzt Wright ein wundervolles Quellengenre, nämlich Poesiealben, welche Einblicke in die seltenen, da ungern gesehenen, Freundschaften zwischen Schwarzen und weißen Mädchen geben. Die Analyse der Poesiealben verdeutlicht das Ringen um Nähe und Distanz in den Freundschaften zwischen weißen und Schwarzen Schülerinnen. Wichtige Ergänzungen zu den Beiträgen über die Geschichte der oft schmerz- und gewaltvollen Kindheit Schwarzer Mädchen sind die Aufsätze von Tara A. Bynum, Dara Walker und S.E. Duff, die Genuss, Freund*innenschaft, kleine Freuden des Alltagsleben oder die Kraft der Black Power-Bewegung hervorheben. Die Benennung persönlicher, liebevoller, politischer Akte, wie etwa das

Zelebrieren von Freund*innenschaft oder Freizeitgenuss in der Öffentlichkeit, die trotz der rassistischen Strukturen weißer Vorherrschaft stattfinden konnten, zeigt die Möglichkeiten auf, die Schwarze Mädchen trotz systemischer Unterdrückung für sich fanden. Diese Akte zeugen von der Kraft Schwarzer Mädchen und Frauen, die Risse im System weißer Dominanz zu finden und für sich zu nutzen.

Manche der Essays greifen eine vieldiskutierte Frage der Black Studies auf, die Frage nach dem Archiv, seinen Lücken und der Schwierigkeit, die Geschichte Schwarzer Subjekte zu schreiben, ohne diese zu Fragmenten einer Gewaltgeschichte zu reduzieren.[3] Tara A. Bynum schreibt in „Sarah and Bess" über die Freundschaft zweier versklavter Frauen in der zweiten Hälfte des 18. Jahrhunderts in Newport, Rhode Island. Sie adressiert die besondere Ungewissheit, die entsteht, wenn wir versuchen aus dürftigen Fragmenten Schwarze Geschichte zu rekonstruieren, zumal im Kontext des Versklavungshandels, wo Schwarze Körper im Archiv als „Waren" gelistet wurden, ihr Tod als Verlustgeschäft, nicht als menschliche Tragödie gehandelt wurde. Diese Ungewissheit ist unbehaglich. Aber dies sei, so Bynum, die eigene Ungewissheit als Leser*in, als Historiker*in, und nicht die Ungewissheit der historischen Subjekte. Die beiden Mädchen aus Bynums Beitrag, Sarah und Bess, seien „alive and living despite the limits of the so-called ‚archive'", sie sind komplexe und vielschichte Figuren, obwohl das Archiv sie so nicht erinnert. Bynum lehrt uns, die Ungewissheit nicht zu fürchten, sondern sie anzunehmen als eine „valide Art des Wissens" (S. 49 f.). Ungewissheit als valides Wissen kann also einen konstruktiven Raum der Imagination eröffnen.

Wenn wir unseren Archivbegriff erweitern, können wir auch S.A. Smythes Essay „Black Girlhood Remains" als einen Beitrag zur Archivfrage verstehen. Smythes konzeptueller und gleichzeitig sehr poetischer Text thematisiert die Temporalität von *Black girl*hood* für Personen, deren Gender falsch gelesen oder nicht anerkannt wird – nichtbinäre Personen, Intersex- und Transpersonen. „Black Girlhood Remains" ist vielleicht das Theorieherz des ganzen Bandes. Für Smythe, auch beeinflusst von Spillers, ist *girl*hood* nicht einfach ein Altersabschnitt, der, je nach rechtlicher Definition oder historischem Kontext irgendwann enden muss, sondern eine verkörperte Erinnerung, die in den erwachsenen Körpern fortlebt. Dieses Körperwissen muss für Smythe, positioniert als *Black transmasculine nonbinary adult*, nicht verschwinden, sondern darf und kann bleiben. Smythe lehnt jedes kompetitive Gerangel um die beste oder richtige Form eines Selbst und damit die Temporalität von Gender (vorher falsch, jetzt richtig) ab. „Our attachments and affections for our past selves may take on different meanings, different values, and differential modes of desire and recognition. However, they need not be discarded or fixed to our past in order to have a coherent present take shape. We can continue to return to ourselves and cobble together makeshift parts of our lives that

---

3 Vgl. Saidiya Hartman, Venus in Two Acts, in: Small Axe, 12, 2 (June 2008), 1–14; Marisa J. Fuentes, Dispossessed Lives. Enslaved Women, Violence, and the Archive, Pennsylvania 2016.

might galvanize us into generously indeterminate futures." (S. 106) Um genau das zu zeigen, nutzt Smythe den Cento, eine Gedichtform, die Verse anderer Autor*innen in eine neue Form gießt. Smythes Cento besteht aus Zitaten aus den Essays des Sammelbandes. Der Cento ist ein Beispiel dessen, was Smythe als „reading as an extension of the act of creation" (S. 106) bezeichnet. In dem Sinne, dass Lesen ein Akt des Schaffens ist, ist Lesen auch das Schaffen eines Archivs oder Kanons, und für Smythe ist dieser Kanon einer, der Schwarze und queere Stimmen privilegiert in einer (Wissenschafts-)Welt, die von weißem Wissen strukturiert ist. Smythes Auswahl ist eine, die Dichotomien in Frage stellen will, sich positioniert, diejenigen Personen ins Zentrum rückt, die durch rassistisch markierte Dichotomien oder normative Gender-Dichotomien unsichtbar gemacht werden (wie etwa nicht-binäre Personen), oder diejenigen, die durch jene Dichotomien, die Transfeindlichkeit und Rassismus Vorschub leisten, in Gefahr kommen.

Der Sammelband bringt Perspektiven aus Kunst, Aktivismus und Wissenschaft unter einen Hut. Eine große Bereicherung ist etwa Nastassja E. Swifts Kunst zu Black-Girl-Ästhetik und Körperlichkeit, die im Sammelband abgedruckt ist, sowie der *Roundtable* namhafter Schwarzer feministischer/queerer Aktivist*innen, die über Kindheiten, politische Mobilisierung und Aktivismus von Mädchen* diskutieren. Der Appendix, in dem Casidy Campell und LaKisha Simmons Schwarze Mädchen dazu aufrufen, eigene (digitale) Archive zu schaffen, ist nicht weniger als ein Akt des *Empowerments*. Schwarze Mädchen*, die sich nicht im Archiv repräsentiert fühlen, bekommen damit eine konkrete Handlungsmöglichkeit gereicht, diesen Zustand aktiv zu verändern. Leider gibt es in dem Sammelband nur jeweils einen Text zu *Black Europe*, einen zum afrikanischen Kontinent und keinen einzigen zu *Black Asia*. Der Hauptfokus des Bandes bleibt Nordamerika und die Karibik.

„The Global History of Black Girlhood" ist ein weiteres Beispiel für das große Potenzial der Black Studies, fixe Dichotomien von *race* und Gender anders zu denken. Der Sammelband reiht sich in eine Tradition kluger Texte dazu ein, von Spillers bis Zakkiyah Iman Jackson.[4] Vielleicht kann das ein Ansporn sein, die leider noch wenig rezipierten Black Studies auch in Europa stärker ins Zentrum zu rücken, gerade im Hinblick auf die deutschsprachige Forschung zur Vergleichbarkeit von Gewaltgeschichten.

Stephanie Lämmert, Berlin

---

4 Zakiyyah Iman Jackson, Becoming Human. Matter and Meaning in an Antiblack World, New York University Press 2020.

Christa Hämmerle, **Ganze Männer? Gesellschaft, Geschlecht und Allgemeine Wehrpflicht in Österreich-Ungarn (1868–1914)** (= Krieg und Konflikt 16), Wien: Campus Verlag 2022, 600 S., EUR 50,40, ISBN 9783593514918.

"Ganze Männer?" by Christa Hämmerle addresses the topic of universal conscription as one of the defining features of human (and not just male) experience in the late nineteenth century. She challenges the reader to see it as a social institution that formed an underlying current in the European collective psyche, one that found its ultimate fulfilment in late July 1914. While historiography has already produced numerous works on the topic from a European perspective, a book that focuses on the workings of the conscription system in the Habsburg monarchy after 1868 is more than a welcome addition, as Habsburg military history remains surprisingly under-researched in this area.

Christa Hämmerle's take is also highly innovative in its approach, going far beyond a mere overview of the political and military considerations that led to new institutional structures, frameworks and practices. Building on the long tradition of *new military history*, her aim is to analyse the broadest possible social repercussions of universal conscription, thus making an important contribution to the ongoing debate on the degree of societal militarisation of Central Europe in the late Habsburg era. It brings further support to the argument that, despite comparatively low levels of military spending, the term "military monarchy" is not an exaggeration when thinking of the old empire.

Not surprisingly, the book does this by analysing the central role of universal conscription in this process, but also – emphasising the perspective of the individual actor ‚from below' – by showing how much influence its very existence had on the lives of individuals and communities, how much the state depended on the associated discourses, symbols and rituals in its quest for legitimacy – and how these were often highly contested. Even more inspiring, Christa Hämmerle builds on her impressive body of work by using gender as a key to her analysis. In doing so, she proves once again that military history is a field ripe for gender analysis and that its study remains incomplete without a full understanding of its gender dimension. At the same time, she shows that the study of such heavily gendered social institutions as the military also offers plenty of research material for gender history. Put simply, the book argues convincingly that gender as an analytical category is inseparable from the study of military history, because modern military institutions are a masculine social space where gender is "being done" on a daily basis through manifold social practices, (re)producing specific forms of masculinity embodied in ideas such as the "citizen soldier" or the "nation in arms". Moreover, as Hämmerle repeatedly demonstrates, the universal nature of "universal conscription" makes this process felt far beyond the confines of the barracks and the male bodies enclosed within them, the institution becoming a fulcrum for the reshaping of cultural and social norms, practices, hierarchies, collective and individual bodies, as well as minds and power structures throughout society.

The basic question of the book is how "full manhood" was conceptualised by the Habsburg military elites, and what role it was perceived to play in shaping military service. Perhaps even more importantly, it asks how this concept was registered in society at large, and what the process of "doing gender" looked and felt like on "parade grounds, in the barracks and on the exercise yard" (p. 37). Drawing on a wide range of sources, from public debates to regulations, statistics, court files and personal accounts, the text is divided into three distinct parts. In the first one, the author covers the decision-making process behind the introduction of universal conscription after the defeat in the war with Prussia in 1866. She follows the debates and analyses the ideological positions of both supporters and various groups of critics, ranging from liberals and financiers to pacifists and anti-militarists. Although the analysis is mostly focused on the centre, with little attention given to the Habsburg peripheries (lower-level political, geographical, social or linguistic), it is very effective in showing how the reform changed the relationship between the state and the soldiers, with a constant ambivalent tension between the concepts of "service" (implying obedience of "men in the ranks") and "civic duty" (implying rights of "citizens at arms"). The book also shows how through the introduction of military tax and the *Landsturm* reserve, the reform became truly all-encompassing, allowing its underlying discourse to spread throughout society. This includes women, who by the end of the period under study were already being considered for a similar process of societal militarisation, a debate that shows how gendered the whole notion of service actually was, as "militarised femininity" was always thought of as a strictly separate construct from its masculine counterpart.

The second part of the book focuses on the discourse of universal conscription, namely on how the *idea* of soldiering was reinterpreted and how it was linked to various state ideologies, such as the cult of dynasty, to the multi-ethnic structure of the army, and ultimately to the gender order and hegemonic concepts of masculinity. Here the gender perspective is truly embodied in specific notions of discipline, the ideal male physique and aesthetics. The changing nature of modern combat paralleled the new social composition of the army, producing new discourses of drill, discipline or punishment applied to bodies understood less as tools and more as spaces of individual performance that needed to be constantly shaped and trained (from childhood) to literally fit the uniform. Through further analysis of a wide range of debates, the book shows how expansive the discourse of manhood produced in this new "school of the nation" was, arguing that it actually helped military elites to eliminate – to some extent – the conflict potentially arising from its multinational nature. This, of course, raises the question of how influential and individually internalised these discourses actually were in practice, that is whether hegemonic masculinity was genuinely militarised throughout the monarchy before 1914. However, the book is very convincing in pointing to the importance of militarised discourses in the way hegemonic masculinities were configured in the late Habsburg monarchy up to 1914.

The third part of the book focuses on the social acceptance of militarised masculinity. Using accounts written by German-speaking soldiers from various decades, the author shows that the military discourse of masculinity was indeed deeply ingrained in various social practices, strategies and dilemmas – such as whether to avoid service and face the judgment of peers, or to accept an unwelcome disruption to one's life in order to take a step closer to "full manhood". Despite these seemingly common dilemmas, conscription gradually became a perhaps unwelcome but accepted rite of passage on the path to manhood, influencing many other patterns of behaviour, such as marriage strategies and parenthood, with consequences not only for men but for families and entire communities. Here the source base is perhaps too limited for us to fully accept universal answers, and it would be highly interesting to see how militarised concepts of masculinity and gender relations interacted with the wide range of ethno-linguistic, class and religious identities that arguably defined the whole monarchy (and its army). While the book addresses some of these issues, such as the urban-rural dynamics, national stereotypes or the specificity of the Jewish experience, it ends up opening more doors than it enters.

On the other hand, there are numerous experiences of the "gender-making/genderdoing" practices of universal conscription that may very well be universal, be it the very physicality of defining, shaping and violently abusing male bodies through the "normative tyranny" of service, or the all-important process of creating unique and often informal – and highly gendered – homosocial hierarchies of age groups, roles, jobs and tasks in the army, often resulting in a specific form of what gender theory defines as the "patriarchal dividend", that is perks and status privileges. One of these, access to sexual experience, was indeed seen as an almost integral part of attaining "true manhood" during one's stint in the service, further integrating the military's "school of manhood" into the intimate life experience of soldiers. However, as this process of masculine socialisation was often quite random, violent, oppressive and ultimately inaccessible to most, it was efficient in producing both "full men" and plenty of trauma, which the author sees reflected in the uniquely high suicide rates in the Habsburg army. As she has shown, it actually undermined individual motivation, leading even those who nominally subscribed to the notion of this hegemonic masculinity to hate their military experience. Thus, the project of transforming recruits into "full men" remained highly ambivalent in terms of results, and for most men it was at best a closed chapter in their individual masculine life stories.

Indeed, one might ask whether it is not the very nature of (militarised) masculinity to undermine itself through constant clashes with the lived reality of its own practices, producing disillusionment or trauma as often as it makes men into *men*. This question is made all the more pressing by the book's epilogue, which projects the key conclusions of the previous chapters into the war years. As Hämmerle shows, the original "legislative militarisation", which became the "societal militarization" of the pre-war period, paved the way for the ultimate "total militarization" embodied in the Emergency Laws and the *Kriegsleistungsgesetze*. These measures applied the militarising logic of the "nation in arms", or rather the "nation in the army", to society as a whole, leading to a brief period in which the symbiosis between "full manhood" and the warrior role reached its apogee, only to be shattered by the realities of industrialised mass warfare.

As with all inspiring works, Christa Hämmerle's book offers many answers and raises many questions. In fact, the important contribution of her conclusions, listed above, is to provide a springboard to further research. As already mentioned, we can continue to ask how gender interacted with ethnicity, linguistic identity and class at the intersection of the military environment. While many of the conclusions presented by the author may arguably prove to be universal across the society of the Habsburg Empire, a stronger intersectional perspective may very well offer a potential qualifying lens. How did the pervasive discourse of military masculinity interact with other masculinities? Was the militarised discourse as widely accepted in the Habsburg peripheries as it was in the political/cultural centre? The book points to some of these issues, and it would be worthwhile nice to see these avenues explored. And speaking of peripheries, what about marginalised masculinities and behavioural patterns, such as homosexuality, which – as the author herself rightly points out – remains an under-researched topic when it comes to the Habsburg military. It is also an area that could provide highly interesting insights into the way masculinities and gender were made in the army.

"Ganze Männer?" is a unique and important book that successfully combines the fields of military and gender history in an exciting analysis, mixing various perspectives in an effort to show universal military service as an institutional, social, mental as well as deeply physical, bodily experience with implications far beyond the limited "space" of military history. It will undoubtedly become a point of reference for anyone with a serious interest in Habsburg military and social history, as well as nineteenth-century military and social history in general, and I would happily recommend it as a source of inspiration for any historian of gender, masculinity, the body and/or war and warfare.

Jiří Hutečka, Hradec Králové

Valérie Dubslaff, „**Deutschland ist auch Frauensache**". **NPD-Frauen im Kampf für Volk und Familie 1964–2020** (= Quellen und Darstellungen zur Zeitgeschichte 131), Berlin/Boston: De Gruyter Oldenbourg 2022, 404 S., EUR 59,95, ISBN 978-3110756661.

Die französische Historikerin Valérie Dubslaff legt mit „Deutschland ist auch Frauensache" eine umfassende Studie über die Rolle und die Aktivitäten von Frauen in der Nationaldemokratischen Partei Deutschlands (NPD) von ihrer Gründung 1964 bis in die Gegenwart (2020) vor. Die Arbeit ging aus einer an der Universität Paris eingereichten Dissertation hervor, die die Autorin selbst in arbeitsintensiver und vorbildhafter Weise ins Deutsche übertragen hat.

Die NPD wurde 1964 als Sammelbecken für verschiedene rechtsextreme Kleinparteien – Deutsche Reichspartei (DRP), Sozialistische Reichspartei (SRP) – und Akteur*innen gegründet und erlebte in den 1960er Jahren einen Aufschwung mit bemerkenswerten Wahlerfolgen: Sie war in sieben Landesparlamenten vertreten und verfehlte 1969 nur knapp den Einzug in den Bundestag. In den 1970er Jahren vollzog sich ein allmählicher Niedergang der NPD; sie fristete ein Dasein in der politischen Marginalität, geprägt von Richtungskämpfen und – nach einem kurzen Wiedererstarken nach der „Wende" und einer Öffnung hin zu Neonazis – von Wahlerfolgen vor allem in Ostdeutschland. Die NPD gilt aufgrund ihres völkischen Weltbildes und ihrer rassistischen und antisemitischen Positionen als eindeutig rechtsextreme Partei, gegen die es seit Jahrzehnten mehrere (bisher erfolglose) Verbotsanträge gab. Ein Verbot der Partei wurde vom Bundesverfassungsgericht 2017 mit dem Argument abgelehnt, dass sie aufgrund ihres geringen Zulaufs keine Bedrohung für die freiheitlich-demokratische Grundordnung darstelle, auch wenn man ihr ein demokratiefeindliches, rassistisches Weltbild und eine „Wesensverwandtschaft zum Nationalsozialismus" bescheinigte.

Vor diesem Hintergrund zeichnet Dubslaff die Geschichte der NPD von ihren Anfängen bis in die 2000er Jahre nach, wobei ihr Fokus auf den bisher vernachlässigten Frauen in der NPD liegt. Rechtsextremismus, so die Autorin, werde vielfach als männliches Phänomen wahrgenommen, wohingegen rechte Frauen in der Forschung kaum oder nur am Rande behandelt würden. Zum Themenfeld „Frauen und Rechtsextremismus" liegen zwar einige sozialwissenschaftliche Studien zu aktuelleren Entwicklungen vor, allerdings sei die zeithistorische Dimension von Frauen im Rechtsextremismus nach 1945 bisher kaum erforscht. Die „doppelte Marginalisierung" (S. 3) rechter Frauen aufzuheben, ist ein Forschungsziel der vorliegenden Studie. Dubslaff möchte die Parteigeschichte der NPD nicht neu, sondern anders schreiben – das heißt, es geht ihr um eine geschlechterfokussierte Perspektive, wobei Gender als „nützliche" Analysekategorie dient, um die in der NPD vorhandene „Geschlechterdifferenz zu historisieren, Weiblichkeitsbilder und -diskurse zu dekonstruieren, Geschlechterdynamiken, Machtverhältnisse und entsprechende Aushandlungsprozesse [...] sowie die agency von NPD-Frauen im männlich-hegemonialen Parteikontext" zu hinterfragen (S. 4). Dubslaff untersucht in ihrer Studie die Rolle und die Aktivitäten der Frauen in der NPD, die Motivationen und Wirkungen ihres politischen Engagements, aber auch mögliche Beschränkungen und Marginalisierungen innerhalb ihrer männlich-dominierten Partei.

Nach einer instruktiven Auseinandersetzung mit dem Forschungsstand und einer theoretischen und methodischen Rahmung der Studie gliedert sich das chronologisch strukturierte Buch in drei große Teile, die unterschiedliche Phasen der Parteigeschichte näher beleuchten. Der erste und – aus zeithistorischer Sicht vermutlich interessanteste

– Teil beschäftigt sich ausführlich mit den „Frauen in der Blütezeit der NPD" von ihrer Gründung 1964 bis 1969. Der zweite Teil zeichnet den Weg der NPD in die politische Bedeutungslosigkeit von 1970 bis 1989 nach, von Dubslaff als „Hibernationsphase" (S. 25) bezeichnet, worunter sie einen Zustand der politischen Agonie versteht. Diese Phase des Stillstands war gekennzeichnet von einer zunehmenden innerparteilichen Isolation der NPD-Frauen. Der letzte Teil stellt die Entwicklung der NPD im wiedervereinigten Deutschland dar, wo es zu einer radikalen Kursänderung und zu (vorübergehenden) Wahlerfolgen in den neuen Bundesländern kam. Dubslaff konstatiert für diese Phase eine „Nazifizierung und Feminisierung" (S. 237) der wiedererstarkten Partei und verweist damit auf die Öffnung der NPD zum Neonazismus, an der Frauen in aktivistischer und ideologischer Hinsicht wesentlich beteiligt waren. Am Ende jeden Kapitels steht ein kurzes Resümee, in dem die verschiedenen Fäden und Argumentationen noch einmal kurz und prägnant zusammengefasst werden.

Parallel dazu arbeitet Dubslaff verschiedene Frauen-Generationen in der NPD heraus, wobei in der der ersten Phase die „Gründerinnen", also jene Frauen, die zur Etablierung der NPD wesentlich beigetragen haben, genauer beleuchtet werden; in der Hibernationsphase der Partei (1970 bis 1989) treten schließlich die sogenannten „Erbinnen" ihre Nachfolge an. Die erste Generation der NPD-Frauen war biografisch und politisch noch stark im Nationalsozialismus verankert („Erlebnisgeneration") und versuchte, den „nazistischen Kampf" unter den neuen politischen Gegebenheiten fortzuführen (S. 49–59). Unter den „Gründerinnen" waren sowohl ehemals aktive Nationalsozialistinnen als auch Vertreterinnen einer etwas jüngeren Generation, die sogenannten NS-Töchter, wie am Beispiel der Himmler-Tochter Gudrun Burwitz oder Holle Grimm (Tochter des NS-Schriftstellers Hans Grimm) deutlich wird. Diese Frauen waren als fester Bestandteil des rechtsextremen Milieus unter anderem im Unterstützungsnetzwerk für ehemalige Nationalsozialist*innen „Stille Hilfe", bei der Organisation von einschlägigen Tagungen oder als rechte Rednerinnen und Publizistinnen aktiv.

Auch wenn in der männlich dominierten NPD Frauen eindeutig unterrepräsentiert waren, finden sich einige hervortretende Frauen, deren biografische Herkunft, Generationenlage, politische Sozialisation im Nationalsozialismus und ideologischen Schwerpunkte Dubslaff am Beispiel der NPD-Funktionärinnen Anneliese Bläsing (Jg. 1923) und Gertraude Winkelvoß (Jg. 1917) nachzeichnet. Neben diesen beiden exponierten NPD-„Gründungsmüttern" (S. 53), die sogar im Bundesvorstand der NPD vertreten waren, stellt Dubslaff eine Vielzahl von NPD-Funktionärinnen vor, die oft auf niederer Hierarchieebene und im Hintergrund tätig waren. Auch wenn Vorzeigefrauen wie Winkelvoß und Bläsing nie als Spitzenkandidatinnen aufgestellt wurden, erhielten sie mit dem Einzug der NPD in einigen Landesparlamenten konkrete Positionen und damit auch Macht. Als NPD-Landtagsabgeordnete agierten sie meist nicht explizit extremistisch, sondern traten eher gemäßigt auf, eine Strategie, die

Lutz Niethammer als „angepassten Faschismus" bezeichnete.[1] Als NPD-Bundesfrauenreferentinnen wurden ihnen von der männlichen Parteiführung klassische Rollen und thematische Beschränkungen (auf Frauen- und Familienagenden) zugewiesen, die typisch für die extreme Rechte waren – die Politikwissenschaftlerin Sieglinde Rosenberger spricht (in Bezug auf die FPÖ) von einer paradoxen „integrierten Separierung" von Frauen innerhalb der eigenen Partei (S. 64).

Offiziell gab es in der NPD keine „Frauenpolitik", trotzdem versuchte man im Wahlkampf 1969 durch dezidert „weibliche" Mobilisierungsnarrative auch Frauen als Wählerinnen anzusprechen, wie im Kapitel „Frau und Familie: die Politisierung des ‚Frauenbereichs'" aufgezeigt wird. Die NPD vertrat eine extrem konservative, auf „Sitte, Zucht und Ordnung" aufgebaute Familienpolitik, die zudem auch völkisch, antiliberal, antisemitisch und antiamerikanisch ausgerichtet war. Mit ihrem Kampf gegen die Gleichberechtigung sowie der Propagierung und Hervorhebung der Gleichwertigkeit der Geschlechter, das heißt ihrem Beharren auf Differenz, propagierte die NPD eine stark essentialistisch aufgeladene Geschlechterpolarität, die in rechten Kreisen bis heute vertreten wird.

Die NPD-Frauen ließen sich aber keineswegs nur auf den Bereich der „Frauenpolitik" festlegen. Stattdessen standen auf ihren Frauenkongressen unter anderem auch darüberhinausgehende Themen wie die „Gefahr des Kommunismus", die Vertriebenenthematik, die „deutsche Frage" etc. am Programm. Sie vertraten einen strikten Antikommunismus, Antiamerikanismus und – besonders stark nach der „Wende" in den 1990er Jahren – eine rassistisch aufgeladene und militante Ausländerfeindlichkeit. Kurz, sie agierten immer auch als rechtsextreme Ideologinnen. Was die Vergangenheitspolitik der NPD betraf, standen die NPD-Frauen den männlichen Narrativen ebenfalls in nichts nach: Der Nationalsozialismus wurde auch von ihnen über Generationen hinweg verklärt, die NS-Verbrechen relativiert beziehungsweise mit dem alliierten Bombenkrieg aufgerechnet und die Forderung nach einer Generalamnestie für NS-Täter*innen wurde im Laufe der Zeit von der aggressiven Forderung nach dem Ende eines „Schuldkults" abgelöst.

Valerie Dubslaff hat mit ihrer umfassenden Studie einen wichtigen Beitrag zur Geschlechtergeschichte und zur zeithistorischen Rechtsextremismus-Forschung in Deutschland geleistet. Das Buch bietet einen exzellenten Überblick über die innerparteiliche Bedeutung und Rolle der NPD-Frauen in Deutschland und könnte auch für Österreich ein wichtiger Impuls für die bisher kaum existente zeithistorische Forschung zum Rechtsextremismus im Allgemeinen und zu Postnationalsozialistinnen und rechten Frauen im Besonderen sein.

Margit Reiter, Salzburg

---

1 Lutz Niethammer, Angepasster Faschismus. Politische Praxis der NPD, Frankfurt am Main 1969.

Grit Bühler, **Eigenmächtig, frauenbewegt, ausgebremst. Der Demokratische Frauenbund Deutschlands und seine Gründerinnen (1945–1949)**, Frankfurt/New York: Campus 2022, 525 S., EUR 50,40, ISBN 9783593516028.

Grit Bühler arbeitet in ihrem Buch „Eigenmächtig, frauenbewegt, ausgebremst" die Anfangsphase des Demokratischen Frauenbundes Deutschlands (DFD) auf und leistet mit der umfang- und materialreichen Darstellung einen längst überfälligen Beitrag zur Frauenbewegungsgeschichte der unmittelbaren Nachkriegszeit in Deutschland.

Der Demokratische Frauenbund Deutschlands war jene Organisation, die als *die* staatliche Frauenorganisation der DDR bekannt wurde. Die Funktion des DFD als „Transmissionsriemen" und „Akklamationsorgan" (S. 409) für den SED-Parteiapparat ist es, die bis heute die Wahrnehmung des Demokratischen Frauenbunds bestimmt. Bühler lenkt jedoch den Blick auf einen DFD jenseits von fast vierzig Jahren Staatstreue, nämlich auf die Organisation in den ersten Jahren nach dem Zweiten Weltkrieg.

Denn gegründet wurde der Demokratische Frauenbund schon im März 1947, also vor der Staatsgründung der DDR 1949. Diese Gründung, das kann Bühler überzeugend darlegen, erfolgte keineswegs *top down* auf Befehl der Sowjetischen Militäradministration (SMAD), sondern *bottom up* aus den antifaschistischen Frauenausschüssen der unmittelbaren Nachkriegszeit heraus, die als Graswurzelbewegung vor allem, aber nicht nur in Berlin relevant waren (S. 64, S. 68). Bühler geht es um ein Herausschreiben der Akteurinnen und des DFD aus einer letztlich paternalistischen Darstellung, die die SMAD an den Anfang allen frauenpolitischen Engagements in der sowjetisch besetzten Zone setzt. Die Gründungszeit des DFD wird so in ihrem eigenen Recht untersucht, also ohne die spätere SED-gelenkte Organisation vorwegzunehmen: Bühler betont den feministischen Anspruch der Frühphase des DFD. Die Monografie ist damit nicht nur ein Beitrag zur Geschichte des DFD, sondern zielt auch darauf ab, die Nachkriegsjahrzehnte in Deutschland in eine Geschichte der Frauenbewegung einzuschreiben.

Das Buch ist in zwei Teile gegliedert und chronologisch aufgebaut: Der erste Teil handelt auf etwa 150 Seiten von der Gründungsphase des DFD 1945 bis 1947, eigentlich der Vorgeschichte der Organisation als Frauenbund: Hier wird der Weg bis zum Gründungskongress, dem „Deutschen Frauenkongress für den Frieden" im März 1947, beschrieben. Der zweite, mit knapp 200 Seiten etwas längere Teil, stellt die Etablierung des DFD zwischen 1947 und 1949 dar. Dabei geht die Autorin vor allem auf die von ihr sogenannte „feministische Phase" ein, deren Ende sich bereits ab Dezember 1948 andeutete, vor allem durch eine personalpolitische Umgestaltung auf Druck der SED. Spätestens 1953, als wiederum auf das Drängen der Partei hin der DFD-Vorstand ausgetauscht wurde, war der DFD in den SED-Staat integriert.

Die große Stärke des Buchs liegt in seinem quellennahen und quellengesättigten Vorgehen. Bühler hat sich in Organisationsquellen aus dem Bundesarchiv sowie in die Nachlässe von zentralen Protagonistinnen und Gründerinnen vertieft. Sie hat aber auch Hördokumente im Deutschen Rundfunkarchiv Potsdam-Babelsberg erschlossen und Zeitschriften wie „Für Dich" oder „Neues Frauenleben" (DFD Sachsen) ausgewertet. Dadurch ergeben sich ganz neue Einblicke in die Geschichte der Nachkriegsfrauenpolitik. So suggeriert zum Beispiel ein von Bühler ausgewertetes Hördokument, eine Aufnahme aus der Berliner Stadtverordnetenversammlung vom 14. Februar 1947 (S. 250), dass sich die Frauenzusammenschlüsse nicht selbst auf karitative Aufgaben festlegten, was in der Forschung bisher oft als Beleg für das politische Desinteresse von deutschen Frauen nach 1945 gewertet wurde. Vielmehr wurde ein derart eingeschränkter Wirkungskreis von außen und insbesondere von Seiten der Parteien gefordert, die den (überparteilichen) Frauenzusammenschlüssen misstrauisch bis feindselig gegenüberstanden (S. 252).

Die über hundert Seiten Anhang mit Dokumenten und Biografien von Akteurinnen legen ein beeindruckendes Zeugnis von der umfangreichen Quellenarbeit der Autorin ab und bieten zudem einen guten Ausgangspunkt für weitere Forschungen zur Frauenbewegung der Nachkriegszeit. Viel Material und interessante Anschlüsse packt Bühler außerdem – manchmal leider etwas auf Kosten der Übersichtlichkeit – in ausführliche Fußnoten; so zum Beispiel zum personellen Zusammenhang der Nachkriegsfrauenbewegung und der Frauenbewegung nach 1968 in Berlin (siehe Fußnote S. 255).

Bühlers Fokus liegt hauptsächlich auf Berlin. Vor allem im ersten Teil ihres Buches bezieht sie jedoch auch frauenpolitische Initiativen aus Thüringen mit ein. Thüringen nahm eine Art Vorreiterrolle ein; so wurden dort schon früh progressive Forderungen zum Beispiel nach einem bezahlten Haushaltstag in der Woche vertreten (S. 31, S. 88). Im ersten wie im zweiten Teil blickt die Autorin mit ihren Akteurinnen jedoch auch über den deutschen Tellerrand hinaus: zum einen ins französische Ausland, wo die Union französischer Frauen (UFF), eine aus der Résistance entstandene Nachkriegsfrauenorganisation, als Vorbild für Organisationsform und inhaltliche Ausrichtung der zu gründenden deutschen Frauenorganisation fungierte – und nicht etwa eine sowjetische Organisation (S. 120–125) – und zum anderen auf die (1948 bereits erfolgreichen) Bemühungen des DFD, in die 1945 gegründete Internationale Demokratische Frauenföderation (IDFF) aufgenommen zu werden, um Anschluss an eine internationale, ja eine „Weltfrauenbewegung" zu finden.

Im Wesentlichen kann Bühler das historiografische Bild des DFD an zwei Stellen neu perspektivieren: Erstens argumentiert sie überzeugend dafür, die unmittelbare Nachkriegszeit als Frauenbewegungsgeschichte zu schreiben und den frühen DFD als feministische Organisation zu verstehen. „Bewegung", so zeigt sie zum Beispiel am Nachlass Maria Rentmeisters, ist ein Quellenbegriff (S. 45, S. 179 f.). Die Protagonistinnen begriffen sich selbst als in der Tradition der (ersten, Vorkriegs-)Frauenbewegung stehend. Dieses Geschichtsbewusstsein drückte sich zum Beispiel in frühen Bemühungen aus, Bibliotheken und Archive der Frauenbewegung (wieder) zu gründen (S. 276, S. 308, S. 312).

Zudem waren viele der Gründerinnen des DFD bereits in der Weimarer Republik frauenpolitisch aktiv gewesen. Im Hinblick auf die Alterszusammensetzung des DFD spricht Bühler dennoch von „[a]ltersheterogene[n]" Gruppen (S. 56), wenngleich sie bemerkt, dass die „jüngste Generation", nämlich die der „‚BDM-Mädchen' der ca. 25- bis 33-Jährigen", zumindest unter den Protagonistinnen „bis auf wenige Ausnahmen praktisch völlig" fehlte (S. 57). Die daher relativ alte Führungsriege des frühen DFD, die seine politische Ausrichtung stark prägte, war also schon rein biografisch/personell mit der Vorkriegsfrauenbewegung verbunden.

Das Buch schreibt so auch gegen das verbreitete Vorurteil an, dass Kommunistinnen einen rein „taktische[n] Feminismus" (S. 178) vertreten hätten. Ausführlich schildert die Autorin zum Beispiel auch die intensive Auseinandersetzung der DFD-Frauen mit Rechts- und Verfassungsfragen und zeigt, wie der DFD die Verankerung des Gleichberechtigungsprinzips in der DDR-Gesetzgebung gegen Widerstände vorantrieb und sicherstellte (S. 281–299).

Zweitens kann Bühler zeigen, dass das Prinzip der Überparteilichkeit, der Anspruch, eine gesamtdeutsche, überparteiliche Frauenbewegung zu sein, nicht „kommunistische Tarnerzählung" war, sondern die im DFD engagierten Frauen unbenommen ihrer verschiedenen Parteizugehörigkeiten „Frauen als Frauen" zusammenbringen wollten und die Gemeinsamkeit des Geschlechts höher werteten als die Parteizugehörigkeit (S. 193). Der DFD sollte nicht eine bestimmte Parteilinie, sondern den „fortschrittlichsten Teil der deutschen Frauenbewegung" (S. 316) repräsentieren.

Die Autorin lotet die Schwierigkeiten und Konflikte aus, die der Anspruch der Überparteilichkeit unter den Mitgliedern im Demokratischen Frauenbund auslöste, aber vor allem, wie sie in den Reaktionen von außen sichtbar wurden – zum Beispiel untersagte die CDU ihren Mitgliedern eine gleichzeitige Mitgliedschaft im DFD, da die „weltanschauliche und politische Aufklärung der Frauen […] in der Hand der Parteien verbleiben" müsse (Quellenzitat, S. 191).

Zusammenfassend lässt sich festhalten, dass Grit Bühler mit ihrer Studie zum Demokratischen Frauenbund Deutschlands ein sorgfältig recherchiertes Buch vorgelegt hat, das seine Materialfülle souverän regiert und durch das Heranziehen wenig beachteter und ungewöhnlicher Quellen glänzt.

Anna Leyrer, Basel

Abstracts

Yurii Zazuliak, Abducted Women and Anxious Patriarchs. Abduction of Women and Ambiguities of Noble Honour in Galicia during the Fifteenth Century

This article investigates the cases of women's abduction before local courts in Galicia (Red Ruthenia) during the fifteenth century. It focuses on the shifting meanings and ambiguities of the practice of abduction and ravishment in local contexts of gender relations, violence and law. The article situates the abduction of women within a wider spectrum of concepts and practices of contemporary gender and social relations, approaching it as a specific form of gendered violence as well as a means of regulating familial conflicts and matrimonial behaviour. The practice of abduction shows the complex and dynamic interplay between women's agency and the institutional and normative constraints of the legal system and the patriarchal order, imposed on women to categorise and control their behaviour. The analysis suggests the crucial importance of the concept of female honour and gender symbols in the discourse and practice of hostile relations among local noblemen.

Nataliia Starchenko, "Treacherous" Women or Opportunistic Men. Volhynian Gentry Women Accused of Murdering Their Husbands in the Eastern Region of the Early Modern Polish-Lithuanian Commonwealth

This article analyses the discourse about noblewomen in the Polish-Lithuanian Commonwealth based on specific sources: accusations of murdering their husbands made against wives. The trial narratives, which have been used as sources for this study, are a distinctive construct with at least three parties involved in its creation: the accuser, the accused and the scribe who compiled the story according to certain clichéd formulas. The construction of the story was primarily modelled on the expectations of society. The way a murder was described always mobilised the socio-cultural resources of its time and place. Despite the fact that these texts have a very tenuous relationship to reality, their authors hoped to use them to influence reality and succeeded in doing so by using the resources offered by the community. The trial of Nastasia Okhlopovska, which occupies a central position in the article due to its extensive documentation in the sources, highlights the performativity of murder accusations against wives. The microhistorical analysis of this case allows broader conclusions to be drawn about the status of noblewomen in the eastern regions of the Polish-Lithuanian Commonwealth (now Ukraine).

Olha Posunko, The Protection of Women's Property Rights in the Courts of Southern Ukraine from the End of the Eighteenth to the Mid-Nineteenth Centuries

Southern Ukraine is a region that was completely subordinated to the Russian Empire only in the last quarter of the eighteenth century. Processes of ennoblement and the acquisition of landed property by nobles and officers in the region enabled women to become active participants in social and economic life. Court records illustrate the implementation, consolidation and struggle for women's property rights. They also show that the extension of the economic rights of noblewomen was primarily a means of protecting the interests of the noble corporation. A principle of separation of marital property was introduced, which was also observed in the legislation of European countries. Women did not become equal to men in their rights as property owners, but their opportunities were greatly increased. The article examines cases of inheritance by women, women as guardians and women as owners. Particular attention is paid to a new understanding of the maternal duty to protect the property interests of children. Court records also reveal the presence of local traditions and legal norms.

Nataliia Kolb and Nataliia Mysak, The Daughters of Greek Catholic Priests in Galicia in the Late Nineteenth Century. Between Conservatism and Emancipation

This article analyses the transformation of the social position of Ukrainian Greek Catholic priests' daughters in Galicia under the influence of the advancing feminist movement in the late nineteenth century. The authors emphasise the factors that caused a gradual change in the social roles of women (increase in educational opportunities, participation in public life, activation of the Ukrainian national movement, etc.). A peculiar dichotomy in the interpretation of gender roles by the Greek Catholic clergy, in particular that of a woman as a wife, mother and public figure, had a noticeable impact on this process. The article examines how gender relations in the family, parents' attitudes towards girls' education and careers, and the dominance of conservative or liberal education influenced the personality formation of priests' daughters. The family was often the centre for the crystallisation of a clear civic position and national identity of women from the clerical community. The attitudes of the priests' daughters themselves towards changes in their social position, the struggle for gender equality and the breaking of gender stereotypes are analysed.

Viktoriia Ivashchenko and Yulia Kiselyova, "I Am Stronger Now, I Know I Can Do So Much". Women Academics in Conditions of Forced Migration during the Russian-Ukrainian War

The article aims to identify growth points in the gender self-consciousness of Ukrainian women academics in forced migration caused by the Russian-Ukrainian war, particularly with regard to their professional, social and personal lives. The source base is a set of semi-structured interviews conducted as part of the oral history project "Moving West", which explores survival and career-building strategies among Ukrainian humanities scholars from the first (2014) and second (2022) waves of war-related migration. The article argues that the impetus for new practices of gender self-identity is given not only by changes in the social experience of women academics, who have been key beneficiaries of European institutional efforts to support the Ukrainian academia, but also by a rethinking of moral obligations in response to external challenges and internal value conflicts. The authors suggest that these developments may lead to a shift from quantitative to qualitative feminisation in the Ukrainian academic community.

Anschriften der Autor*innen

Susanna Burghartz, Departement Geschichte, Universität Basel, Hirschgässlein 21, 4051 Basel, Schweiz – susanna.burghartz@unibas.ch

Dietlind Hüchtker, Fakultätszentrum für transdisziplinäre historisch-kulturwissenschaftliche Studien, Universität Wien, Kolingasse 14–16, 1090 Wien, Österreich – dietlind.huechtker@univie.ac.at

Jiří Hutečka, Historický ústav, Filozofická fakulta, Univerzita Hradec Králové, Rokitanského 62, 500 03 Hradec Králové, Czech Republic – jiri.hutecka@uhk.cz

Tetiana Isaieva, Gendermuseum Kharkiv, 124 A Moskovskiy Ave, 61037 Kharkiv, Ukraine – gender.museum@gmail.com

Viktoriia Ivashchenko, V. N. Karazin Kharkiv National University, Svobody Sg., 61022 Kharkiv, Ukraine – ivashchenko@karazin.ua
Address in Poland: Adjunct Museum of the Eastern Territories of the Old Polish Republic, Litewske Sg., 20-080, Lublin, Poland

Yulia Kiselyova, V. N. Karazin Kharkiv National University, Svobody Sg., 61022 Kharkiv, Ukraine – yu.a.kiselyova@karazin.ua

Nataliia Kolb, Department of modern history, Ivan Krypiakevych Institute of the National Academy of Sciences, Kozelnytska Street 4, Lviv, Ukraine – nata_kolb@ukr.net
Second address: Institute of Religion Studies – a branch of Lviv Museum of Religion History, Muzeina Street, 1, Lviv

Claudia Kraft, Institut für Zeitgeschichte, Universität Wien, Unicampus, Spitalgasse 2–4, Hof 1.13, 1090 Wien, Österreich – claudia.kraft@univie.ac.at

Stephanie Lämmert, Max-Planck-Institut für Bildungsforschung, Lentzeallee 94, 14195 Berlin, Deutschland – laemmert@mpib-berlin.mpg.de

Anna Leyrer, Departement Geschichte, Universität Basel, Hirschgässlein 21, 4051 Basel, Schweiz – anna.leyrer@unibas.ch

Nataliia Mysak, Department of modern history, Ivan Krypiakevych Institute of the National Academy of Sciences, Kozelnytska Street 4, Lviv, Ukraine – natalia_mysak @ukr.net

Claudia Opitz-Belakhal, Departement Geschichte, Universität Basel, Hirschgässlein 21, 4051 Basel, Schweiz – claudia.opitz@unibas.ch

Olena Petrenko, Fakultät für Geschichtswissenschaft, Historisches Institut, Universitätsstrasse 150, 44801 Bochum, Deutschland – olena.petrenko@yahoo.de

Olha Posunko, Department of Ukrainian history at Oles Honchar Dnipro National University, 72 Haharin Avenue, Dnipro city, Ukraine – olgaposunko70@gmail.com

Margit Reiter, Fachbereich Geschichte, Paris Lodron Universität Salzburg, Rudolfskai 42, 5020 Salzburg, Österreich – margit.reiter@plus.ac.at

Nina Seiler, Zürcher Hochschule der Künste, Departement Darstellende Künste und Film, Toni-Areal, Pfingstweidstr. 96, Postfach, 8031 Zürich, Schweiz – nina.seiler @zhdk.ch

Gabriela Signori, Universität Konstanz, Fachbereich Geschichte und Soziologie, Fach 2, 78457 Konstanz, Deutschland – gabriela.signori@uni-konstanz.de

Nataliia Starchenko, Hrushevsky Institute of Ukrainian Archaeography and Source Studies of the National Academy of Sciences of Ukraine, 4 Triokhsviatytelska Str., 01001 Kyiv, Ukraine – interregnum@ukr.net
Second address: Institute of History of Ukraine, 4 Hrushevskoho Str., 01001, Kyiv, Ukraine

Maria Tranter, Departement Geschichte, Universität Basel, Hirschgässlein 21, 4051 Basel, Schweiz – m.tranter@unibas.ch

Katharina Wiedlack, Anglistik und Amerikanistik, Universität Wien, Unicampus, Spitalgasse 2–4, Hof 8.3, 1090 Wien – katharina.wiedlack@univie.ac.at

Yurii Zazuliak, Department of History, Faculty of Humanity, Ukrainian Catholic University, Vul. Kozelnytska 2, Lviv, Ukraine – yuriy_zazuliak@yahoo.com

Weitere Hefte von „L'Homme. Europäische Zeitschrift für Feministische Geschichtswissenschaft"

34. Jg., Heft 2 (2023)
Natur
hg. von Caroline Arni, Anna Becker
und Claudia Opitz-Belakhal

174 Seiten, kartoniert
€ 25,– D / € 26,– A
ISBN 978-3-8471-1591-5
eBook: € 23,–
ISBN 978-3-8470-1591-8

34. Jg., Heft 1 (2023)
Kinder in Heimen
hg. von Anelia Kassabova
und Sandra Maß

158 Seiten, kartoniert
€ 25,– D / € 26,– A
ISBN 978-3-8471-1534-2
eBook: € 23,–
ISBN 978-3-8470-1534-5

Vorschau:

35. Jg., Heft 2 (2024)
vor Gericht
hg. von Maria Fritsche
und Ulrike Krampl

Erscheint im Herbst 2024

36. Jg., Heft 1 (2025)
MACHT(ver)HANDELN
hg. von Julia Burkhardt
und Christina Lutter

Erscheint im Frühjahr 2025

L'Homme Schriften

Bd. 29: Maximiliane Berger /
Mirjam Hähnle / Anna Leyrer (Hg.)

Männer über sich
Wissenschaft – Biografie – Geschlecht
2024. 166 Seiten mit einer Abbildung, gebunden
€ 45,– D / € 47,– A
ISBN 978-3-8471-1688-2
Open Access
ISBN 978-3-7370-1688-9

Bd. 28: Veronika Helfert

Frauen, wacht auf!
Eine Frauen- und Geschlechtergeschichte von
Revolution und Rätebewegung in Österreich,
1916–1924
2021. 399 Seiten mit 15 Abbildungen, gebunden
€ 50,– D / € 52,– A
ISBN 978-3-8471-1184-9
eBook: € 50,– D
ISBN 978-3-8470-1184-2

Vandenhoeck & Ruprecht Verlage

www.vandenhoeck-ruprecht-verlage.com

Ältere Ausgaben von „L'Homme. Z. F. G." (1990 bis 2015) sind im Böhlau Verlag erschienen und über die Redaktion erhältlich: https://lhomme.univie.ac.at/ und lhomme.geschichte@univie.ac.at

Heft 26, 2 (2015)
Maria Fritsche, Anelia Kassabova (Hg.)
Visuelle Kulturen

Heft 26, 1 (2015)
Ulrike Krampl, Xenia
von Tippelskirch (Hg.)
mit Sprachen

Heft 25, 2 (2014)
Gabriella Hauch, Monika Mommertz,
Claudia Opitz-Belakhal (Hg.)
Zeitenschwellen

Heft 25, 1 (2014)
Margareth Lanzinger, Annemarie
Steidl (Hg.)
Heiraten nach Übersee

Heft 24, 2 (2013)
Claudia Ulbrich, Gabriele Jancke,
Mineke Bosch (Hg.)
Auto/Biographie

Heft 24, 1 (2013)
Ingrid Bauer, Christa Hämmerle (Hg.)
Romantische Liebe

Heft 23, 2 (2012)
Almut Höfert, Claudia Opitz-Belakhal,
Claudia Ulbrich (Hg.)
Geschlechtergeschichte global

Heft 23, 1 (2012)
Mineke Bosch, Hanna Hacker, Ulrike
Krampl (Hg.)
Spektakel

Heft 22, 2 (2011)
Sandra Maß, Kirsten Bönker, Hana
Havelková (Hg.)
Geld-Subjekte

Heft 22, 1 (2011)
Karin Gottschalk, Margareth
Lanzinger (Hg.)
Mitgift

Heft 21, 2 (2010)
Caroline Arni, Edith Saurer (Hg.)
Blut, Milch und DNA. Zur Geschichte generativer Substanzen

Heft 21, 1 (2010)
Bożena Chołuj, Ute Gerhard, Regina
Schulte (Hg.)
Prostitution

Heft 20, 2 (2009)
Ingrid Bauer, Hana Havelková (Hg.)
Gender & 1968

Heft 20, 1 (2009)
Ulrike Krampl, Gabriela Signori (Hg.)
Namen

Heft 19, 2 (2008)
Christa Hämmerle,
Claudia Opitz-Belakhal (Hg.)
Krise(n) der Männlichkeit?

Heft 19, 1 (2008)
Ute Gerhard, Karin Hausen (Hg.)
Sich Sorgen – Care

Heft 18, 2 (2007)
Caroline Arni, Susanna Burghartz (Hg.)
Geschlechtergeschichte, gegenwärtig

Heft 18, 1 (2007)
Gunda Barth-Scalmani,
Regina Schulte (Hg.)
Dienstbotinnen

Heft 17, 2 (2006)
Margareth Lanzinger, Edith
Saurer (Hg.)
Mediterrane Märkte

Heft 17, 1 (2006)
Ingrid Bauer, Christa Hämmerle (Hg.)
Alter(n)

Heft 16, 2 (2005)
Mineke Bosch, Hanna Hacker (Hg.)
Whiteness

Heft 16, 1 (2005)
Ute Gerhard, Krassimira
Daskalova (Hg.)
Übergänge. Ost-West-Feminismen

Heft 15, 2 (2004)
Erna Appelt, Waltraud Heindl (Hg.)
Auf der Flucht

Heft 15, 1 (2004)
Caroline Arni, Gunda Barth-Scalmani,
Ingrid Bauer, Christa Hämmerle, Margareth Lanzinger, Edith Saurer (Hg.)
Post/Kommunismen

Heft 14, 2 (2003)
Susanna Burghartz, Brigitte
Schnegg (Hg.)
Leben texten

Heft 14, 1 (2003)
Gunda Barth-Scalmani, Brigitte Mazohl-Wallnig, Edith Saurer (Hg.)
Ehe-Geschichten

Heft 13, 2 (2002)
Mineke Bosch, Francisca de Haan, Claudia Ulbrich (Hg.)
Geschlechterdebatten

Heft 13, 1 (2002)
Karin Hausen, Regina Schulte (Hg.)
Die Liebe der Geschwister

Heft 12, 2 (2001)
Waltraud Heindl, Claudia Ulbrich (Hg.)
HeldInnen?

Heft 12, 1 (2001)
Susanna Burghartz, Christa Hämmerle (Hg.)
Soldaten

Heft 11, 2 (2000)
Ute Gerhard, Edith Saurer (Hg.)
Das Geschlecht der Europa

Heft 11, 1 (2000)
Christa Hämmerle, Karin Hausen, Edith Saurer (Hg.)
Normale Arbeitstage

Heft 10, 2 (1999)
Hanna Hacker, Herta Nagl-Docekal, Gudrun Wolfgruber (Hg.)
Glück

Heft 10, 1 (1999)
Erna Appelt (Hg.)
Citizenship

Heft 9, 2 (1998)
Christa Hämmerle, Karin Hausen (Hg.)
Heimarbeit

Heft 9, 1 (1998)
Susanna Burghartz, Edith Saurer (Hg.)
Unzucht

Heft 8, 2 (1997)
Waltraud Heindl, Regina Schulte (Hg.)
Höfische Welt

Heft 8, 1 (1997)
Hg. vom Herausgeberinnen-Gremium der L'Homme. Z. F. G.
Vorstellungen

Heft 7, 2 (1996)
Andrea Griesebner, Claudia Ulbrich (Hg.)
Gewalt

Heft 7, 1 (1996)
Gunda Barth-Scalmani, Ingrid Bauer, Christa Hämmerle, Gabriella Hauch, Waltraud Heindl, Brigitte Mazohl-Wallnig, Brigitte Rath (Hg.)
Tausendundeine Geschichten aus Österreich

Heft 6, 2 (1995)
Gudrun-Axeli Knapp, Edith Saurer (Hg.)
Interdisziplinarität

Heft 6, 1 (1995)
Erna Appelt, Verena Pawlowsky (Hg.)
Handel

Heft 5, 2 (1994)
Susan Zimmermann, Birgit Bolognese-Leuchtenmüller (Hg.)
Fürsorge

Heft 5, 1 (1994)
Herta Nagl-Docekal (Hg.)
Körper

Heft 4, 2 (1993)
Christa Hämmerle, Bärbel Kuhn (Hg.)
Offenes Heft

Heft 4, 1 (1993)
Hanna Hacker (Hg.)
Der Freundin?

Heft 3, 2 (1992)
Waltraud Heindl, Jana Starek (Hg.)
Minderheiten

Heft 3, 1 (1992)
Hg. vom Herausgeberinnen-Gremium der L'Homme. Z. F. G.
Krieg

Heft 2, 2 (1991)
Brigitte Mazohl-Wallnig, Herta Nagl-Docekal (Hg.)
Intellektuelle

Heft 2, 1 (1991)
Erna Appelt, Edith Saurer (Hg.)
Ernährung

Heft 1, 1 (1990)
Christa Hämmerle, Edith Saurer (Hg.)
Religion

Diese Hefte sind Open Access unter https://lhomme-archiv.univie.ac.at abrufbar.